Slumming in New York

Slumming in New York

FROM THE WATERFRONT TO MYTHIC HARLEM

Robert M. Dowling

UNIVERSITY OF ILLINOIS PRESS

URBANA AND CHICAGO

© 2007 by Robert M. Dowling
All rights reserved
Manufactured in the United States of America
1 2 3 4 5 C P 5 4 3 2 1
♾ This book is printed on acid-free paper.

Library of Congress Cataloging-in-Publication Data
Dowling, Robert M., 1970–
Slumming in New York : from the waterfront to mythic Harlem /
Robert M. Dowling.
    p.   cm.
Includes bibliographical references and index.
ISBN-13: 978-0-252-03194-6 (acid-free paper)
ISBN-10: 0-252-03194-6 (acid-free paper)
1. American fiction—New York (State)—New York—History and criticism.
2. American fiction—19th century—History and criticism.
3. American fiction—20th century—History and criticism.
4. New York (N.Y.)—In literature.
5. New York (N.Y.)—Social conditions.
6. Slums in literature.
7. Outsiders in literature.
8. Immigrants in literature.
9. Literature and society—New York (State)—New York—History—19th century.
10. Literature and society—New York (State)—New York—History—20th century.
I. Title.
PS374.N43D69   2007
813'.009327471—dc22   2006100925

CONTENTS

ACKNOWLEDGMENTS

THE OLD JOKE IS THAT I BEGAN researching this project in my teenage years, meandering as I did with my oldest friends Alex Smith and Chris Francescani, both journalists now, through the Lower East Side, Alphabet City, Chinatown, the Meatpacking District, Hell's Kitchen, and Harlem (though I can scarcely afford visiting those neighborhoods today). Practically speaking, the seeds of this book were planted during my second year of graduate school in California, when the sensation of homesickness was so extreme I found it infinitely therapeutic to write about New York City. For their encouragement and non-native insights, I would first like to thank the faculty of the American Studies graduate program at California State University, Fullerton—in particular, John Ibson, Karen Lystra, Allan Axelrad, and Jesse Battan. They were a group to write about home for, and to write home about.

I would never have entered the Ph.D. program in English at the Graduate Center of the City University of New York had it not been for my early discovery of David S. Reynolds and his work. Until that time, I never thought such research—deeply probing "beneath" the American literary canon as he does—appropriate for "serious" academic discourse. Since then, he has been a continual source of enthusiasm and inspiration. Morris Dickstein was my official faculty mentor at CUNY, and from our first conversation on the phone, before I had even attended a doctoral seminar, I have found his to be a model intellect. Morris is the person most responsible for bringing the diverse vitality and historicizing potential of the realist movement to my attention. Marc Dolan, also at CUNY, has been my guide, my sponsor, and in many ways, my conscience. Without him, I would never have explored roads that appeared at a distance to be blind alleyways, but were, upon further investigation, grand concourses. My other great influences at CUNY were Louis Menand, William P. Kelly, Catherine Lavender, Sondra Perl, and Norman Kelvin. While there, I also made friends and contacts with emergent scholars such as myself, friends who have provided unflagging and mutually beneficial intellectual stimulation and support, most importantly Tom Cerasulo, Matthew Gold, Jean Murley, and James Groom.

Since that time, I have taught full-time in two remarkable faculties—the Department of Humanities at the U.S. Coast Guard Academy and Central Connecticut State University, where I am now an associate professor of English. I would like thank everyone at the Academy who helped me along through revision after revision of this book and closely related projects: Bruce Dalcher, Gary Donato, Pat Newman, Julie Johnson, Alex Waid, Faye Ringel, Jose Gonzalez, Anne Flammang, Laurel Goulet, Jon and Laura Heller, Craig and Sue Corl, and Sean Carroll. At CCSU, for their warmth and welcome, I would like to thank Gil Gigliotti, Katherine Sugg, David Cappella, Ravi Shankar, Matthew H. Ciscel, Christine Doyle, Barry Leeds, Robert Dunne, Candace Barrington, Laurence Petit, Jaclyn Geller, and, for reading through many chapters and his encouragement along the way, Tony Cannella, along with all the others I wish I had space for. The CCSU College of Arts and Sciences, under the leadership of Dean Susan Pease, deserves many thanks for their generous course releases and research grants that secured crucial time for revision and expansion. Debbie Herman of the Elihu Burritt Library at CCSU was, and continues to be, a marvel—her help securing photographs and attending to technological crises was indispensable.

Next are a group I call my "great patrons," scholars, friends, and editors who have held indefatigable faith in me and my research over the past few years: these include, but are by no means limited to, Bruce Kellner (who originally suggested the University of Illinois Press for this project), Jerome Loving, Jay Parini, Robert Paul Lamb, Barbara McCaskill, Paul Sorrentino, James Nagle, Julie Rivkin, John Christie, Mary Papke, my Partner in Crime, Wilfred D. Samuels, and my editors, Joan Catapano, Angela Burton, John Bealle, and Louis Simon. Here's to the Rhodes Scholars of City Island, the Bronx—Dick Bach, "Tall Paul" Westermeier and Fred Freder—and to my lifelong friends and fellow travelers, Adam Kroshus, Sara Duffy, Sheila Power, Tim Raycroft, Rob Cowan, Brian Nicholson, and John Iskander.

I also acknowledge the efforts of the library staffs at CSU Fullerton's Pollack Library, the CUNY Graduate Center's Mina Rees Library, Fordham University's Walsh Library, Wesleyan University's Olin Library, the U.S. Coast

Guard Academy Library, Connecticut College's Charles E. Shain Library, CC-SU's Elihu Burritt Library, the New York Public Library, and Yale University's Collection of American Literature/Beinecke Rare Book and Manuscript Library. I thank Peggy Porter Poole and David Poole, the novelist Ernest Poole's daughter-in-law and grandson, for their heartfelt enthusiasm in this project and for sending on the elusive image of Ernest Poole now in these pages.

Thanks especially to my mother, Janet B. Kellock, for her intellectual influence, her brilliance, and her editorial acumen; and my sisters Elisa Olds and Susanne Magee and my grandmother Evelyn Dowling for their undying affection and support. This book is dedicated to my father, the late Richard O'Rahilly Dowling, who unfortunately will not be able to read this, and my daughter Mairéad Huber Dowling, who is just learning how to.

Slumming in New York

Introduction

IN THE HALF-CENTURY BETWEEN 1790 and 1840 the population of Manhattan grew from roughly thirty-three thousand to over ten times that size. Coming into existence at the island's lower tip, the settlement expanded northward, swallowing up farmland and exploiting any usable resource for the growing needs of transportation, commerce, and housing. By the 1850s, Manhattan was a major international port city; by the 1890s, a metropolis; by the 1920s, the cosmopolitan capital of the world. The 1890 U.S. Census reports that a third of the city was foreign-born and that it housed as many Germans as Hamburg, double the number of Irish in Dublin, and two and a half times the number of Jews in Warsaw (Martin 5), figures that lent new meaning to Walt Whitman's earlier rhapsody of the United States as a "teeming nation of nations." Only a part of these immigrants were actually from Hamburg, Dublin, or Warsaw, however. Most arrived from rural-based villages and *shtetls,* from societies that considered cities morally corrupt and impossibly complex. The future of the United States was no longer one of manifest destiny across the continent, but of furthering the frenzied processes of urbanization, immigration, and industrialization.

Slumming in New York attempts to give shape and form to one of the most intriguing discourses to materialize from New York's tempestuous ascent: mainstream, or "outsider," interactions with marginalized "insider" voices. The term "outsider" has been variously applied in contemporary scholarship and popular culture but most often signifies immigrant populations, racial minorities, and the urban poor. I invert the popular usage, however, so that "insider" replaces "outsider," as sociology has it, to indicate voices that emerge from marginalized districts within the larger city. "Marginalized," in kind, is distinct from "marginal," which signifies someone in between insider and outsider, settling vagabond-like in a variety of cultures, but belonging nowhere.

One of the most revolutionary developments in American literary history was the mounting awareness, born of the realist movement, that for the "real thing" to be fully realized in American writing, insider authors must supply their own idiosyncratic perspectives, on their own terms, in their own vernacular, and from their own ground. As early as 1894, Hamlin Garland, one of the leading promoters of American realism, boldly called for an "indigenous literature" in his seminal treatise on postbellum American fiction *Crumbling Idols:* "We have had the figures, the dates, the bare history, the dime novel statement of pioneer life, but how few real novels! How few accurate studies of speech and life! There it lies, ready to be put into the novel and the drama, and upon the canvas; and *it must be done by those born into it*" (16, emphasis mine). The truth was, however, that most foreigners and working-class migrants were straddled with more pressing concerns than finding a publisher for their latest memoir or short story, inconvenient as that must have been for promoters of realist writing. They first had to learn "proper" English, navigate the bureaucracy of American institutions, earn money to support their families back home, and, most important for the long-term, provide schooling for their children.

As a result, first-generation immigrant and working-class fiction from the turn of the twentieth century is not readily available in your local or college library, though there may be some exceptions—perhaps a dusty first edition of Hjalmar Hjorth Boyesen's *Vagabond Tales* (1889), Mary Antin's upbeat assimilationist memoir *The Promised Land* (1907), the ghetto tales of Abraham Cahan (the immigrant cynosure of the period), or the Irish publisher S. S. McClure's *My Autobiography* (1914, ghostwritten by Willa Cather). Thanks to recent scholarship, however, we now know that there exists an as-yet-undiscovered reservoir of ethnic and working-class writing from this period that deserves to be funneled into the larger U.S. literary tradition.[1] But by addressing the changing *representations* of insider voices in the focal years of New York realist and naturalist writing, from 1880 to 1930, we can take a fresh look at urban writing by mainstream outsiders about "those born into it." Outsider narratives, I will show, are not exclusively vehicles for moralistic middle-class values or purely subversive expressions of radical or transnational democracy. Neither are they strictly avenues for race, class, or gender antagonism or affirmation. Taken as a whole, they reveal a more open pattern of social transformation and moral experimentation.

In *Slumming in New York* I argue that the triple threat of modernity—urbanization, immigration, and industrialization—amplified Victorian ethnocentrism to such an extent that it forced a counter-ethnocentric backlash. By looking at sources emblematic of this remarkable trend, the goal of this book is to consider new ways of reading realist narratives by outsiders, narratives that helped alleviate this social conflict by gradually freeing the insider voice from neighborhoods like the East Side waterfront, the Bowery and thereabouts, the Tenderloin district's "black Bohemia," the Jewish Lower East Side, and Harlem. The interface between culture and urban space in New York writing becomes increasingly significant as this narrative unfolds: up from the representational twist at the turn of the twentieth century—first with literary naturalism's foregrounding of the consciousness of the "other half," then heading skyward via the Jewish Lower East Side into the Harlem Renaissance. The celebratory nature of 1920s Harlem writers might be considered the top of the narrative arc. But the final act is the decided victory of the insider voice over that of the outsider observer. In short, representations of marginalized districts since the 1930s have been turned inside out.

Most of the writing I cover here is fiction, but it is an ethnographic fiction fuelled by a strong desire, as Dominika Ferens succinctly defines the incipient field of ethnography, to realize "a set of changing rationales for and styles of knowing and representing the other" (2). Naturally, both urban neighborhoods and their affiliate populations were and continue to be compelling subjects for authors mining provocative insights from the American scene, men and women alternatively called "down and outers," "participant observers," "epistemological scouts," "genteel interlopers," "friendly visitors," or "slummers." And of course canonical literary realists like William Dean Howells, Henry James, and Edith Wharton reveal a great deal about their own genteel lives and drew on their insider middle- and upper-class status to voice the concerns of other insiders in their milieu. But their ability to ingratiate audiences in this way, to "belong" on a conventional level, gave literary realists more leverage to probe marginalized subjects as well.

❖ ❖ ❖

Charles Dickens's notorious chronicle of antebellum life *American Notes* appeared in 1842, notably the same year Walt Whitman published *Franklin Evans,* his moralistic temperance novel responding to the timely demand for anti-alcohol agitprop. *American Notes* was a highly circulated travel narrative with a blistering chapter on conditions in the notorious Five Points area of New York City. But rather than the backhanded brickbats that targeted alcohol as the number one scapegoat, a temperance genre New Yorkers were well-accustomed to by the 1840s, Dickens's was a sweeping assault. Soon after the book's publication, the Five Points paradoxically became New York's most alluring tourist attraction.

Dickens's damning critique of the United States left many Americans feeling profoundly betrayed—he was, after all, the most celebrated novelist in the Western world. But a large cohort of popular American authors soon followed suit. The so-called city-mysteries writers of the late 1840s and '50s, including George Lippard, Ned Buntline, George Foster, and John Vose, to name only a few, broadened their focus from the confines of intemperance to include gambling houses, brothels, street walkers, groggeries, police corruption, and rat-worrying, among other carnalities. The mushrooming proliferation of city-mysteries novels through the 1850s set in motion what Leslie Fiedler has called "the provincial image of the city as Babylon" (483–84). Their off-putting image of city space, Fiedler suggests, "presides over the main line of American city novels from Whitman's *Franklin Evans*, through Crane's *Maggie*, up to the fiction of Dreiser and the 'muckrakers'" (484). The urban historian William Taylor adds that New York "exercised a veritable tyranny of place over the sensibilities of these artists. Even in their moments of repugnance, they are drawn back repeatedly to attempts at defining its aesthetic uniqueness . . . the city possessed . . . a kind of terrible beauty" (xvii).

Popular antebellum city writing, as we see in the journalistic urban exposés of John Vose, the bizarre cosmology of George Foster, the gothic world of George Lippard, and the cynically immoral pamphlet novels of George Thompson, brought with it a new obsession—telling the story of New York "as it is." On the one hand, however, as Timothy Gilfoyle explains in his comprehensive work on New York prostitution *The City of Eros*, "the popularity of these fictional and non-fictional accounts did not rest upon their pornographic imagery alone. . . . There were the images of New York's antebellum nightlife, scenes residents and visitors witnessed daily. The inclusion of such a readily recognized geography gave these stories a sharp sense of realism, a resonance of authenticity, so often absent from earlier accounts of the metropolis" (155). On the other hand, if "authenticity" is a resonant concern in city mysteries, it is alternately not, strictly speaking, what scholar Amy Kaplan calls a "fiction of the referent" (8). Though they were written with a naturalistic sensitivity to the material realities of the city, most go no further than, as George Foster himself phrased it, "an irresistible wind" (135).

Kaplan opens her book *The Social Construction of American Realism* with this premise: "The urban-industrial transformation of nineteenth-century society did not provide a ready-made setting which the realistic social novel reflects, but . . . these changes radically challenged the accessibility of an emergent modern world to literary representation" (8). If this was true in Kaplan's focal years, the 1880s and '90s, in the antebellum period, when urban American life was in its adolescence, the challenge of referential analysis proved even more difficult, since models of urban realism were not yet available. As Foster implies in the preface to his novel *Celio: or, New York Above-Ground and Under-Ground* (1850), if his readers are confused by his book's tentacular moral and spatial geographies, they should blame the bizarre convolutions of the city itself (4). City-mysteries novels dealt more abstractly with morality and space than their successors, who will be treated at length in the following chapters, but they triggered what became a New York tradition—venting moral and environmental anxieties by writing about them.

The anxieties born of New York's growth exploded at the turn of the century, due in large part to the influx of immigrants from southern and eastern Europe and black migrants from the South and the West Indies in the 1910s and '20s; these new groups permanently transformed the older, racially mixed "slum" to the modern ethnically cohesive "ghetto."[2] Economically speaking, as Eric Schocket has pointed out, the horrendous effects of the great depression of 1893 led moral reformers to "[shift] from moralism to environmentalism, a move that highlighted the importance of these contained residential spaces" (116). Of course, moral crusaders had already begun to circulate horrifying and often tantalizing accounts of both the traditional slum and the modern ghetto in popular sociological treatises like Charles Loring Brace's *The Dangerous Classes of New York* (1872), Helen Campbell's *The Problem of the Poor* (1882), and Jacob Riis's widely read *How the Other Half Lives* (1890). Brace, Campbell, Riis (an assimilated Danish immigrant himself), and other reformers hoped to improve the living conditions of the working poor while at the same time firmly establish ethnic identity as "otherness" in the mainstream American mind. Their conclusions rarely flattered their subjects—mainly Irish, eastern European Jews, Chinese, and African Americans—nor did they calm native-born Anglo-Saxon Americans. The rhetoric of reform affirmed the preexisting view that, as their titles imply, newly investigated ethnic groups were "dangerous," "problematic," and "other," and thus threatened the nation's democratic institutions and economic prosperity from within.

Conversely, a group of liberal-minded idealists, including the ghetto journalist Hutchins Hapgood, the muckraking reporter Lincoln Steffens, and the "Dean" of American letters William Dean Howells, rose up from genteel circles to champion the cultural legitimacy of the disenfranchised "other." These more liberal "crusaders" regarded immigrant and working-class urban life as both an education in cosmopolitanism and a modern diversion at the turn of the twentieth century, a Progressive-era tactic often regarded as the exploitation of disenfranchised insiders by privileged outsiders. But Hutchins Hapgood, one of the most strident radical voices of the era, regarded this modernist perspective as a kind of philosophical anarchism: "It means a willingness to receive hospitably whatever dawning forces there may be in the submerged; a refusal to deny their possible validity in a more complex society. . . . It is deeply sympathetic with the psychology of the underdog" (*Victorian* 277).[3]

In kind, when Lincoln Steffens worked the street beat as a young reporter for the *New York Post,* he learned many Jewish customs and rituals because he became "as infatuated with the Ghetto as eastern boys were with the wild west." "You are more Jewish than us Jews," his new friends told him. When Steffens later traveled through Europe, he came to recognize the "absurdity of the American who is more French than the French, more German than the Kaiser." By the early 1900s, Lower East Side Jews reached what the sociologist Robert K. Merton calls a "critical measure of success" in that they now had rightful sway over how their group was interpreted, and in Steffens and Hapgood, the success was "at the extreme": "The converted Outsider validating himself, in his own eyes and in those of others, by becoming even more zealous than the Insiders in adhering to the doctrine of the group with which he wants to identify himself, if only symbolically . . . He then becomes more royalist than the king, more papist than the pope" (335).

Steffens mastered the labyrinth of alleyways and cafes on the Lower East Side so well, in fact, that on a visit to New York, the British playwright Israel Zangwill chose Steffens as his insider informant in that district (Steffens 244). Zangwill then returned to London and composed the now mythic drama of ethnic America, *The Melting Pot* (1908). In other words, perhaps the most resonant immigrant text of the period, whose title entered the American vernacular with terrific force, is a third-hand account from a gentile source. At the same time, well-known Anglo-Saxon novelists such as Henry Harland, Edward W. Townsend, and Ernest Poole were writing about immigrant groups with remarkable success. Poole wrote on the Italians and the Irish to such acclaim that he won the first Pulitzer Prize for fiction in 1918. In their audience's eyes, these authors were "in the know," explorers of ethnic terrains notoriously alien to their own kind.

Outsider penetrations into the unknown of this sort reveal the impact of "otherness" on the priorities and motivations of wandering outsiders like Steffens—a fact that sheds light upon the interstices between realism and modernism. The modernist philosopher and critic Alain Locke, an instrumental architect of the Harlem Renaissance, makes this connection in his essay "American Literary Tradition and the Negro" (1926). Locke believed that the realist movement proved a liberating force from the odious ethnic caricature of nineteenth- and early-twentieth-century melodrama; and he later argued in his 1933 essay "The Saving Grace of Realism" that the use of realism in future treatments of black America might put an end to the "propagandist," "exhibitionist" writings of modernist-era black authors and the "hectic faddist," "superficial," "commercialized" books of white writers on black subjects (221; see Wonham 4–6 for the complications that arise by accepting Locke's premise in toto).

Locke's retrospective from 1933, regardless of its cutting scrutiny of white authors on black subjects, still acknowledges the importance of understanding "that little known zone of interracial cultural collaboration between black and white intellectuals and artists which starting with the vogue of Negro art in New York is spreading gradually throughout all liberal culture centers of the nation" (223). But an emergent school of contemporary criticism has begun to argue that only negligible mutual faith could have been won at the turn of the twentieth century between ethnic and working-class insiders and the outsiders who represented them. By virtue of ethno-racial dominance, the argument goes, Anglo-Saxons enter relationships with traditionally underrepresented groups only to symbolically conquer and colonize them. Eric Schocket discusses these "discursive acts of imperialism" (127) in the context of socioeconomic class. Once the concept of "class" is replaced by "culture," he insists, the middle-classes effectively dissemble class struggle and deny "revolutionary visions of transcendence" (127). But the colonial aspects of slumming narratives are particularly salient in mainstream representations of ethnicity. As critic Berndt Ostendorf interprets it, "the literature of dominant groups about their ethnics is based on the deep myth of the 'voyage into the unknown,' the 'descent into the underworld,' 'going slumming,' and 'the search for the primitive.' . . . The lower folk ran into the melodrama, the upper strata melodramatized their emotions at the symbolic expense of the victims" (583–84). He targets Hutchins Hapgood, along with Carl Van Vechten and Jane Addams, as guilty parties in this incursion. On its face, this perspective has some merit, but it tends to ignore insider responses to their more genuine outsider co-workers in culture.

Both James Weldon Johnson and Langston Hughes publicly praised and privately collaborated on Carl Van Vechten's portrait of Harlem life, *Nigger Heaven* (1926), in the face of scathing criticism from fellow insider critics who probably did not read the book at all. Abraham Cahan, the Jewish American author, labor leader, socialist agitator, longtime editor of the *Jewish Daily Forward*, and subject of a full chapter in Hutchins Hapgood's *The Spirit of the Ghetto* (1902), might also disagree with Ostendorf's assertion that Hapgood, as a member of the "upper strata . . . melodramatized [his] emotions at the symbolic expense of the victims [Jews]" (584). Indeed, long after Hapgood published his study, Cahan praised him as "the only Gentile who knows and understands the spirit of the Ghetto" (qtd. in Rischin, Introduction xxviii); and in one of dozens of intimate letters to Hapgood, he wrote, "I have never had a chance to make a declaration of love to you, Hutch, but there are really very few people within my vast range of acquaintance whose company I so keenly enjoy" (February 1, 1918).

Hapgood's participant observation, what Chicago sociologist Robert Park called "taking on the role of the other" and Schocket has now termed "class transvestism" (though this designation specifies a certain level of "passing" in the vestments of the other, "cross-dressing" across class lines [119]), is unlikely to have stemmed from any inclination to convert Cahan and other Jewish "actors" into grotesque caricatures or inhibit their ability to achieve "revolutionary visions." The artist Jacob Epstein's darkly reverent illustrations in the book might alone preempt such readings. Hapgood's explicit purpose was to introduce New York's "respectable" society to the Jewish Lower East Side without the anti-Semitic lip service we find in Jacob Riis's *How the Other Half Lives*. Indeed, Jewish studies scholar Moses Rischin reflects that "geographically, Riis' 'Jewtown' and Hapgood's ghetto were identical worlds. Spiritually, however, they were worlds apart" (Introduction xxiv). Two years before Hapgood's death in 1944, this representative of the "upper strata," buried in debt and out of work, wrote a revealing plea to Cahan in the form of a personal letter left unsigned and unsent. He begged his old friend, now a major political force, to offer him a position in any activist Jewish organization during the Second World War. His dead letter reads, "You know as well as anybody what my past record has been in this respect, and what my state of mind is [toward the Jews]" (October 22, 1942).

Balancing the line between insideness and outsideness not only allowed writers admittance into their subjects' worlds, and thus the opportunity to more accurately render the "other" in a mainstream ethnographic discourse, but it also helped alleviate many of their audiences' fears while at the same time subversively revising conventional moral wisdom. It was a law enforcement officer, ironically enough, who entertained both the popular novelist John Vose and (according to Vose) Charles Dickens by leading them through the rat pits and gambling dens of lower Manhattan in the 1840s and '50s; urban activist Helen Campbell, a prep school graduate and home economics maven, lectured widely to students and philanthropists on the subject of waterfront prostitution; Stephen Crane, the son of two leading middle-class evangelists from New Jersey, acted as a Bowery guide for visiting luminaries in the 1890s; Hapgood, a Harvard graduate from Puritan New England stock, wrote the first book-length study of the Jewish Lower East Side based on several years of reporting in that district; and Carl Van Vechten, a gay white man from Cedar Rapids, Iowa, was a kind of freelance cabaret promoter to the white elite during the Harlem Renaissance of the 1920s. J. Gerald Kennedy has reflected on these seemingly contradictory notions of belonging in his remarkable study *Imagining Paris,* in which he maintains that "feelings of 'insideness' and 'outsideness' occur as more or less conscious responses to milieu; but we can also experience place as space which has penetrated to the level of the unconscious" (7). These penetrations into the unconscious reveal the effect of place on the priorities and motivations of wandering outsiders—for my purposes, literary slummers in New York City.

Cultural historian Vernon L. Parrington wrote at length about the sociological turn in American literature in his social history *Main Currents in American Thought* (1927). What Parrington calls the "school of sociological fiction" was on the rise at the turn of the twentieth century, and he contends that "such a development was in the nature of things": "The artist would not sit forever in his ivory tower, content to carve his statuettes while the country without was turmoiled with revolution. . . . It was in the nineties that the sociological novel expanded into a great movement that in the next decade and a half was to engulf pretty much all American fiction and bring it into service to the social conscience. . . . *It was the city that played havoc with our older fictional methods, as it played havoc with our traditional social philosophy.* . . . The change was no less than revolutionary (178, 179, 180, emphasis mine). Parrington attributes this watershed to a singular shift in both the realities of the new urban scene and in the art of fiction writing itself, a shift that "may be summarized in the word *background*" (180). Cultural backgrounds, along with distinctly American "types," take on a new significance from this period onward, as compared to "the older city of literature [that] had been a polite world wherein ladies and gentlemen drank tea and made love and talked proper scandal—a pleasant background of clubs and drawing-rooms, against which moved well-dressed figures" (179).

Thus, although Parrington only treats Victorian practitioners like Edith Wharton and Hjalmar Hjorth Boyesen, the sociological quality of both insider and outsider writing on the margins of urban space—the worlds which "rose to challenge the respectability of the romantic city" (179)—is impossible to ignore. The documentary realism I bring to bear often reflects the work of early twentieth-century social scientists who had a hand in wedding sociology and literature in the United States, early anthropologists and sociologists like Robert E. Park (Booker T. Washington's ghostwriter), Franz Boas (Zora Neale Hurston's mentor), and Charles Lummis (Sui Sin Far's most encouraging editor). Alluding to this merger of social theory and art, James Weldon Johnson's protagonist in *The Autobiography of an Ex-Colored Man* (1912) remarks of his adventures in the Tenderloin's "black Bohemia" of the 1890s that "more that I learned would be better suited as a book on social phenomenon than to a narrative of my life" (79); and his friend H. L. Mencken later assessed the novel as "not, at bottom, a novel at all, but a sort of mixture of actual biography and fantasy, with overtones of sociology" (320). This ethnographic mode demonstrably humanized the ethnic and working-class "other" in American fiction and belied mainstream typecasts by including straightforward documentary prose as a vehicle for disclosing the realities of urban life.

❖ ❖ ❖

Mid-nineteenth-century writing about New York's cultural landscape is often disjointed, confused, and frustratingly lacking in detail. But as the century moved forward, writers singled out marginal districts that Robert Park coined in 1925 "moral regions," definable areas that the larger society imagines are characterized by deviant social behavior. These areas, according to Park, attract "eccentric and exceptional people" who are bravely determined to "emancipate themselves from the dominant moral order" ("The City" 45, 43). Park's use of "morality" does not signify notions of right or wrong exactly. It is a term he applies to the "tastes and temperaments" of distinctly organic social milieus that are divorced from, though necessarily contingent upon, the "occupational interests or economic conditions" of the city (43). New York moral regions proliferated at a fantastic rate at the turn of the twentieth century, while at the same time becoming increasingly self-contained and foreign. Commercial regionalism as seen on the East Side waterfront and the Bowery in the 1880s and early '90s gave way to ethnic isolationism—the Tenderloin's "black Bohemia" in the 1890s, the Jewish Lower East Side from the 1890s to the 1910s, and Harlem in the 1920s. Soon enough, urban ghettoes wielded more influence on the regulators of decency than moral reformers ever had on them. There exists an "if you can't beat 'em, join 'em" sensibility in much urban realism, and therefore slumming narratives become a means of unifying, for better or worse, an otherwise fragmented urban environment.

Amy Kaplan argues that literary realism was often as not "a strategy for imagining and managing the threats of social change, not just to assert a dominant power but often to assuage fears of powerlessness" (8). Revising Frederic Jameson's "strategy of containment," the mainstream's deliberate isolation of a working-class culture in order to destroy it, Kaplan asserts that "by containing the threats of social change, realistic narratives also register those desires which undermine the closure of that containment" (10). As such, the forbidden nature of slumming in moral regions affords the practice a stinging potency and so has the potential to transform conventional morality: the more the moralizing middle-class American impulse condemns moral regions and their entertainments, the more rigorously curiosity seekers will explore them; the more socially abhorrent an illicit act, such as interracial sex, the more actively it will be pursued; the more a musical genre is criticized by the public—ragtime, blues, bebop, punk rock, gangsta rap—the more popular and often creative it will become; and so on. But only insiders are capable of giving voice to these advancements, and only marginalized districts, or moral regions, can transmit that voice.

So many bogus categories exist to call out threats to the establishment—race, ethnicity, sexual orientation, occupation, and so on, particularly in a trade city like New York—that the only (seemingly) reliable means by which insiders and outsiders are capable of defining themselves is to investigate who belongs in what moral region within the mosaic of the city as a whole. Paul Laurence Dunbar does not identify black characters in his Tenderloin novel *The Sport of the Gods* (1902) as "black" so much as they are rural southerners from tight-knit communities who are transformed utterly by life in the Tenderloin. As the range and depth of New York neighborhoods swelled, access to cultural difference became a vital feature of the modern sensibility. Outsiders and insiders are clearly distinguished by the length of their exposure to that district, and this perhaps typically New York stress on regional identity extends into our own day. In the mise en scène of recent-day

Manhattan, a long-time resident of Harlem, Chelsea, or Hell's Kitchen would be characterized as such within Manhattan's social taxonomy significantly more than as an African American, a homosexual, or an Irish Catholic.

By the 1920s, Park's "Chicago school" of sociologists announced that the urban environment was the ideal laboratory for studying the dynamics of social interaction, given the generally understood fact that moral regions do not thrive in rural America to any significant degree. Rural communities rely principally on "primary" sources of cultural knowledge—that is, face-to-face social relations that depend on the church, the family, and the school for guidance. In fact, social relations in New York itself were largely "primary" before the rise of immigration, mass marketing, and industrial capitalism. In the modern world, then, these relations become more "secondary," as individuals increasingly find their information in mass market books, newspapers, advertising, lectures, or simply by taking a walk.

In a 1925 interview with the *New York Herald Tribune*, Theodore Dreiser told the interviewer that New York "is the last refuge of the free, truthful man in America. Here the intelligent artist, the man who resents the rigorous regimenting of life going on elsewhere, can huddle into a group and express himself without regard to his neighbors or the Ku-Klux Klan or the corner banker. . . . [intellectuals in small towns] have no one to talk to; if they express ideas contrary to the ones prevailing in their community they are hunted down savagely" (Rusch and Pizer 99, 100). More recently, *New York Times* journalist and postmodern critic John Leland, in his prepossessing chronicle *Hip: The History* (2004), argues that the roots of postmodern "hip" music scenes like punk rock and gangsta rap pass through the early twentieth-century American city: "Because urban populations [at the time] were [already] new and often transient, they enjoyed a protective anonymity; unlike small towns, nobody could tell your parents or spouse or clergyman if you were acting up. Cities' disorder also provided cover for marginal or radical ideas. You could cultivate your iconoclasm and expect to meet other iconoclasts more freely than in provinces. Density was everything: a book or play that shocked mainstream sensibilities could find a constituency in a city, spark debate and beget even more radical works; in a small town it would just be weird" (63).

Characters who migrate to cities from the ordered communities of the countryside experience powerful mental transformations in urban fiction, what Blanche Gelfant in her groundbreaking study *The American City Novel* calls "personal dissociation." Referencing characters from Dreiser's *Sister Carrie* (1900), John Dos Passos's *Manhattan Transfer* (1925), James T. Farrell's

Studs Lonigan trilogy (1932, 1934, 1935), and Nelson Algren's *The Man with the Golden Arm* (1955), Gelfant identifies "personal dissociation" as an ever-present motif in urban literature, describing a symptom where, wrenched from the solid foundations of a localized community, the alienated individual becomes morally and emotionally unbalanced (21–24). A former professor of mine, Jesse Battan, once related a "first day in New York" anecdote to our "Culture and Emotion" graduate seminar: Within an hour of arriving in the city, Jesse, a studious young greenhorn from the Midwest, spotted a woman in her late forties jumping up and down on the hood of a taxi cab. Kicking the windshield and screaming obscenities at the man behind the wheel, the woman had gone berserk, ranting that the driver had almost run her over as she crossed the street. Such a scene would be less plausible in a community where the two actors car-pooled their children, had attended the same high school, or were otherwise acquainted on a first- or even last-name basis. But since we can sustain relative anonymity in a big city, accountability for our actions is substantially undermined.

What might be interpreted as ghetto resourcefulness today was often mistaken for the kind of louche behavior or "personal dissociation" Gelfant considers central to urban narratives. Thanks to John Kasson, Karen Halt-tunen, Richard Butsch, and others, we know that outsider observers before the purview of Gelfant's study (the first half of the twentieth century) relied on "morals and manners" to understand group identity at a time when urban psychology was nebulously understood. Progressive reformers in the 1890s, for example, saw the aptitude of eastern European Jews to successfully challenge Broadway's garment industry as demonstrable proof of the unruly influences brought in by non-Anglo-Saxon immigrants. Ghetto reporters like Jacob Riis regarded aggressive business practices on the Lower East Side as an ill-mannered means by which the Jews took advantage of vulnerable market conditions. Though pre-Progressive era free-market dogma encouraged such practices among Anglo-Saxons, in the case of the Jews it was admonished as an unacceptable abuse of the entrepreneurial spirit.

Reformers also accused Irish Catholics of agitating an unsettling brand of political fanaticism in an already tenuous democratic state. Not only were the Irish a clear threat to the cities, but the slums had begun hemorrhaging them into the countryside as well. Helen Campbell, whose complex perspective on immigration and New York's East Side waterfront district will be the subject of my first chapter, professed in her exposé *The Problem of the Poor* that Irish immigrants "form a larger portion" of her titular problem, whereas "German or French paupers [are] almost an anomaly." She upholds the prevailing

Protestant American view that once in the United States, Irish Catholics as a group abandoned any redeeming qualities they may have had in the Old World: "They are a class apart, retaining all the most brutal characteristics of the Irish peasant at home, but without the redeeming lightheartedness, the tender impulses and strong affections of that most perplexing people. Sullen, malicious, conscienceless, with no capacity for enjoyment save in drink and the lowest forms of debauchery, they are filling our prisons and reformatories, marching in an ever-increasing army through the quiet country, and making a reign of terror wherever their footsteps are heard" (215). Similarly, William Dean Howells observed that Italians, once they arrived in Greenwich Village from their homeland, transform "from the friendly folk they are at home to the surly race they mostly show themselves here" ("New York Streets" 279). More often than not, reformers of this period presented ethnic transplants as moral deviants in this way, whether they were discussing politics, economics, race, or sexuality. Authors like Riis, Campbell, and, though far more evenhandedly, Howells, represent a largely reactionary response to urban identity, one ripe for attack by modernist social critics in the decades that followed.

But literary realists slumming at the turn of the twentieth century were the forerunners of the post–World War I moderns, already probing what June Howard calls the "crucial difference between omniscience and omnipotence" (x). It was one thing to investigate life on the margins, and even to write about it, but if there was to be any change in moral perspective, it was the privileged spectators even more than the objectified "other" that now did the changing. Howard elaborates on this notion, professing that

> the author and reader and the characters who represent them inhabit a privileged location . . . assuming a kind of control over forces and events through their power to comprehend them. Yet the privilege of the spectator, constructed by contrast, is necessarily vulnerable; fear and desire—sexual passion and violence, the fatal spell of the commodity, the fascination of the Other—constantly disrupt the design of safety. To venture any dealings with the powers that inhabit causality proves hazardous; *characters who go slumming in the realm of determinism risk their freedom and expose themselves to the dangers of paralysis and proletarianization.* (x, emphasis mine)

Paul Laurence Dunbar and William Dean Howells are two examples of realists who consciously rendered the impact of New York's neighborhoods on outsider sensibilities—Dunbar demonstrating "paralysis," Howells "proletarianization." Dunbar sardonically warns in his naturalistic novel *The*

Sport of the Gods (1902) that after a short time in New York, outsiders unaccustomed to the city become intoxicated by "the subtle, insidious wine of
New York." Singling out the Bowery, Broadway, and Central Park, Dunbar
entreats the wise traveler to avoid such temptations; they might even consider
going "over to Jersey" (71). In contrast, Howells welcomes the new aesthetic
offered by working-class street life, such as that which his character Basil
March in *A Hazard of New Fortunes* (1890) observes from the window of a
Third Avenue elevated train—the "shapeless, graceless, reckless picturesque-
ness of the Bowery" (159). Later, in his essay "An East Side Ramble" (1896),
Howells similarly professed that "I believe a single week's sojourn [on the
Lower East Side] . . . would make anarchists of the best people of the city"
(139). And in a meditation on his Bowery theater experience in 1904, Henry
James too expressed this preoccupation among Anglo-Saxon New Yorkers,
that they may fall into the hands of what was generally known as "'damned
foreign impudence'" (148). During the show, James observed Yankee symbols
emanating down from the stage into the minds of the "exotic" immigrant
audience of Jews, Galicians, Moldovans, and so on: "The sense of the business
[resides] in our ineradicable Anglo-Saxon policy, or our seemingly deep-
seated necessity, of keeping, where 'representation' is concerned, *so far away
from the truth and the facts of life as really to betray a fear in us of possibly doing something like them should we be caught nearer*" (148, emphasis mine; on
James's "pragmatic pluralism," that "perpetually provisional," or marginal,
authorial position—lying as it does, somewhere between "revulsion" and
"subterranean identification"—see Posnock 229 and Wonham 108–9).

Outsiders habitually enter urban neighborhoods that are not only and
not always impoverished but, in some ways more importantly, considered
morally depraved by society at large. Realist outsiders knew this, that the
appeal of vicarious reports from inside unknown spaces was not exclusive
to squalid conditions downtown. Considering the relationship between morality and space, "respectable" middle-class citizens in a Fifth Avenue salon
were slumming among the "other" as surely as if they were loitering in a
tenement stairwell on the Lower East Side. William Dean Howells's fictional
editor Basil March from *A Hazard of New Fortunes*, for instance, ascertains
that his subscribers are equally scandalized and intrigued by a millionaire's
folly as they are by the goings on in a downtown brothel. As the editor of
a struggling New York magazine, Basil is thinking outside the box when
he remarks to a colleague, "true . . . those phases of low life are immensely
picturesque. Of course we must try to get the contrasts of luxury for the
sake of the full effect. That won't be so easy. You can't penetrate the dinner

party of a millionaire under the wing of a detective as you could to carouse in Mulberry Street, or to his children's nursery with a philanthropist as you can to a street boys' lodging house" (129).

Stephen Crane also notes that slumming occurs among the very rich as well as the very poor, contrasting the two respectively in his 1894 sketches "An Experiment in Misery" and "An Experiment in Luxury." In the original version of "An Experiment in Misery," first published as a feature story for the *New York Press*, a young journalist's confidante inquires whether through his experience in lower Manhattan slumming among the homeless he discovered any idiosyncratic "point of view." "I don't know that I did," the autobiographical journalist rejoins, "but at any rate I think mine own has undergone a considerable alteration" (164). In "An Experiment in Luxury," a sketch that in his first sentence he labels a "social study," Crane smartly deconstructs the traditional middle-class American assumption that "each wealthy man was a miserable wretch" (556). The youth attends a dinner at his well-to-do friend's extravagant townhouse on Fifth Avenue, where it soon becomes clear that what he had been taught about the rich—essentially the Dickensian Scrooge model—was misleading. What he found instead was a surprisingly well-adjusted nuclear family (aside from the mother, perhaps, whose "terrible pride" stonewalls any meaningful happiness). As in "Experiment in Misery," the narrator experiences a cultural conversion: "There were influences, knowledges that made him aware that he was idle and foolish in his new state, but he inwardly reveled like a barbarian in his environment. It was delicious to feel so high and mighty. . . . For a time, at any rate, there was no impossible" (553).

I propose that such work invites us to challenge popular morality irrespective of which social strata is under the microscope. James Weldon Johnson's vagabond narrator in *The Autobiography of an Ex-Colored Man* is unmistakably slumming when he plays ragtime piano at cocktail parties on Fifth Avenue, Carl Van Vechten's enamored Harlemites Mary Love and Byron Kasson in *Nigger Heaven* first meet at an upscale Long Island resort, and Claude McKay's Pullman porter Jake in *Home to Harlem* (1928) finds his way into elitist Midtown nightclubs, not to mention the sizable array of modernist slumming sequences involving conspicuous consumption in the 1920s and '30s that will not be covered in this study, most famously Jay Gatsby's ritzy affairs in West Egg. As such, the neighborhoods I explore in the chapters that follow do span the socioeconomic scale, though most are situated in working-class neighborhoods or ethnic ghettoes.

❖ ❖ ❖

This book samples a range of New York slumming narratives, narratives attempting to describe marginalized neighborhoods and the insiders who inhabited them, to help clarify the perplexing relationship between New York writing and the city's cultural environment. Taken from the post-Reconstruction era to the Great Depression, these narratives are squarely placed in the context of other forms of cultural production, including plays, poetry, folklore, music, and moral reform tracts. Questions will surely arise about the connections among such incongruent genres. But I argue that the symbolic act of outsiders slumming in New York City has produced a large and infinitely telling body of literature that speaks to parallel literary and thematic concerns: the tenet of class, race, and gender inclusiveness according to the prescriptions of founding literary realists like Balzac, Zola, Garland, and Howells; individual relationships to social space; an evolving sense of cultural difference; an ambiguous take on the rewards of cosmopolitan heterogeneity; an almost spiritual connection to the pathos of the "real"; and an innovative literary perspective that makes the urban neighborhood the most roundly developed character of all.

City writing involves ordering and reordering the chaotic pace of everyday living, and the same is true for the process of nurturing and adapting to a city's growth. Realist slumming narratives from the 1880s to the Great Depression helped alleviate urban divisiveness by gradually foregrounding insider voices from marginalized New York neighborhoods. Whether liberal or conservative, paranoid or complacent, subversive or complicit, one striking trait that each writer I cover shares is a profound respect for the impact New York City had on their lives and on the lives of their subjects. More importantly, they had the courage (and naiveté) to attempt both textually and socially to order and reorder this fragmented, perilously alluring place. The guiding question of this study, then, is the extent to which the "penetrations" of cultural consciousness that inevitably follow slumming expeditions are realized consciously and unconsciously in both the New York outsider narratives they produced and the moral landscape of New York City as a whole.

My chronology takes into consideration the years in which these narratives take place more than their dates of publication, a crucial method for studying the historical and ethnographic nature of urban writing. Some scholars, for example, mistakenly read James Weldon Johnson's Tenderloin

novel *The Autobiography of an Ex-Colored Man* as taking place in Harlem,
though Harlem was a German and Irish neighborhood in the 1890s, the decade in which the novel is set. *Slumming in New York* also treats a spectrum
of canonical and noncanonical New York authors, including shining stars
like Stephen Crane, James Weldon Johnson, Abraham Cahan, Claude McKay,
and Paul Laurence Dunbar, lesser lights like Carl Van Vechten, Ernest Poole,
and Hutchins Hapgood, and authors who have fallen into total obscurity like
Helen Campbell, whose book *The Problem of the Poor* I am uncovering for
the first time since it fell out of print in 1882. I also explore texts that have
been largely overlooked by writers whose reputations are otherwise firmly
entrenched, like Stephen Crane's unduly forgotten Bowery novel *George's
Mother* (1896). Some authors are introduced with more biographical detail
than others, depending on their degree of obscurity and the importance of
their backgrounds to the texts in question. And by expanding the traditional
periodicity of the realist movement, I am free to compare working-class Irish,
Jewish, African American, and other ethnic voices from eras as seemingly
distinct as the antebellum period and the Harlem Renaissance. In the epilogue,
we will see the extent to which these investigations are related to the recent
boom in Old New York studies, and how the twentieth-century legitimacy of
the insider voice drove outsider authors back in time where they "belong."

1 "Under the Bridge and Beyond"

HELEN CAMPBELL, JERRY MCAULEY, AND ERNEST POOLE ON THE EAST SIDE WATERFRONT

> I did not know how deeply I had felt the nobility and harmony of the great European cities till our steamer was docked in New York. . . . I remember once asking an old New Yorker why he never went abroad, and his answering: "Because I can't bear to cross Murray Street." It was indeed an unsavoury experience, and the shameless squalor of the purlieus of the New York docks in the 'seventies dismayed my childish eyes . . .
>
> —Edith Wharton, 1933

> If Jesus were here I could quite imagine him walking the streets of New York by day and by night going down into subcellars and climbing rickety stairs into high attics, making his way into dens of iniquity and reaching down into the depths to save the lost.
>
> —J. Wilbur Chapman, 1906

MANHATTAN'S MAJOR WATERFRONT AREA in the late nineteenth century was located in the Fourth Ward, a district that formed an apron around the Manhattan side of the Brooklyn Bridge. In 1885, the Fourth Ward contained thirty acres of tenements that housed around seventeen thousand people. The area had been awash with cheap groceries, rat pits, and stale-beer dives for years, and due to the growing population of transient sailors, prostitute traffic thickened exponentially; at this time in New York history, the Fourth Ward was, as historian Timothy J. Gilfoyle describes it, "the most significant and the poorest waterfront zone of prostitution" (218). But the waterfront was also the centerpiece of an international trade city, signifying plurality and opacity. The vortex of sailors and longshoremen from all parts of the globe swelling into and out of the shops and bars along the East River was in continuous motion. Significantly, the district appealed to no one ethnicity, class, race, or gender. Ethnically cohesive neighborhoods, or "ghettoes," would only emerge when jobs and industries became associated with specific ethnic groups—garments for the Jewish, cigars for the Bohemians, and so on. But through the 1870s and '80s, the East Side waterfront region of New York, though perhaps mainly Irish, was still composed of workers and unemployed groups that largely allied themselves with trade and the lifestyle of the wharves rather than with any particular language, religion, or national origin.

Class divided Manhattan more than anything else through the postbellum period, and wealthy neighborhoods formed a corridor down the middle of the island while the poorest neighborhoods straddled the river banks. Luc Sante astutely remarks in his *Low Life: Lures and Snares of Old New York* that "Fifth Avenue was, after all, the farthest one could get from either river" (50); William Dean Howells affirms the deliberateness of the avenue's location in his cartographic essay "New York Streets" (1896), where he contrasts the center of the island with its margins along the rivers: "It is Fifth Avenue which divides the city length-wise nearest the middle, and it is this avenue which affords the norm of style and comfort to the other avenues on either hand. . . . on the east, they lose their genteel character; their dwellings degenerate into apartment-houses, and then into tenement houses of lower and lower grade till the rude traffic and the offensive industries of the river shores are reached" (248, 249).

But rather than emphasizing class distinctions, middle-class reformers maintained through the 1880s that the slum was an inevitable symptom of deviant lifestyles as opposed to group identity or even collective class consciousness. Social historian David Ward reports that "popular indictments emphasized moral and personal relationships rather than structural and social conditions" (48). The underprivileged, therefore, became predominantly associated with both geographic space and individual interactions within that space. One all-night missionary on Baxter Street vividly renders the culturally diverse nature of the waterfront population in this way: "The audience was gathered from neighboring alleys, narrow streets, saloons, dance-halls, and dives. Jews, Gentiles, olive-skinned Italians, and almond-eyed Chinamen, sat side by side. Sailors were in the majority. Dissolute women, both white and black, and a few loafers. . . . A scattering of beggars and tramps sought refuge from the wintry blast. Several boys and girls, attracted by the singing, helped to fill the room" (Campbell, *Darkness* 194).

Reinforcing this image during a walk along the waterfront, moral reformer Helen Campbell, the subject of the following two sections, discovers "one of the most curious features of night life in New York,—the sidewalk restaurants." In these odd venues, "no one is turned away, and sailors, negro longshoremen, marketmen, and stray women, come and go, and fare alike" (*Darkness* 215). If New York was the quintessential American trade city, with all of its side streets and subcultures, the waterfront was at its pitiless core the ideal location for proving the effectiveness of immersing oneself in the climate of poverty and moral laxity—comprehend it and the remainder of the city would be an open book.

New York writing after the Civil War reflected the growing popularity of the social sciences over Protestant evangelicalism to address the issue of New York's increasingly identifiable and morally problematic "lower" districts. The corollary in literary history is the transition from sentimentalism to realism, from a preoccupation with plot-driven pathos to social concerns, material referents, deterministic scientific theories, and unheroic character play. Sentimental and sensational modes of representing New York life spliced with the social sciences during America's Gilded Age into a new mode that might be called "moral realism," a fusion of the romantic and the pragmatic practiced by such reform writers as Charles Loring Brace, Helen Campbell, and Jacob Riis, a group whose explicit aim was nothing less than to change the face of urban America. What comes into focus in the 1880s and '90s is the conviction that moral systems are inherent to specific regions, that in order for mainstream outsiders to overcome the problem of urban representation in their documentary-style writing, they must adopt new methods of investigation and engage the "lower million" more objectively on their own ground, in the streets, missions, and tenements of New York neighborhoods that had thrived and developed mythologies and mysteries of their own.

Brace, Campbell, and Riis intermingled Protestant gospel with sociology, stark melodrama with appalling statistics, romantic characterization with interviews, and caricatured settings with specific sites of inquiry—urban neighborhoods that outsider audiences were encouraged to explore for themselves. Poverty then became a provable, tangible lifestyle that had deeply rooted and seemingly irreversible effects. Like the sentimental or sensational text, characters in the new mode were rewarded for choosing the right moral path after experiencing a series of temptations, but the stories were "real" and the characters could be literally sought out at a neighborhood mission or downtown saloon. Moral realists condemned "low class" neighborhood cultures in favor of cultural assimilation. But rather than passively observing their subjects, they immersed themselves in the society of each site by exercising an inductive process of investigative journalism.

Although outsider texts like Campbell's *The Problem of the Poor* (1882) and Riis's *How the Other Half Lives* (1890) reflect an altruistic middle-class concern for the inhabitants of lower Manhattan, New York society and its urban investigators still retained their "moral interpretations of poverty" (Ward 43). A process of polarization was at work, regarded as both necessary and repugnant by uptown New Yorkers. This division was precipitated by increasingly isolated job sites, inadequate housing, and neighborhood displacement, and reformers mobilized to manage the crisis. The slums both emerged and were transformed from the 1850s to the Civil War, and by the late 1880s, the distinctive qualities of many neighborhoods that had been singled-out by moral suasion efforts were effectively incapacitated. If Paula Rabinowitz theorizes that "slumming" in the 1930s was "more likely the regulation of working people's desires than the expression of middle-class pleasures," a practice manifested in "ritual encounters between those whose lives were privileged to observe, regulate, and detail the behaviors of others" (188), the 1870s and '80s were, in fact, the heyday of slumming as social regulation. By 1895, to give one high-profile example, the notorious Five Points area had been, as Helen Campbell recalled, "long ago reduced to order and decency by forces working for good" (51).

"Only a Zola": Helen Campbell and the New Method of Immersion

Helen Campbell was born Helen Campbell Stuart on the fourth of July, 1839. Her father, Homer Stuart, was a New York lawyer for fifty years running and served for a time as the president of the Continental Bank Note Company. Stuart insisted his daughter receive the finest education available to a young girl in mid-century America, so she dutifully attended both New York public schools and two elite private institutions for girls, the Gammell School in Rhode Island and Mrs. Cook's Seminary in New Jersey. She was married in 1862 to Grenville Mellen Weeks, a surgeon who served aboard the U.S. ironclad *Monitor* during the Civil War (an experience that may have effected their divorce in 1871). Starting in the first years of her marriage, Campbell began publishing children's stories, a few popular novels, short stories in *Lippencott's, New England Magazine,* and *Harper's,* and one home economics textbook, *The Easiest Way in House-Keeping and Cooking* (1881).

Her reputation as a writer, however, would culminate in a series of outsider studies on the economic polarization and moral distinctiveness of the urban poor: *The Problem of the Poor: A Record of Quiet Work in Unquiet Places* (1882), *Prisoners of Poverty: Women Wage-Workers, Their Trades and Their Lives* (1887), and a sizable contribution to the co-authored exposé, *Darkness and Daylight, or, Lights and Shadows of New York Life* (1895).[1] Campbell attracted the attention of many literary and political luminaries over her lifetime, including the renowned feminist and realist fiction writer Charlotte Perkins Gilman, who shared living quarters with her for a number of years in California and New York City, respectively. A realist in form if not always in spirit, Campbell directly compared herself to the radical French journalist and fiction writer Emile Zola, well before Frank Norris, whose impact on American realism (more specifically, naturalism) was prodigious, and she collected the bulk of her data for her books firsthand.

As a reform writer, Campbell tangled with and fell victim to the central paradox of the urban industrial environment—the disjunction between social unification and individual agency. "Society has no right to absorb the individual," Campbell asseverates in her waterfront exposé *The Problem of the Poor*, "any more than the individual has a right to be absorbed or supported. His right is to his own personality and its best means of development, and all we can ask of society is that those means be made easier of attainment" (113–14). But the "means of attainment" Campbell discovers to promote the characters of disaffected New Yorkers involved incorporation and assimilation, what Campbell called "absorption." Rather than allowing New York neighborhoods to crystallize into distinct and isolated sites, she was determined to co-opt them into a unified moral fold. By writing about the East Side waterfront district of the 1880s, Campbell attempted to reconstitute the area into her outsider society's image, regardless of some misgivings she may have had concerning that society: "They [the poorer classes] are with us. The burden is ours and cannot be cast aside. It remains with us to train them into decent members of society, or to fold our hands and let the crowd of imbeciles and drunkards and criminals and lunatics increase years by years, till suddenly some frightful social convulsion opens the eyes that have refused to see, and disaster brings about what moderate effort could long before have accomplished" (244). The mingling sentiments of repulsion and concern created a contradiction in the consciousness of New York's middle class. The "frightful social convulsion" could manifest itself in many forms—a socialist state, a nation of drunkards—and unless concrete, pragmatic actions were taken, "decent members of society" would be corrupted beyond repair.

A precursor to the more celebrated "slum journalist" Jacob Riis, Helen

Campbell, again, balances on the threshold between sentimentalism and realism in American literary history. On the one hand, she is a persistent Protestant moralizer, and her parabolic tales of lower-class woe come straight from the altruistic preacher Lyman Abbott's pulpit. On the other, she is a part of the growing literary realist movement in the United States, one dedicated to rendering the lower classes in a humanistic light. In Campbell, prostitutes can be tough-willed fighters in a terrifying urban environment rather than "scarlet whores of Babylon," convicts can be reformers not lost souls, and immigrants can be nonparochial. In some ways, like her contemporary William Dean Howells, Campbell "defected" from her middle-class foundation as a result of "dissatisfaction with reigning genteel conventions" (Burrows and Wallace 1179), and she did so by adopting insider voices for outsider consumption.

From the outset of her investigations, Campbell grapples with ideological dilemmas: "One *ism* after another presented itself, seeming at first to meet the demand for truth; then paling and fading away under the light of investigation. Church people were stupidly intolerant; Radicals equally so. Where I had belonged had long been a mystery to myself" (7). But this admission, set down in the introduction to *The Problem of the Poor,* does not prevent her from adopting the most familiar discursive mode to her own milieu—the gospel of the Protestant church. Hers is a moral realism that widens the parameters of the middle-class discourse of the slums, but maintains its inherent premise that the lower classes must adopt cultural codes from above in order to actuate salvation.

While writing *Prisoners of Poverty,* four years after *The Problem of the Poor,* Campbell consciously attempted to strip her writing of sentimental rhetoric. She insists that "the one aim in the investigation has been and is to tell the truth simply, directly, and in full, leaving it for the reader to determine what share is his or hers in the evil or in the good that the methods of to-day may hold" (10). Recognizing the growing taste for realistic literary expression, she foregrounds interviews and mimetic detail and deliberately tones down the romantic portrayals of insider heroism on which *The Problem of the Poor* depends. At the same time, she eschews strict "scientific philanthropy," which had become an increasingly popular mode for outsider investigators in the 1880s (Burrows and Wallace 1176). Instead, she humbly affiliates herself with continental European naturalism, just then drawing the rapt attention of the American literati: "Only a Zola could describe deliberately what any eye may see, but any minute detail of which would excite an outburst of popular indignation. Yet I am by no means certain that such detail has not far more right to space than much that fills our morning papers, and that the bald statement of facts, shorn of all flights of fancy or play of facetiousness, might not rouse the public to some sense of what lies below the surface of this fair-seeming civilization of to-day" (129). Though divergent modes of expression, Emile Zola's literary naturalism and Campbell's moral realism follow contiguous trends in their stylistic concerns and subjective conclusions. "Flights of fancy" are being replaced in nineteenth-century American literature by "bald statement[s] of facts" while at the same time, as Frank Norris noted of Zola, maintaining a "vague note of terror" that smacks of romanticism (1107). Her nod to Zola may refer to his journalism, not his fiction, but many of the urban journalist's concerns were shared by writers of urban fiction as well. Campbell understood the need for artists of any stripe to accommodate the tastes of the age.

Like many privileged women of the period, Campbell discovered that the only means by which to "reverse or to modify the effects of the polarization of urban society" was through "friendly contact" (Ward 57) or "friendly visiting." Setting down the historical context of women's philanthropic novels of the 1870s, Deborah Carlin argues that "perhaps the most important and influential venture female philanthropists undertook was that of 'friendly visiting' in the slums and tenements" (208). "Friendly visiting" was a popular activity among frustrated, dynamic women tired of the subjugations the codes of domestic respectability imposed. It was a means to head off impending ennui, and at the same time an attempt to generate some spiritual uplift in an increasingly cynical urban environment. David Ward writes of this phenomenon that "the search for community was ultimately a search for order. . . . efforts to distinguish the poor on the basis of their deviancy were intended to bring the rich and the poor into friendly contact in order to reverse or modify the effects of the polarization of urban society" (57).

Campbell's work mostly presents the waterfront district along the East River, the notorious Fourth Ward, as harboring a well-established culture that agitates the moral order of Victorian New York. Her writing is both a call for responsible citizens to immerse themselves in the society of New York's lowest socioeconomic ranks and, paradoxically, a vicarious means for them to do so without dirtying their hands. She believed, however, that for the active reformer to enact any meaningful social response, one or two cursory visits to those problem areas with "smoldering elements" is insufficient. *The Problem of the Poor* in particular is a collection of galling statistics and depraved scenes designed to shock a concerned but complacent middle-class audience out of their fireside wing chairs and onto the streets of lower Manhattan. Throughout the 1880s, Campbell assiduously collected provocative material in New York's opprobrious East Side waterfront district, and an overview of the waterfront's spatial and moral distinction appears in her 1895 sketch, "A Region of Vice and Crime":

> Side by side with warehouse and factory are dens given over to all abomina-
> tions. Here are sailors' boarding houses, where poor Jack [a typical seaman]
> is fleeced and turned loose to ship again and earn painfully the wages that
> he will return to use in the same fashion. Stale-beer dives are in every other
> basement; and from shaking old houses—once the home of old New Yorkers
> who knew this as fashionable and aristocratic ground—come the jingle of
> cracked pianos and the twanging of cheap fiddles. Women hideously painted
> and bedizened are here, their faces bearing an imprint of vice unspeakable;
> and here also children swarm at every point, *drinking in the influence of all
> phases of a life which even to look upon for a fleeting moment carries pollution
> with it. (Darkness 51, emphasis mine)

The transformation of this previously "fashionable and aristocratic ground" is one of apocalyptic proportions. Urban growth had effectively transformed the stylish homes and churches of Old New York and replaced them with sailors' boarding houses, brothels, and stale-beer dives. The waterfront's polluting agency is not solely restricted to its inhabitants, but affects New Yorkers from all walks of life: "Often respectable men and women out of work drift into the neighborhood, falling always a little lower and lower" (*Darkness* 108).

Campbell describes the outer limits of the Water Street district in a way a New Yorker might characterize the same neighborhood today—the weekdays overrun by financiers, the weekends deserted (although this is beginning to change as the Manhattan real estate market continues to swell): "On week-days the whirl of business life; the hurrying masses of preoccupied men . . . indicate only the American devotion to its god, the dollar. And on Sunday the utter absence of all ordinary sights and sounds; the deserted streets and warehouses, would seem to evidence the most careful keeping of the fourth commandment" (40). But then, Campbell the outsider crosses the line into the Fourth Ward, and the atmosphere dramatically transforms: "Only as Peck Slip is passed does a suggestion of what is to come suddenly dawn upon one, as the whole character suddenly changes, and the sound of music from a sailors' boarding house is heard. . . . With Dover street and the great pier of the East River bridge ends the dominion of trade in its higher forms and a new trade, old as the foundations of the world—the trade in men's souls—takes place" (40–41).

The boarding-house sailor in Campbell is the antithesis of the cult of domesticity and respectability. He is, after all, transient, homeless, and often unmarried. Sailors' boarding houses were located at the center of waterfront life, and there was nothing, or more exactly no one, to prevent the lodgers from spending long hours and large paychecks during their time ashore. The waterfront boarding house is the sailor's only permanent residence, hardly a respectable venue for moral guidance. But "Jack's life" (slang for maritime culture) would be less likely to arouse middle-class anxieties if it wasn't contagious: "Women crowded here, sitting in rows on benches, or out on the sidewalk, waiting the return of sailors, for those were the noted 'sailors' boarding houses' and for blocks around, far up Cherry street to the police station-house, and out into a region of dark alleys festering with filth, and narrow streets alive with masses of people, *spread the influence of these foul lives*" (10, emphasis mine).

If prostitution was a viable alternative to starvation wages for work-ing-class women, and it subsequently engendered a popular association of waterfront women as "scarlet whores of Babylon," for men, the symbolic occupation that bonded their identities to the Fourth Ward, the cultural and economic mainstay of the district, was the maritime industry. Heroism and dissolution meshed in the picaresque figure of the sailor, and these attributes influenced a great many waterfront youths to follow suit. "In spite . . . of all knowledge to the contrary," Campbell finds, "nothing convinces the average boy that Jack's life is anything but a series of marvelous adventures in which he is generally the victor, and where the hardship is much more than made up for by the excitement and glory" (*Darkness* 434).

The push and pull of cultural counteractions are most starkly embedded in a child's fecund imagination. Campbell posits children, like her better-known predecessor Charles Loring Brace, as a group particularly susceptible to the allure of the adventuresome, free-wheeling maritime lifestyle. One case involves a teenage boy whose lifetime goal was to become a physician. In his formative years, a high-minded urge to "make everybody well" (436) compelled him to volunteer at a hospital, where he "followed the daily round of hospital physicians and surgeons with unflagging interest" (436). One day, he visited an elderly sailor, a "bronzed, wrinkled weather-beaten wreck" (436), who had just survived a near-death experience on his last voyage. The youth was captivated:

"Tell me about it, please," the boy said. "Tell me every word of it," and the
old sailor began.

"More, more," the boy urged at any stop,—his shining eyes intently fixed
on the old Sinbad's face. "I want to know everything about it."

"You can't unless you tries it yourself," said Jack at last. "An' I wouldn't
say as anybody'd better do that." (436)

But the lad persists, and the sailor's warnings give way to boastful enthusiasm:
"'That's the right kind of boy! . . . I shall [disembark] as soon as this thing is
knit an' I'm set up enough to pass muster. You come along too, an' I'll make
a sailor out o' you fit to command anything as floats" (437). The impressionable youth subsequently rejects his vocation for medicine, and "to-day he is
captain of a great ship and happiest when in mid-ocean" (437). Campbell
warns her readers against succumbing to such capriciousness: "Something
like this is the story of thousands who are drawn from remotest distances,
and who answer the call once for all. Yet there is no life among workers that
holds more certain hardship and privation, or often more utter brutality of
treatment" (438). Campbell posits the clash between middle-class domesticity and the transient maritime lifestyle as a discouraging hindrance to the
moral reform effort on the waterfront. "Jack's life" is tough competition for
outsiders born into the claustrophobic security of middle-class domesticity,
as well as for a boy raised as a waterfront insider in the cramped quarters
of the tenements.

Campbell illustrates a typical sailor's outlook as he disembarks in New
York in this way: "Jack's heart warmed as he saw the familiar names over the
doors on South and Water Street: 'The Flowing Sea,' 'The Mariner's Home,'
and the like. In these dens, where foul women waited and the bar offered
every temptation, Jack found a home such as it was till he shipped again"
(440). In his early study of urban communities *Metropolis* (1938), Howard
Woolston depicts the East Side waterfront in another way: "Sailors and fisherman, dock laborers and ship builders, chandlers, commission men and
agents make their homes there. These people, together with their families
and neighbors, have an interest, not merely in the business of shipping, but
also in the pleasure of living" (205). Campbell, in contrast, provides few af-
firmative insider utterances from the waterfront; though in one, a crusty old
salt does respond, if mulishly, to a chaplain lecturing him on reform: "Oh,
don't talk about them things to me! I've been without 'em sixty year, an' I
reckon I kin stan' it for a year or two longer" (*Darkness* 449). This is but one
short burst of contentment from an otherwise muffled insider voice.

Earlier on, in the 1860s and '70s, middle-class New Yorkers became exasperated by the lowering moral standards on the waterfront, and expectations for reform there were high. Always responsive to popular demand, moral reformers soon poured into the area; but they abruptly found themselves ill-equipped to restrain the denizens of Water and Cherry Streets and eventually resorted to acting out ridiculous publicity stunts to keep up appearances. The *New York Times*, for instance, broke an incriminating story about one group of Protestant reformers led by the Reverend A. C. Arnold. The missionaries, as it turned out, had been bribing dive-bar owners, rat-pit proprietors, and gang members to act as if they had been "saved" by the area's Howard Street Mission, at that time running prayer meetings in the worst dens. One businessman caustically referred to the carnival as "sheer humbug," and the notorious rat-pit proprietor Kit Burns laughed openly after finding out that a local saloon and brothel owner named John Allen was hosting evangelical prayer meetings: "I've known Johnny Allen fourteen years and he couldn't be a pious man if he tried ever so hard. You might as well ask a rat to sing like a canary bird as to make a Christian out of that chap" (qtd. in Bonner 32).

Nevertheless, Allen's initial involvement in this otherwise spurious reform effort appears to have been uncharacteristically genuine. But after a few weeks he found the clergy's evangelical rhetoric offensive. In a public statement on their treatment of prostitutes, he fumed, "I have not lived among them for seventeen years without learning something about them. Some of them have many virtues. They have feelings also, feelings which those missionaries should have respected but did not. . . . One preacher cried, 'Oh, God, we thank thee that these scarlet whores of Babylon have come to seek salvation.' Another pointed them out and exclaimed: 'Behold the harlots whom we are going to take to Jesus'" (qtd. in Bonner 33). Arnold's missionary activity was a desperate fraud, and Luc Sante reports that "the actual congregants at the saloon services were almost uniformly businessmen from other parts of town, and even these were less steadfast in their attendance, being driven out of Kit Burns's, at least, by the overpowering stench of rat and dog carcasses buried under the bleachers" (280).

Kit Burns's rat-pit prayer meetings at 273 Water Street drew a good deal of skepticism, and a public inquiry ensued regarding both Burns and the missionaries; but it was Burns himself who precipitated an end to the meetings. One night after the clergymen and ladies had overstayed their welcome, Burns, the living embodiment of the stereotyped waterfront insider, announced to a group of reporters, "them fellows has been making a pul-pit out of my rat pit and I'm going to purify it after them." "Jim!" he yelled over to his barman, "Bring out the vermin" (qtd. in Bonner 32). Jim heartily responded by flinging rats into the meeting while gamblers howled hymns in grotesque mockery of the choir. Burns soon after mandated a nightly show and referred to his sacrament as one that "*ratified*" the meetings (Bonner 33, emphasis mine). For the police, this was the last straw. Turning a blind eye to an illegal gambling ring that exploited New York's mushrooming rodent population was one thing, but to abuse respectable ladies and popular clergymen in such a foul-mannered way was quite another. Within a few weeks, they shut the place down once and for all.

Outsider reformers on the East Side waterfront clearly required more savvy methods of acculturation. Rather than rent out an immoral venue for moral suasion as Campbell's predecessors had done at Burns's and elsewhere, a method that did little but amuse the insiders it was designed to convert, Campbell chose to engage the waterfront on a more personal level. She saw the disturbing social constructions taking place on the waterfront as an unremitting cycle of destructive behavior that must be stopped dead in its tracks, and she rose to this reformist challenge by working to construct a new method of urban reform. She explains that rather than depend on dusty deductions producing outdated generalizations on the nature of poverty and the poor, she would immerse herself, for better or worse, in the landscape and society of the slums. Thus, her matrix of action was not the industrial school or parlor discussions of the "low classes," but the waterfront district itself.

Consciously or not, however, Campbell could take herself out of the parlor, but could not do the reverse. In her essay in *Darkness and Daylight*, she codifies the distinctions between the progressive modern metropolis and the slums in this way: "Broad Avenues . . . Narrow lanes / Beautiful Parks . . . Fetid Streets with festering filth / Palaces of extravagance . . . Tenements where in defiance of every law, moral and sanitary, people crowd in like maggots in cheese / Great universities . . . Grossest illiteracy / Greatest churches . . . Garish saloons / The noblest men and women who labor for the redemption of their fellows . . . The most hopeless specimens of degraded humanity" (qtd. in Miller and Miller 93).[2] It would be fascinating if such a dichotomy had been authored by an insider, as the extreme subjectivity of the system is revealing: one group is "broad," "beautiful," "extravagant," "great," and "noble"; while the other is "narrow," "fetid," "defiant," "gross," "garish," and "hopeless." All but the last item concerns physical space, and the insiders of each reflect their respective architectural and moral attributes.

Campbell designed her work on the model of a biblical testament. A messianic figure, she devoted years of her life to converting lost souls on the waterfront. After the success of *The Problem of the Poor* in 1882, the *New York Tribune* commissioned her to produce a series of articles on the state of women laborers in Manhattan. One year later, the series was collected in book form as *Prisoners of Poverty: Women Wage-Workers, Their Trades and Their Lives* (1887). Campbell promises in her preface that the articles are "based upon the minutest personal research into conditions described" (i). The "conditions" of the Fourth Ward have improved some, she reports, "Yet here, on this familiar battle-ground, civilization and something worse than mere barbarism still struggle. For which is the victory?" (127).

According to the 1885 report of the Bureau of Statistics for Labor, there were some two hundred thousand working women, not including domestic servants, in ninety-two different trades—generally undesirable trades: "The city which affords the largest percentage of habitual drunkards, as well as the largest number of liquor saloons to the mile, is naturally that in which most women are forced to seek such means of subsistence as may be had" (*Prisoners* 10–11). Their men are mainly longshoreman, whiling away time until their next berth and squandering their earnings "by long seasons of drinking" (128). Waterfront women are a group who, as Campbell reductively sums up their lives, "scrub offices, peddle fruit or small office necessities, take in washing, share, many of them, in the drinking bouts [of men], and are, as a whole, content with brutishness, only vaguely conscious of a wretchedness that, so long as it is intermittent, is no spur to reform of methods" (128). Campbell believed it was because of the severe living conditions of working women that they themselves stubbornly refused to reform. In short, most of the women she met there, to her great consternation, had no wish to be saved.

Campbell thus stresses the moral implications of women working long hours for little money while at the same time providing and caring for large families crammed into tenement flats. One sketch entitled "The Case of Rose Haggerty" demonstrates anecdotally just what those implications are. Rose's parents were Irish immigrants who had both died young of alcoholism, leaving her as a young girl with eleven siblings to support. Like many women in her position, she turned to prostitution to make ends meet. "It was a sailor from a merchantman just in," Campbell relates of Rose Haggerty's first experience as a prostitute, "she took his arm and walked with him toward Roosevelt street" (29). But Rose's decision is not necessarily a moral discrepancy. Campbell does not condone her lifestyle, but in stark contrast to the blood-and-thunder sermonizers at John Allen's, we find a startling new tone in Campbell's report. At least, Campbell admits, Rose Haggerty "has her trade, and it is a prosperous one, in which wages never fail. The children are warm and have no need to cry for hunger anymore" (29).

Like John Allen the insider, she "lived among them," if not for seventeen years. And like Allen, she recognizes that "some of them . . . have many virtues." In Campbell's view, the question is not why waterfront women prostitute themselves, but rather how even "one remains honest when the only thing that pays is vice" (42). "It might be dishonor," Campbell admits of Rose's experience, "but it was certainly food and warmth for the children, and what did it matter? She had fought her fight for twenty years, and it had been a vain struggle. She took his money when morning came, and went home with a look that is on her face to-day" (29).

Crossing such boundaries for an outsider, engaging the "other half" up or down on their own ground, requires leisure time and a disposable income. New York's privileged classes obsessively observed and commented on the rise of the poor, an occupation that both voiced their fears and affirmed their social standing. "To talk of poverty," Campbell writes, "and to take a theoretical interest in the social questions of the day is a fashion at present, and a fashion which has its foundation of good" (77). Campbell, however, insisted that armchair theorizing about urban poverty yields few practical rewards. Rather than simply contributing to relief organizations and attending speeches by popular reformers like herself, the moral majority should immerse themselves in the society of the "other half": "'To know how the other half lives.' That is the demand made upon woman and man alike. Once at least put yourselves in the worker's place, if it be for half an hour, and think her thoughts and live her starved and dreary life." Reporting on a tenement she visits on Water Street, she entreats her audience to follow suit: "Whoever, even once, sets foot in a home like this, carries away a memory that must forever act as spur to lingering action, and keep vivid the thought of these smoldering elements of riot and revolt down among the slums" (77).

Addressing the housing problem in the Fourth Ward, Campbell recounts a conversation with an anonymous newspaper editor whom she refers to as "the Bachelor." The chapter is structured as an argumentative interview in which their dialogue—he as the designated "armchair ethnologist," she as the "participant observer"—concerns various methods of civil service, including Campbell's neighborhood immersion: "'Have you ever been in one of these tenement houses?'" she asks him. "'I have been by them,'" is the reply, "'is not that enough? I feel half poisoned for days afterward. Must I be wholly so, for that would be the result of going in? I am neither architect, builder, nor landlord'" (110). The bachelor's admission suggests that even if he were to visit the tenements, he is not expert enough to draw any valid conclusions. Campbell retorts that regardless of formal training, if you criticize the architecture you must know the laws of "utility" that govern the standards of your criticism, otherwise remove yourself from the discourse:

> For a month I have been among the tenement houses, beginning with the quiet, pleasant 'flats,' both east and west, up town, and ending in the basements and cellars of Cherry and Front and all that labyrinth of down-town streets. I have seen lodging houses where a score of people lay on the floor, paying three cents a night for this shelter. I have been in the old church where they crowd by the hundred at the same rate, and in rooms of a trifle higher pretensions where cot-beds with a pillow and single covering are ranged thick as they can be set. And I have been in rooms where a whole family herded together, seven, eight, or even nine people in a space fourteen by sixteen, eating, drinking, sleeping, performing every office of life in this common space, and their brutalized faces bearing the story of inevitable results, written in letters all may read at will. (111)

The people who live in such conditions, she continues, "have become at last a standing army of menace to the whole political, social and moral life of the city" (114). Anticipating Jacob Riis's work, she emphatically identifies her remedy to the problem of the poor as "immediate legislation, compelling the erection of new houses on sanitary principles, needed alterations in existing ones, and the demolition of all unfit for human habitation" (114). And this conviction, along with the precise form this legislation should take, is informed by her immersion experience as an outsider on the waterfront.

In this sense, the act of slumming or "friendly visiting" often educated the middle class more about the realities of their own communities than about the communities they discovered. Engaging the slums directly, in other words, not only complicated the familiar understanding of poverty, but also the perceived security of their own privileged existence. The trick to New York moral reform was to isolate the desirable attributes of the larger society and spread them outward into morally marginalized districts, or "moral regions"—a method institutionalized in the Progressive era. The only effective means of "training" the poorer classes, Campbell argues, is not from the outside in, but rather from the inside out: "Such work as is done must be from within, out. Methods which touch merely the outside are but of temporary service" (248). By immersing herself in waterfront culture, Campbell accumulates firsthand knowledge that would aid her and her outsider compeers in the struggle to reform the urban poor; looking "from within, out," she discovers an alien moral framework that was to be effectively torn down. In time, she implies, New York would experience a series of cultural implosions, and in their wake the city would emerge a shining moral example to the rest of the nation. One neighborhood at a time, New York would become the city on the hill—it would transform into the model American community, towering and knowable.

Jerry McAuley and the "New Look" of Protestant Reform

Campbell soon found that in order to effect substantial change as an outsider on the waterfront, she needed guidance from a respected insider who might accommodate reform from without. It thus became necessary to ferret out insiders sympathetic to the cause. In his introduction to *Darkness and Daylight,* the Reverend Lyman Abbott praises Campbell's discussion of the Water Street Mission in that volume, specifically for its positive representation of helpful insiders. He emphasizes the importance and evangelical tradition of applying the knowledge of insiders to convert their own people: "Her description of that mission makes evident that our Christian work in the outcast wards will never accomplish what it ought, until the outcasts themselves, who have been converted, are set apart to mission work among their fellows. Jesus ordained to the gospel ministry the twelve fishermen after they had received but a year's instruction from Him, and one of them had not fully recovered from his sailor habit of profanity; and Paul began preaching to the Jews a few days after he was converted to Christianity" (50).

The insider informant with whom Campbell most closely allied herself was an ex-convict Irishman named Jeremiah "Jerry" McAuley. A former waterfront rough, alcoholic, small-time pirate, and Catholic who shared the singular fisherman's taste for bawdy language (all of which Campbell dutifully renders in her text), McAuley converted to Protestant Christianity while serving time at the Sing-Sing correctional facility in Ossining, New York, just north of the city. "There's no sham about it," McAuley testifies to his audience at the Water Street Mission, "I don't tell you I was a thief and a drunkard and a fraud to glory in it, but I want you roughs to understand what Jesus has done for me" (Campbell, *Problem* 18). Importantly, Campbell's waterfront reportage here is entirely dictated by the caprices of an insider voice more than anywhere else in her study. She splits her sympathies between a desire to improve the conditions of the poor in a manner that would substantiate the hegemony of the middle class and a sincere admiration for the occasional waterfront insider like Jerry McAuley. McAuley's voice, after all, would never have been effective had he not been raised on Water Street. Instead of applying dialect as a condescending literary device to deride the "lower million," as so many of her predecessors had done, she designed it to add credibility and authenticity to the only group she thought could truly solve the problem of the poor: the poor themselves. By immersing herself in East Side waterfront culture and writing about her experiences there, Campbell substantiates her outsider audience's a priori perceptions while at the same time positing the figure of the insider hero (a convicted criminal no less) as the "ordained fisherman" of the waterfront. The insider voice of the Fourth Ward tough preaching Protestant scripture is a redemptive thread that provides structure and purpose to her work. Here lies the fundamental logic of her representation. Had she presented the conversion argument in her own voice it would read as one more evangelical sermon from an outsider, an ineffectual method of reform for those who presumably require salvation most.

Jerry McAuley was born in 1837 in County Kerry, Ireland. At the age of thirteen, he and his grandmother emigrated to the United States; like many Irish of the period, they moved into a crowded tenement flat in the Fourth Ward. And like many young Irish in the Fourth Ward, McAuley promptly developed tastes for the criminal life and the inviting atmosphere of the waterfront's lower saloons. After five active years of crime, he landed a fifteen-year sentence at Sing-Sing for "highway robbery" (McAuley *Transformed* 11) and remained there until 1864, when he was abruptly pardoned, possibly as a result of diminishing resources during the war. He converted to Protestantism at Sing-Sing, but upon winning his freedom began drinking again. In no time, he was back on the streets willy-nilly as one of the most feared and respected toughs of the Fourth Ward. His conversion experience proved stronger than his criminal inclinations, however, and McAuley finally and unalterably reformed at the Howard Street Mission.

Eight years after his release from prison, McAuley, with his wife, Maria, opened his own mission in October 1872 at 316 Water Street near the East Side docks. The Water Street Mission was a valuable setting for Campbell, as it was operated by a man who had himself struggled with alcohol, poverty, immigration, and the law. McAuley is the working-class hero of Campbell's *The Problem of the Poor,* one of Reverend Abbott's ordained fishermen, and we are invited to read the book as gospel for the times. Campbell's attitude towards McAuley calls to mind William James's revelation that in our search for heroes, we have forgotten that they are everywhere around us, existing beneficently "in the daily lives of the labouring classes" (290). But Campbell's outsider account does not attempt James's call a decade later to cure the "blindness" of Victorian America. Instead, the "other half" must assimilate into middle-class modes of living in order to "attain," as Campbell had paradoxically phrased it, the "right . . . to his own personality."

Historian Aaron Ignatius Abell describes McAuley as a man who "unlike many men of his type avoided pious pretension and mission cant," and along with his reform efforts within the neighborhood, "his influence upon the cultured classes was no less pronounced [than upon his Water Street converts]. They, too, were 'converted' in the sense that many of them resolved to devote their lives to the welfare of others" (37). To Helen Campbell, insiders like Jerry McAuley—mythic working-class heroes who hold "the key to the regeneration of the masses"—could reconcile contradictions between the romantic and the pragmatic in urban writing, along with the individual and society in a maturing urban space. He is a marginal man, both Irish tough and Americanized Protestant, who exudes streetwise individuality while at the same time preaching the gospel of uptown outsiders for the benefit of the larger society. McAuley is on display at each mission meeting Campbell renders. At one, he proudly booms to the congregation, "Clean, ain't I, an' respectable, ain't I, an' happy, as the blindest eye might see. That's me, an' yet I've been down in the gutter deeper than those fellows over there or one that's here tonight" (55). McAuley, then, is an insider arbiter of Protestant American morality and serves the practical purpose of emboldening outsider reformers to enter the otherwise intimidating landscape of the waterfront.

Frederic Jameson, in his discussion on "Otherness," the novel, and social space, makes the assertion that "these seemingly separate and homogeneous zones of social space become interesting for the novelist only when they are intersected by characters from the other class, by class interlopers or refugees, defectors or missionaries" (197). Campbell's is not a novel, but its intrinsic subjectivity creates a fictional world engulfed in cultural poetics. McAuley represents all of Jameson's marginal voices—the interloper, the refugee, the defector, and the missionary—fused into what McAuley himself considered one "clean," "respectable," and "happy" whole. Campbell singles him out as a model of human potential in her attempt to understand converts and disaffected alike. If in the postwar era the dominant mode of moral suasion was, as Charles Loring Brace contends, "to connect the two extremes of society in sympathy, and carry the forces of one class down to lift up the other" (136), McAuley interlopes upwards as well as being a complicit receptacle for the downward current.

After five years in prison, McAuley confessed to Campbell that he "grew weakly," since he had been "used to the open air always, an' a shut-in life told on me" (81). In desperation he sought refuge in the prison chapel, where services were conducted by a reformed prize-fighter and gambler from the Water Street neighborhood named Orville "Awful" Gardner. Back in his cell, McAuley read the King James Bible, a copy of which the warden allocated to every inmate (McAuley *Transformed* 20), and in time came across a passage that, as he phrases it, "hit the Catholics" (31). It was Timothy, chapter 1:1–4, a passage he recites to Campbell from memory: "Now that the Spirit speaketh expressly that in the latter times some shall depart from the faith, giving heed to seducing spirits and doctrines of devils; having their conscience seared with a hot iron; forbidding to marry and commanding to abstain from meats which God hath created to be received with thanksgiving of them which believe and know the truth" (32). Either he or Campbell significantly leaves out the line in verse 2 that reads, "Speaking lies in hypocrisy." There is no way of knowing whether he makes the slip or she does, but the idea that McAuley is indeed performing religious hypocrisy is not a connection that Campbell would wish her readers to make. The punctuation too does not coincide with the King James, another slip that indicates that Campbell may have committed the passage to memory herself.

The conversion story continues that after some reflection, McAuley impulsively kicked the King James about his cell. Taking up the Catholic version for comparison next, he reluctantly discovered that he preferred the Protestant method of asking God to forgive his sins to the Catholic demands of "'penance an' sayin' so many prayers, an' such like'" (32). The use of dialect here, more pronounced in fact than Campbell makes him sound generally, substantiates his role as an insider hero. Indeed, the extreme transliteration of his argot is sustained throughout the narrative. He denounces Catholicism in the unmistakable voice of the Irish Catholic. And again, when Campbell relates McAuley's description of his mother performing traditional Catholic rituals he finds ridiculously superstitious, she turns up the dialectical heat: "many's the time, when she was tellin' her beads an' kissin' the floors for penance, I'd shy things at her just to hear her curse an' swear at me, an' then back to her knees'" (29). This amalgamation of dialect and "proper" or "sober" English is one of the most common literary conventions in realist writing, a timeless literary topos that locates the speaker in his or her historical past and demonstrates the intrusion of that past onto dominant linguistic and cultural patterns. The uses of dialect are many, but the clearest purpose is to enhance the feeling of cultural exchange and dislocation in the guise of daily conversation. Campbell allows that McAuley's Catholic devotion only

came after he immigrated to the United States, where religion was more a
matter of ethnic identity and personal pride than moral purpose; in other
words, his early defense of Catholicism was in Campbell's estimation the
misguided act of a confused boy.

McAuley first publicized his conversion tale in a slim, privately released
volume entitled *Transformed, or, the History of a River Thief* in 1876. The
book opens with an evangelical preface signed by a Mrs. Helen E. Brown who
refers to the book as a "biography" (5) and, given the high-toned rhetorical style throughout the book, appears to have been McAuley's ghostwriter.
Transformed foregrounds McAuley's earthly connection to Jesus, describing
his conversion experience in prison, subsequent lapse back into alcoholism
(at one point he unsuccessfully attempts suicide by throwing himself under
a subway car, but is saved at the last second), and final acceptance of Jesus
as a benevolent supernatural force and ultimately his personal savior. At
Sing-Sing, a heavenly light streams into his cell, and voices echo in his head
whenever he asks for forgiveness and guidance. Little if any of his dialect is
recorded, though he was the ostensible author, and the rhetoric of Protestant
evangelicalism dominates the "mass of strikingly interesting incidents which
might have made a far more imposing volume" (5).[3] Some waterfront expressions are left intact; for example, after reading the passage from Timothy, he
quotes himself as crying out, "the vile heretics . . . there's the lies. I always
heard the old book was a pack of lies. That's the way they hold us Catholics
up" (22). (Later he realizes that the same passage in Timothy is included in
the Roman-Catholic version as well, more evidence for him that Catholicism is a false theology.) Six years later, however, when Campbell takes on
McAuley's story, the reformed waterfront bandit speaks in the unmistakable
voice of a Fourth-Ward insider.

By the end of Campbell's account, McAuley attributes the "new look" he
discerns in Orville Gardner's countenance to the revelations of the Protestant faith. He decides that he too "'wanted to be different'" (32). It is then
that he becomes the ordained fisherman, Paul among the Jews. Insiders,
specifically the Water Street Irish, do not take his conversion from Catholicism to Protestantism lightly. McAuley is routinely assaulted on the streets
by Irish youths, his community accuses him of being a "turn-coat," and
while accompanying Campbell into a tenement of Irish families he warns
her, "'Look out for your footing. . . . It's dreadful dirty here. The time wasn't
long ago that they'd pitch dirt out on you. I've gone home covered many a
time. They're mostly Romanists, an' very bitter against a turn-coat, an' the
city missionary has a hard time in these places. I'd a kicked one down the

stairs myself, twelve years ago'" (76). Out on the street a few moments later, a gang of young Irish toughs approaches them yelling, "There's McAuley the turn-coat!' . . . 'Hi! McAuley and his band! Give it to them! Hi!'" (79). McAuley gallantly responds by charging "down through the crowd with an Irish whoop," promptly dispersing the assailants (79).

McAuley's street wisdom and selfless loyalty to the city mission reform movement splits the moral imperative of slum reform between "decent," "respectable" outsiders and the insider street toughs themselves. Campbell admits, in fact, that well-meaning middle-class outsiders lack the skills to take on a working-class neighborhood. Outsider reformers, she argues, must ally themselves with insiders like Jerry McAuley if there is to be any hope for moral reform: "Men of this stamp hold the key to a regeneration of the masses, such as organized charities are powerless to effect; and already some who believe in this fact are seeking to make their work easier and to give the substantial aid that it demands. The poor are the best missionaries to the poor, and he who has gone hungry, suffered every pang of poverty and known the sharpest temptation to sin can best speak words that will save men and women entering on the same path" (191). But when she later addresses him as "a priest to his people" (191), Campbell ignores the most significant aspect of McAuley's philanthropy—that it is intrinsically Protestant. And if a thief, gambler, or alcoholic is to "turn honest," it is to be done through the guidance of the Protestant church.

First-generation immigrants like McAuley often abandoned their Old World religions in favor of the "new look" Protestantism offered. In kind, Campbell reports a series of conversion testimonials from the congregation at the mission. Liars, swearers, drunkards, tobacco addicts, gamblers, and thieves all testify in Campbell's account. In one Water Street meeting, a German Jew rises from her seat among the multicultural congregation to condemn her Semitic past. "I hated Christians," she confesses, "I say, dey should be killed every one. I would hurt dem if I could" (51). When a "Bible reader" gave her a copy of the New Testament, she tore out the name "Jesus" everywhere it appeared, a process which "take a good vhile" (51). In time, she came to the mission looking for a clean, forgiving space and the promises of spiritual uplift. Her testimonial makes clear that without the Protestant church, she would have condemned herself to a life of sin: "'Oh, my sins are so big! I want to lose dem. I want to love Jesus! I keep prayin', an' one day dey are all gone. Oh, I am so happy. You vill not believe. I do not ever vant to schvear any more. I do not vant tell lies; no, not any more. Gott is gut to me. I could not be vicket any more. Oh, pray for me, an' help me be gut'" (57).

The presumption, of course, is that swearing and lying are moral iniqui-
ties the Jewish religion had somehow failed to check. Jews must then achieve
salvation, like their Catholic counterparts, through the tenets of the Protestant faith. Immorality is perceptibly linked to Old World belief systems
in these insider accounts, and again Campbell puts dialect to use in each
of the testimonials as proof of redemption. The poor must save themselves,
according to Campbell, but first they need to adopt the "new look," whether
in prison or the missions, and that new look is reserved for readers of the
King James Bible. "Temporary relief for cases like this," Campbell intones, "is
merely palliative, and common sense must work with Christianity, if revolution and anarchy are not to be a national pastime" (79). Alarmist evangelical
rhetoric of this kind was so prevalent in nineteenth-century reform writing
that this comment can only be taken as pandering to audience expectations.
By that logic, the meaning of the words does not always reflect the author's
own sentiments.

Was Campbell really anticipating revolt and anarchy from the waterfront
district? Is her interpretive community less literal than we are in the twenty-
first century? These are interesting questions and worth investigating, but
the pathos of urgency and resolve remains. The immigrant population must
be codified and understood in terms that an audience can appreciate and
act upon. Campbell applies words like "revolution" and "anarchy" to signify
urban disorder at their hands; and if the problem is left unresolved, Irish
Catholics, "with a little added intelligence," could enact a socialist revolution that would make New York its headquarters. The socialist leader on
the waterfront, Campbell insists, "can sound every chord of jealousy and
suspicion and revenge lying open to his touch" (215).

Clearly, demonstrating the effects of poverty, crime, and congestion on
popular morality was Campbell's cardinal contribution to the discourse of
urban reform, though she focuses more on moral issues than economic injustices and condemns waterfront culture as deviant rather than appropriate
to its situation. Deborah Carlin importantly acknowledges this as a general
evasion by middle-class reformers: "If the poor could learn the manners and
customs of the middle class, could they ever attain the leisure to practice
them that only economic security could provide? This question was one
that proponents of 'social amelioration' necessarily ignored, since its answer
would represent a far more radical, and, indeed, threatening program of social uplift than manners alone" (211–12). The difference between Campbell
and many of the "friendly visitors" Carlin discusses, however, is that instead
of being "enclosed within [her] own room of privilege, gazing beyond [her]

windows at the social spectacle outside" (221), Campbell insists that outsider philanthropists should spend long hours of enlightening visitation with waterfront insiders. "No attempt at an understanding of the labor question as it faces us to-day," Campbell writes, "can be successful till knowledge of its underlying conditions is assured. . . . To learn the struggle and sorrow of the workers is the first step toward any genuine help" (*Prisoners* i, ii).

Ernest Poole's The Harbor *and the Industrialization of U.S. Maritime Culture*

Just as Jerry McAuley emulates the Protestant piety and moral standards of middle-class decency while maintaining an insider's waterfront vernacular and behavior, some respectable citizens found the heterogeneous ruggedness of seamanship equally appealing. In 1915, New York novelist Ernest Poole, most notable, perhaps, for being the first recipient of the Pulitzer Prize for fiction (1918) and assisting Upton Sinclair in researching *The Jungle* (1906), boldly assaulted common assumptions among the urban middle class by arguing that the waterfront was at its best a resource for artistic production and at its worst an unhealthy obsession. What Poole articulated in his novel *The Harbor* (1915) covers a time period roughly from the tail end of the sail age in the 1870s to approximately 1911, the year of the Great General Strike by the dockworkers of Great Britain, a strike that inspired "Big" Bill Haywood of the Industrial Workers of the World (commonly known as "the Wobblies") to spur on dock laborers in the United States to join their British union compatriots. Poole's novel is a remarkable treatment of this transitional period in New York maritime cultural history from a culture of diversity to a culture of industrial containment. In it, Poole blames both steam power and maritime industry giants for the dissolution of maritime life.

Steam power began challenging the sailing industry in the 1870s and '80s, even while sailboat designs continued to prove more efficient for trade world-wide. The competition was short-lived, however, once designers introduced triple-expansion engines that lowered the cost of fuel and could reach three times the velocity of sail-powered cargo ships. Add to that the fact that the iron and steel hulls of the steam ships were lighter, cheaper, stronger, and could carry more cargo with less risk of damaging the goods, and sailboat-ing swiftly became a relic of the past, consigned to the leisure world of yacht racing and booze cruises (Labaree 390).

This transition from sail to steam was a fait accompli by the early 1910s.

Sailors were no longer the skilled adventurers of the previous century but instead became associated with the general labor force and by association with labor unrest. The perilous, earsplitting duties aboard a coal-fuelled steamship changed the nature of seamanship along with the social perceptions of sailors. Various efforts were made to alleviate their severe labor conditions, particularly the right to quit if things got to be too much—but in 1895, the U.S. Supreme Court likened the sailors' life to slavery and still unbelievably denied them protection under the Thirteenth Amendment. The court stated that "It can not be open to doubt that the provision against involuntary servitude was never intended to apply to their contracts" (Labaree 425). And with England's Great General Strike of 1911, observed and aided by American labor activists, the American merchant classes had reason for concern.

Poole's novel *The Harbor* incorporates two central narratives, and both are love stories. The narrator, named Bill, falls in love with Eleanor Dillon, the daughter of a prominent engineer heavily involved in developing the port of New York. But at the same time, as an aspiring young writer, Bill finds his best material along the docks of the New York harbor; and ultimately, his obsession with the harbor surpasses his love for Eleanor. Bill's father is a former merchant mariner who establishes himself after retirement as a warehouse owner in Brooklyn. The proximity of the East River to Bill's home enables him to sneak out at night and engage the "Micks" and "Dockers" that he had been warned to avoid at all costs, as his household adhered firmly to the strictures of reform and the protective culture of Victorian New York. But from his first experiences he discovers that "by making friends with 'Micks' and 'Dockers' and the like, you find they are no fearful goblins, giants bursting savagely up among the flowers of your life, but people as human as yourself, or rather, much more human, because they live so close to the harbor, close to the deep rough tides of life" (12).

Bill's music teacher, a modern thinker, teaches his pupil that Beethoven "found his music . . . by listening to the life close around him" (38). "If I were you," he advises, "I should watch the great ships down there below, I should listen to them with an artist's ears. They are here from all over the world, these ships, they are manned by men of all nations . . . you in your city of all nations might gather the folksongs of all the seas" (39). Poole argues through the progressive lessons of the music teacher that the move from sail to steam and the subsequent proletarianization of the sailor figure removed in the eyes of the larger society what cultural legitimacy may have been attributed to the cosmopolitan character of the waterfront. But Poole's enlightened retort to waterfront reform writers was too little too late. "Jack's life" was no longer a threat to the respectable elite; rather, well before 1915, maritime culture had been subsumed by a modernized industrial complex that affected harbors throughout the world.

Poole personifies the harbor in his novel as a muse-like presence that emboldens Bill's calling to be an artist—first in music, then in writing. The harbor is, of course, the title character, and it works as protagonist and antagonist, diversion and obsession, love interest and muse, and it speaks to him as an inner dialogue in its various manifestations. In one of the opening sequences of the novel, the harbor goads him into eschewing traditional romantic and sentimental narrative along with his Protestant upbringing: "When you were little," it tells him, "for you I was filled with thrilling idols—cannibals and condors . . . strange wonder-ships and sailors adventuring to heathen lands. But then I dragged these idols down and made you see me as I am. And as I showed myself to you, so I'll show up all other wonderful places or men that your mother would have you believe in" (33). As Bill grows older he discovers that the docks assemble "all races of men," like Campbell's East Side waterfront missions and sidewalk restaurants. But the terms of engagement have drastically changed. The ships and piers have become factory-like, and the only means by which to gain entry is to either falsify your identity and claim seaman status, or actually become a seaman yourself.

As a brief aside, the latter option is precisely what a young man with a touch of the poet named Eugene O'Neill chose to do, and in 1911 he found himself in the midst of the Great Strike on the Liverpool docks. O'Neill's earliest full-length play, *The Personal Equation* (1915), fictionalizes the American anarchist movement's support of the strike. His experience as a crewman for two months on the Norwegian bark, *Charles Racine,* and the steamships, the S.S. *Ikala,* the S.S. *New York,* and the S.S. *Philadelphia* provided him with firsthand experience on the transition from sail to steam, along with material for well over a dozen of his plays. It was on the waterfront that he found his temperament best suited, and he remained there, drinking himself into that world the way Jack London had a few years earlier in the San Francisco waterfront dives (London chronicled his experiences in *John Barleycorn: "Alcoholic Memoirs"* [1913]). In a poem of O'Neill's that he composed while boarding above Jimmie the Priest's bar in the South Street district, entitled "Ballad of the Seamy Side" (1911), he calls to mind Campbell's image of the waterfront, but with a modernist outsider's passion for the lowlife of the docks.

Where is the lure of the life you sing?
Let us consider the seamy side: . . .
Think of the dives on the waterfront
And the low drunken brutes in dungaree,
Of the low dance halls where the harpies hunt
And the maudlin seamen so carelessly
Squanders the wages of months at sea
And maybe is killed in a bar room brawl;
The spell of these things explain to me—
"They're part of the game and I loved it all."
(qtd. in Gelb 307)

Though Poole's narrator himself does not choose this path among the waterfront's dispossessed, Joe, his college friend and a radical labor activist signs on as a coal stoker, the brutal occupation of the character Robert "Yank" Smith in O'Neill's expressionistic play *The Hairy Ape* (1921), and "for two years [Joe] had shoveled coal in the stokeholes of ships by day and by night, he had mixed with stokers of every race, from English, French and Germans to Russians and Italians, Spaniards, Hindus, Coolies, Greeks. He had worked and eaten and slept in their holes, he had ranged the slums of all the seas" (210).

The sad irony is that the singular attribute that Poole, and to a large extent O'Neill, felt deserving of celebration and fantasy about the waterfront—its diverse, cosmopolitan aspect analogous to that of the "slums"—was not viable in a steam-powered harbor industry that no longer signified worldliness, since its foreign laborers were effectively secured from entry into the city proper. By that time, cosmopolitan American sailors seemed a thing of the past, as the ships now resembled factories, "buried and choked in smoke and steam, in grime, dirt, noise and regular haste" (116). Industrialization restricted its labor and materials to "the cheapest there is," Bill's father tells him, and the laborers no longer handled exotic goods like silks and spices from the East Indies. "Oh no," Poole writes, "They were hoisting and letting down into the hold an automobile from Dayton, Ohio. . . . Gone were the figs and almonds, the indigo, ivory, tortoise shells. Into the brand-new ledgers . . . [were entered] such items as barbed wire, boilers, car wheels and gas engines, baby carriages, kegs of paint. I reveled in the commonplace stuff, contrasting it vividly in my mind with the starlit ocean roads it would travel, the picturesque places it would help spoil" (116–17).

Bill's calling as a journalist is to expose this pernicious transformation as a consequence of greed and ignorance on the part of the architects of world trade. In one self-reflexive moment he writes, "I would have a whack at the place by day. No mystery now, just ugliness. I would show it up in broad daylight, bringing out every detail in the glare. I would do this by comparing it to the harbor of my father's youth" (115). The allusion points to the novel itself, which attempts precisely that task. *The Harbor* occupies a significant fault line between Melvillean romances of the South Seas and the harsh, coal-blackened realities of O'Neill's *The Hairy Ape.*

The diversified and competent crew of Captain Ahab's whaler the *Pequod* in *Moby-Dick* (1851), or Melville's personal experiences as a seaman/tourist in his early travel narratives, combine memoir with romance. O'Neill's Yank and Poole's Joe, on the other hand, and the menacing, coal-stoking world they inhabit makes *The Hairy Ape* and *The Harbor* a combination of reportage and modernist wasteland. It is the nostalgic Irishman Paddy who taunts Yank's fantastic pride in speed and steel by contrasting a sailor's life in the natural past to the demoralizing slavery of their industrial present:

> Oh to be scudding south again wid the power of the Trade Wind driving her on steady through the nights and days! Full sail on her! . . . 'Twas them days men belonged to ships, not now. 'Twas them days a ship was part of the sea, and a man was part of a ship, and the sea joined all together and made it one. (*Scornfully*) Is it one wid this you'd be, Yank—black smoke from the funnels smudging the sea, smudging the decks—the bloody engines pounding and shaking—wid devil a sight of sun or a breath of clean air—choking our lungs with coal dust—breaking our backs and hearts in the hell of the stokehole—feeding the bloody furnace—feeding our lives along with the coal, I'm thinking—caged in by steel from a sight of the sky like bloody apes in the Zoo! (127)

Paddy's monologue makes clear that O'Neill's experience on the Norwegian bark, *Charles Racine,* one of the last of the old square-riggers (Richter 40), was by far a more fulfilling voyage than his work on the industrialized steamers. And in one interview with *American Magazine,* O'Neill criticizes the new industrial order in which Syndicalism and Capitalism are at odds, perhaps justifiably. But at what cost? The days of sail power had celebrated "the spirit of craftsmanship, of giving one's heart as well as one's hands to one's work, of doing it for the inner satisfaction of carrying out one's own ideals, not merely as obedience of orders. So far as I can see, the gain is over-balanced by the loss" (qtd. in Alexander 393). Charting this transition in meaningful ways, Poole also eulogizes the old waterfront culture—that Whitmanic waterfront of "mast-hemm'd Manhattan"—while at the same time, like O'Neill's Paddy, indicts the new, industrialized, steam-powered

factories of the sea. Now the New York harbor stands, Eleanor's father tells
Bill, as a "complicated industrial organ, the heart of a country's circulation,
pumping in and out its millions of tons of traffic as quickly and cheaply as
possible. That's efficiency, scientific management or just plain engineering,
whatever you want to call it" (164). And it is this dehumanization of the
harbor that historically defines maritime culture from the 1910s to our own
time.

The grim realities of steam-driven maritime life cause two fundamental
shifts in Bill's character: he embraces socialism as a political philosophy
(which O'Neill also did, albeit briefly), seeing it as the dockworkers' only
means to regain their nostalgic agency, but as an outsider he becomes terribly
disillusioned by the characteristics of the dockworkers themselves. Reporting
on a strike meeting, he remarks, "I had looked for a [dockworker] army. I saw
only mobs of angry men . . . picketing the docks. . . . [They were] jamming
into barrooms, voicing the wildest rumors, talking, shouting, pounding tables
with huge fists. And to me there was nothing inspiring but only something
terrible here, an appalling force turned loose, sightless and unguided" (231).
His sentiments echo a basic tenet of Leninism, one that proliferated in Russia
at approximately the same time: the proletariat should be granted freedom
from bourgeois domination, but it should do so under the guidance of well-
educated intellectuals. His socialist friend Joe is the outsider hero of the novel
as a Yale graduate "slumming" with the coal stokers, and as such he wields no
authority as a true insider voice. At one point he even rants, "Ignorant? Of
course they are! But that's where you and me come in—we can help 'em get
together faster than they would if left to themselves! You can help that way a
lot—by writing to the tenements!" (231). Laura Hapke, a scholar of working-
class insider writing, argues that regardless of Poole's socialist leanings, the
author provides little opportunity to "hear the rank and file" in their own
voice (*Labor's Text* 127). We do hear what Bill calls "the real thing" from the
"Dockers" and "Micks" from the earlier days in the earlier chapters (25), but
once the sailors have been proletarianized we can only ascertain the crass
roar of an unruly mob.

"Lucky people," one character declares to Bill, "to have all this modern
life condensed so cozily into your harbor before your eyes—and to have
discovered . . . that life is growth and growth is change" (331). Technological
progress in the field of propulsion is clearly not a stoppable force, nor, when
considered carefully, should we necessarily wish it to have been stopped. But
the fact remains that if earlier, evangelical reform efforts failed—those of exposé reporters like Campbell and others—the victory over maritime culture

came as a manifestation of industrialization. Frederic Jameson's phrase "the strategy of containment" is a metaphor for the process of identifying and describing neighborhoods that respectable society finds deviant in order to transform them, to inoculate society from their infectious possibilities. But the real cultural containment was achieved through technological advances and with a device, now well-known in the post-9/11 world, that revolutionized the transportation of trade goods ironically called the "container."

❖ ❖ ❖

The next subject of this study will be Stephen Crane and his more distanced interactions with another objectified New York moral region—the Bowery. Through the 1880s and '90s, more and more writers began investigating marginalized neighborhoods in uniquely introspective and realistic modes. Walt Whitman, Stephen Crane, and Henry James all descriptively revealed the extent to which outsider middle-class influences had affected insiders from immigrant and working-class backgrounds into the Victorian "cult of respectability." All of them slumming on the Bowery—Whitman in the late 1880s, Crane in the early 1890s, and James as late as 1904—found there a milieu in the process of being stripped of its cultural identity. The idiosyncratic Bowery lifestyle of the 1830s and '40s existed only residually by their time. But the moral reform efforts of the 1860s, '70s, and '80s had given way to a culture of consumption. Entertainment venues in particular were guided by the principles of middle-class Victorian conduct. Consumer culture, such as might be found in New York's theaters, dance halls, and museums, proved far more effective for bringing urban "low life" into the "respectable" fold.

On the act of composing "subjective realism through the object," Paula Rabinowitz asks a puzzling question: "To whom do the objects speak, those bourgeois subjects slumming among them?" (197). One obvious answer is that the dialogue goes both ways. Stephen Crane in particular, I will show, portrays this moral and religious absorption by McAuley-like insiders on the Bowery as a pernicious solution to the problem of the poor by illuminating the destructive psycho-cultural effects of uptown outsider interference on downtown insider morality.

2   A Culture of Contradictions

WALT WHITMAN, STEPHEN CRANE,
AND THE TRANSFORMATION OF
THE BOWERY

I stood upon a high place,
And saw, below, many devils
Running, leaping,
And carousing in sin.
One looked up, grinning,
And said, "Comrade! Brother!"

—Stephen Crane, "The Black Riders," 1895

IN THE LATE SEVENTEENTH CENTURY, a rural path known as Bowery Lane, from the Dutch word *bowerij,* or farm, was put to use as the main postal route from New York to Boston. The lower mile of this, situated in the heart of Manhattan's Lower East Side, became known simply as the Bowery. Due to its heavy commercial traffic and proximity to immigrant neighborhoods, "the Bowery" rapidly swelled into a celebrated urban boulevard, rivaling the already famous Broadway to its west. And with the construction of the Great Bowery Theater in 1826, the Bowery and thereabouts became New York's theatrical center, both on the stage and off. The area was packed to the point of bursting with cheap theaters, burlesque shows, dance halls, brothels, basement-level dives, and beer halls that seated up to two thousand patrons. It competed with Broadway, but did not cater to a Broadway crowd; it was notoriously flamboyant and alive with action; it was the epicenter of working-class culture and openly advertised itself as such, basing its appeal for outsiders on picaresque urban experience and melodramatic spectacle as performed by Bowery insiders.

By the 1890s, evangelical reform efforts had born some fruit, but the subsequent "cult of respectability" turned Helen Campbell's religious gospel into the far more marketable gospel of consumption. New York entertainment spots, including saloons, dance-halls, and popular theaters had begun to accept the trappings of genteel respectability. If conversion to evangelical Protestantism was too much for Campbell and her contemporaries to ask of marginalized neighborhoods, "low life" haunts on the Bowery and throughout the city ultimately adopted, if in a bogus and distorted way, a public face of gentility. Stephen Crane's Bowery tales signal a move away from mere soundings of urban morality toward a more realistic and ultimately naturalistic representation of the insider voice. A culture comparatively unaffected by middle-class outsider influences would be simply too alien to represent without resorting to caricature. But when Crane met Bowery insiders firsthand, he apprehended a cartoonish reflection of himself.

The year Stephen Crane was born, 1871, the Bowery as it was known worldwide had all but vanished. And with the construction of the Third Avenue elevated train seven years later, the boulevard was transfigured beyond recognition. The sun was blocked out by the tracks, and the streets were showered with hot oil and coal. By 1893, the year Crane published the vanity edition of his first novel, *Maggie: A Girl of the Streets*, the Bowery was already the infamous Bowery, once again conspicuous in the outsider imagination but now for alcoholism, poverty, homelessness, and crime. The streets were filled with hoboes and rival gangs. The number of prostitutes drew sailors by the thousands. The area was no longer a bastion of republicanism, and Bowery insiders were inveigled into accepting an oppositional system of social behavior, helplessly caught in a vicious cycle of cultural prostration seemingly indefinite in origin. As T. J. Jackson Lears postulates in "The Concept of Cultural Hegemony," "most people find it difficult, if not impossible, to translate the outlook implicit in their experience into a conception of the world that will directly challenge the hegemonic culture" (596). For Bowery insiders, grappling as they were with the city's unrelenting challenges to their self-esteem, admitting defeat to the hegemonic culture was as unimaginable as absorbing culture from outside was subconscious. The indisputably dominant Victorian culture, distinguished by an allegiance to the cult of respectability and traditionally associated with Broadway and Fifth Avenue, had effectively wiped out any staying power its working-class counterpart on the East Side might have summoned up.[1] But the region still captivated outsider audiences: as Crane's first biographer Thomas Beer wisecracked in 1923, "New York was proud of the Bowery precisely as a child is proud of a burned thumb" (78).

Timothy J. Gilfoyle argues that Crane's "treatment of the Bowery varies little from that of the literary 'slumming' missions found in the earlier 'mysteries and miseries' [or, city mysteries] of New York" (271). But Crane, the son of evangelicals from New Jersey, renders the Bowery and its insiders with surprising impressionistic adroitness. Though city-mysteries writers like Ned Buntline and George Foster confronted the challenge of "the accessibility of an emergent modern world to literary representation" (Gilfoyle 8), they rarely concerned themselves with understanding the insider point of view or with complicating their own. Ned Buntline's novel, *The B'hoys of New York* (1850), for example, has few referents to the Bowery and its cultural makeup. Indeed, the most remarkable aspect of this novel is its failure to describe the popular New York type, the Bowery B'hoy. As late as 1850, Foster asked his audience, "Who are the B'hoys and G'hals of New York? The answer to this question, if it could be completely efficient, would be one of the most interesting essays on human nature ever written" (*New York by Gas-Light* 169). Distinctive moral regions did, of course, exist in the 1850s, the most obvious cases being the Five Points and the Bowery district. And although Bowery culture was well-represented in working-class theaters during the 1840s and '50s, respectable outsiders mainly stayed home.

One of the finest commentaries on the cultural transformation of the Bowery has been furnished by, of all people, the expatriate "master" novelist Henry James. While slumming on the Bowery at the age of sixty, following his return to the United States in 1904 (and the untimely death of his friend and fellow expat Stephen Crane in 1900) James attended a theater matinee that closely resembled the Bowery scenes Crane wrought so well the previous decade. James observed there a "vertiginous bridge of American confectionery," which he identified as a bridge that transverses the gap between outsiders and insiders, between the Victorian codes enacted on the stage and the level of the audience's assent. He speculated that these "almost 'high class' luxuries, circulating in such a company, were a sort of supreme symbol of the promoted state of the aspirant to American conditions" (196). Most enthralling for James was not what took place on the stage but rather the unwritten dialogue between the audience and the notions of respectability the theater and, more importantly, American society was peddling to its "laboring classes": "Nothing (in the texture of the occasion) could have had a sharper interest than this demonstration that, since what we pretend to do with them is thoroughly to school them, the schooling, by our system, cannot begin too soon or pervade their experience too much. Were they going to rise to it, or rather fall from it—to our instinct, as distinguished from their own, for picturing life?" (199).

James observed a new social lesson that midwinter afternoon on the Bowery, but it was one diametrically opposed to what Walt Whitman had referred to as "great lessons of nature" in his republican tract *Democratic Vistas* (1871), lessons of cultural integrity that we might now call "multiculturalism." "Were they to take our lesson submissively," James asks, "in order to get with it our smarter traps and tricks, our superior Yankee machinery?" (199). Venues of popular entertainment such as the one James witnessed, ones boldly sworn to elevating Bowery life, did not answer Whitman's call in *Democratic Vistas* for "variety and freedom"; rather they enforced, as James attested, "blank conformity to convention" (198).

Victorian culture in New York was in its infancy when Bowery insiders began promoting their cultural distinctiveness. Richard Butsch, in his comprehensive essay "Bowery B'hoys and Matinee Ladies," acknowledges that "middle- and upper-middle class Americans wished to distinguish themselves from the uncultivated working class at the very time when the working class was politically ascendant, at least rhetorically" (385). Proper social markers for Americans with "respectability" included certain clothes, levels of education, and speech patterns, along with infinite other social graces. These were all learned behaviors, however, that the "vulgar" masses could successfully adopt. As a result, manners became increasingly rarefied and more difficult to interpret. Once firmly established, middle-class New Yorkers became obsessed with protecting the status of Victorian respectability at the expense of the indecorous rabble. And in due course, to ensure social order, they proliferated respectable morals and manners to satisfactorily regulate working-class behavior. By the 1890s, Victorianism became so entrenched in New York's social consciousness that the notion of respectability would have a sizable impact on the actions and value structure of the very working-class culture that openly despised it.

Crane's novel *Maggie: A Girl of the Streets* (1893) does not sound a beginning for Bowery culture, but rather an ending; Bowery insiders were stifled by their own acceptance, however subconscious, of codes of behavior conceived of by outsiders, and Crane's characters are prostrated by the psycho-cultural contradictions that ensued. Though Crane does give lip service to the new consumer culture Bowery dwellers enjoyed, he does not present theaters, dance halls, and taverns as vehicles for cultural dissent; any such dissent, on the Bowery at least, would have been vestiges of a former time. *Maggie,* in short, is a story not of rebellion, but of "blank conformity to convention."

Taking into account the profound transformation of Bowery culture over the course of the nineteenth century, Crane's insider actors, Maggie Johnson, her brother Jimmie, and her lover Pete, symbolize fragmented relics of a culture drowned out by rampant commercialization and its effects on working-class Bowery culture in the form of middle-class Victorianism. Indeed, Crane's characters are highly indicative of many Bowery issues. Christopher Benfey, in his exemplary biography *The Double Life of Stephen Crane,* argues that Crane's knowledge of New York and the Bowery culture he represents is secondhand, taken from Jacob Riis and the mass of Methodist moral reform tracts that abounded during that period (63). I will show, however, that Crane's Bowery tales are charged with a social energy that could only have come from an artist who, though an outsider, was significantly familiar with the Bowery and its past. Crane began writing *Maggie* in Syracuse, before he had experienced Manhattan life to any significant degree, but in every chapter there are salient references to the city's signature "respectable" outsider culture and how it was both loathed and emulated by Bowery insiders.

Victorians are not meant to be portrayed here as hobgoblins or bugaboos. Crane certainly points to no group or individual as inherently evil; they are all products of a naturalistic environment that is beyond reason. As a likable character from Crane's sketch "An Experiment in Luxury" wisecracks, "Nobody is responsible for anything. I wish to heaven somebody was, and then we could all jump him" (550). Though there was no doubt a very real cultural conflict between vying groups, there is an aura of inevitability in the effect of urbanization on the Bowery, whether it be at the hands of the Victorians or some other cultural force from without.

What follows is a brief account of the development of the historically resonant subculture that Walt Whitman, Crane, and others have drawn from for their portraits of New York life, the Bowery B'hoys and G'hals. Following that, I will demonstrate how Crane's Bowery tales, along with some other Bowery writing, including Whitman's elegiac essay "The Old Bowery," reflect the suppression, not the ascendance, of that singular culture.

"The Greatest Lessons of Nature": Frank Chanfrau, Walt Whitman, and the B'hoys and G'hals of the Bowery

While still a teenager, actor Frank Chanfrau ate regularly at the Broadway House, a small eatery on Grand Street in the middle of Manhattan's Lower East Side. At lunch one afternoon, Chanfrau overheard a boisterous young man howl to the waiter, "*Look a heah! Gimme a sixpenny plate ev pork and beans, and don't stop to count dem beans . . . !*" This was Mose Humphreys, a printer at the *New York Sun* and one of the "fire boys" of the mid-1830s. Over a decade later, the playwright Benjamin A. Baker would catch wind of Chanfrau's comical mimicking of the then famous Bowery B'hoy's style of speech. Baker promptly composed a dramatic sketch for Chanfrau to perform on the popular stage. They showed it to William Mitchell, the proprietor of a Lower East Side venue, Mitchell's Olympic Theater. Mitchell criticized the play or, more specifically, Baker's writing, remarking that "the characters are good, but what a bad piece!" Months later, coming up short for a new idea, he consented to let Chanfrau give Baker's play, then entitled "New York As It Is," a trial performance (Brown 284).

When Chanfrau first strolled onto the stage with a swagger and a sneer, the clamorous audience plunked into a hushed silence. This might have been discomfiting for Chanfrau, since they generally greeted their favorite actor with lusty applause, but the fact is, as drama historian Allston T. Brown notes, the audience "didn't recognize Chanfrau. He stood there in his red shirt, with his fire coat thrown over one arm, the stovepipe hat . . . drawn over one eye, his trousers tucked into his boots, a stump of cigar pointing up from his lips to his eye, the soap locks plastered flat on his temples, and his jaw protruded into a half-beastly, half-human expression of contemptuous ferocity" (284). Chanfrau ripped the cigar from his mouth, spat on the stage, and bellowed, "*I ain't a-goin' to 'run wid dat mercheen no more!*"[2] The audience was no longer tongue-tied. As reported in the *New York Herald* the next day (April 18, 1848), the crowd "climbed up to the stage boxes, and all seemed bent on genuine frolic. The police and officers connected with the theater were rendered powerless." A mob of people pushed in from the street, but at length the police got it under control; they "hereupon commenced to clear the front of the stage amid the most deafening cheers," the *Herald* continued, "and some of the B'hoys were to be seen springing forward on the heads of their different groups of friends, from the stage, whom they joined in the pit, amid continued laughter" (qtd. in Buckley 392).

Under its new name, "A Glance at New York in 1848," the play was performed for forty-eight consecutive nights, selling over forty thousand tickets, making it, up to that point, the most popular play in American history (Buckley 392–93). William Dean Howells later admitted to feeling wholly beguiled by its reception: "Some actor saw and heard things spoken with the peculiar swagger and whopperjaw utterance of the B'hoy of those dreadful old days . . . and he put them on stage and spread the poison of them all over the land, so that there was hardly anywhere a little blackguard boy who did not wish to act and talk like Mose" (*Criticism* 271). Though this appears to be crotchety disapproval from a hopeless traditionalist, Howells appreciated the long-lasting effect the play had on his own consciousness: "Other things have come and gone," he grants, "things of Shakespeare, of Alfieri, of Cervantes, but those golden works of a forgotten dramatist poet remain with me" (271).

The Baker sketch was, in short, an unintentional power play of cultural credibility. The Mose character empowered Bowery insiders with both a defiant attitude and a comic voice. The B'hoy thereafter became a widely known character type on the American stage, and the stage was one of the most important cultural vehicles of the time. Gay Wilson Allen, in his critical biography of Walt Whitman, demonstrates how the role of the B'hoy's "bravado" was a powerful influence on the Long Island-born poet and shows this characteristic as highly reflective of early American culture: "In fact the Americans as a whole were a swaggering, brawling nation of exhibitionists, as the folklore of the period plainly reveals" (63). Along with Captain Stormalong, "the Sea-going Yankee"; Daniel Boone; Mike Fink, "King of the Mississippi Boatmen"; Davy Crockett, "King of the Wild Frontier"; Paul Bunyan; and Pecos Bill, Mose "the Fireman" became a figure of mythic proportions.

Invoking these antebellum subalterns makes it possible to decipher Crane's cryptically impressionistic image of Bowery culture. As William Dean Howells rightly observes, Jimmie Johnson, Maggie's younger brother in *Maggie,* was "an Ishmaelite from the cradle, who, with his warlike instincts beaten back into cunning, is what the B'hoy of former times has become in our more strenuously policed days" ("New York Low Life" 154). Indeed, contrary to some recent scholarship that views Crane's characters as demonstrative of a new urban type, most of the traits shared by Jimmie and Pete in *Maggie* were typical of the B'hoy of the 1830s and '40s. In Keith Gandal's essay "Stephen Crane's 'Maggie' and the Modern Soul," for instance, Gandal is somewhat less attuned to Crane's historical perspective than Howell's. Gandal writes that, "Crane perceives in the turn-of-the-century slums, not vice, but an alternative morality and moral inspiration. The slums had generally appeared to the middle class as a moral foil, an ethical morass short on character; Crane discovers there instead a more advanced culture of consumption and a heterodox hero of self-esteem, the swaggering Bowery tough" (759).

The attributes of Bowery culture resonant in Crane's characters have roots over fifty years old. Pete, like the B'hoys, is described as having "an enticing nonchalance," with his hair "curled down over his forehead in an oiled bang," and a red scarf tied around his throat (25),[3] while Maggie, like her G'hal counterparts, is a seamstress infatuated with the theater. If one recalls Chanfrau's performance while reading the following scene from *Maggie*—Crane's dramatic introduction of the character Pete—the comparability between stage and fictional characters is even more vivid: "Down the avenue came boastfully sauntering a lad of sixteen years, although the chronic sneer of an ideal manhood already sat on his lips. His hat tipped over his eye with an air of challenge. Between his teeth a cigar stump was tilted at the angle of defiance" (8).

The analogy Howells proffers, likening Crane's Jimmie to the B'hoys is, then, perhaps even more applicable to Pete, who, unlike the B'hoys, ensures Maggie's metamorphosis from seamstress to street walker. At the same time, Crane makes Jimmie an admirer of fire engines, which testifies to the author's intention to evoke Bowery history, as the B'hoys were extreme in their fascination with fire fighting. "A fire engine," Crane writes, "was enshrined in [Jimmie's] heart as an appalling thing that he loved with dog-like devotion. It had been known to overturn a streetcar" (23). To the B'hoys, fighting fires was a contact sport. Any activity, including socializing with their female counterparts, the G'hals, was immediately broken off by the sound of a distant fire signal. Insiders on the Lower East Side would know at that point to keep their heads about them, while outsiders inauspiciously caught on the street would be run down.

The B'hoy became a recognizable "type" in the popular consciousness of mid-nineteenth-century New York at a time when the establishment of urban "types" was vital to the evolution of the city's identity (Buckley 359). As historian Peter Buckley writes, "types became convenient building blocks both for new forms of cultural production and for a new knowledge of the city" (359). But much like the case with the rich and visible New York gay culture in the 1920s (Chauncey 335), the famed Bowery B'hoys of the 1840s would gain too much press in the eyes of the dominant culture and face a subsequent backlash.

Reporting directly after the Astor Place Riots for *The Home Journal* (May 12, 1849), journalist N. P. Willis complains of the personal affronts men of "good society" had to endure at their hands: "If the English tragedian wishes to see the company that he offends, he has only to follow the well-dressed idler down the Bowery and observe the looks he gets from Mose and the soap-lockery as he goes along. . . . Let but the passive aristocratic party select a favorite, and let there be but a symptom of a handle for the B'hoys to express their dissent and the undercurrent breaks forth like an uncapped hydrant" (qtd. in Buckley 296). The antagonism, not surprisingly, was not one-sided. A B'hoy character in Ned Buntline's *The G'hals of New York* (1850) rails in disgust against the Victorian lack of respect for his position in society. Complaining to his sister about their bad financial luck, their father having lost everything, he is dumbfounded by the general lack of compassion: "Gas! Will our rich 'quaintances recognize us in our rags as they used to do when we were proud and dressed like them? Will they even speak to us? No! They turn from us as though they thought we were going to rob 'em; and if you meet 'em in the street, they turn their eyes another way, and hurry past you as if you had the small pox, and they were afraid o' ketchin' it!" (16). Parodying B'hoys irreverence in *The B'hoys of New York* (1848), one of Buntline's characters—a newspaper editor, like Whitman self-styled as "The B'hoy of New York"—decides to change the title of a proposed article on lewd female exhibitionism from "SHAMEFUL" to "Chaste and Beautiful Representations of Ancient Statuary" in order to, he vociferates over half a century before H. L. Mencken, "Give the Puritans a dash!" (11–15).

Few writers of that period, however, including Buntline, captured the spirit of life among the B'hoys on the inside. Writing nearly a decade after Ned Buntline wrote his *The B'hoys of New York,* George Foster pleaded to literary men to write about them with more determined authenticity: "Nothing has been adequately done to begin imparting to our literature the original and rich wealth lying latent in the life and history of Mose and Lize." "New York As It Is," he felt, had a "slight" plot and he refers to the staged events as "meager" and "commonplace" (177). Buntline's novels also stigmatized the B'hoy as a confidence man and the G'hal as a "painted woman," or prostitute. And John Vose in his *The B'hoys of Yale, or, The Scraps of a Hard Set of Collegians* (1878) depicts the B'hoys as an immature fraternity trying to drink as much and learn as little as possible. Vose describes the one B'hoy in the novel actually from the Bowery neighborhood as a "bully" who only wanted to "get tight!" "go on a time!" and "raise the d—l somewhere" and "similar spirited propositions peculiar to that lively locale. . . . He was 'awful papers'" (3). Even Walt Whitman, writing as late as 1888, acknowledged the lack of authentic literary representations of this singular group:

> For types of sectional New York those days—the streets East of the Bowery, that intersect Division, Grand, and up to Third Avenue—types that never found their Dickens, or Hogarth, or Balzac, and have passed away unportraitured—the young ship-builders, cartmen, butchers, firemen (the old-time "soap-lock" or exaggerated "Mose" or "Sikesey,"[4] of Chanfrau's plays), they, too were always to be seen in these audiences, racy of the East River and the Dry Dock. Slang wit, occasional shirt sleeves, and a picturesque freedom of

looks and manners, with a rude good-nature and restless movement, they were generally noticeable. ("The Old Bowery" 1214)

Whitman confirms that New York had always been "sectional," but there were no insider accounts of the phenomenon, particularly for the B'hoys. "Behavior at the Bowery," Richard Butsch bluntly concludes his essay on the topic, "was cited by middle-class newspapers and magazines as examples of how not to behave" (386). But the expansive characteristics of the B'hoys had been appropriated in the fictions of both Melville and Whitman, who discovered in the B'hoy a refreshingly American articulation. Indeed, Melville describes the character Henry Jackson in *Redburn* (1849) as dressing like a Bowery B'hoy (Reynolds, *Beneath* 285), and much of the credit for the characteristics of Whitman's "I" in *Leaves of Grass* can be attributed to the B'hoy. Whitman's "whole persona," David S. Reynolds argues, "wicked rather than conventionally virtuous, free, smart, prone to slang and vigorous outbursts—reflects the b'hoy culture" (*Walt* 155). Nineteenth-century reviewers labeled Whitman the "Bowery B'hoy of Literature," and he used "Mose Velsor," the name most commonly associated with the B'hoys in the popular press, as a pseudonym for many of his newspaper articles (Reynolds, *Walt* 105, 103). Whitman's affiliation with them characteristically disregards the period's increasingly virulent modes of cultural discrimination.

In *Democratic Vistas,* written in the year of Crane's birth, Whitman foresees a future America that is hyper-democratic "—the main thing being the average, the bodily, the concrete, the democratic, the popular, on which all the superstructures of the future are to permanently rest." Whitman was well aware of the prodigious power cultural dissemination afforded the rising middle-class, a power that worked against the hyper-democratic state he longed for. "The convertibility of America and democracy," Alan Trachtenberg relates in his essay, "American Studies as a Cultural Program," "represents for Whitman a definite (though not an inevitable) historical process. It also represents, that mutuality of terms, a role for culture, a role Whitman is able to articulate as a 'distinct cultural programme,' a 'programme of culture' (as he calls it) based upon 'a radical change of category,' 'in the distribution of precedence.' He would redeem the world by purging of its discriminations, its class distinctions, its disdain for the low and vulgar" (175).

Whitman implied that American culture had a very narrow base, and he records this notion in his sketch "The Old Bowery" (1885). Reminiscing about his Bowery theater experiences in the halcyon days of the B'hoys (the 1830s and '40s), he writes,

> Recalling from that period the occasion of either Forrest or Booth [two
> popular actors of Bowery affiliations], any good night at the old Bowery,
> pack'd from ceiling to pit with its audience mainly of alert, well dress'd,
> full-blooded young and middle aged-men, the best average of American-
> born mechanics—the emotional nature of the whole mass arous'd by the
> power and magnetism of as mighty mimes as ever trod the stage—the whole
> crowded auditorium, and what seeth'd in it, and flush'd from its faces and
> eyes, to me as much of a part of the show as any—bursting forth in one of
> those long-kept-up tempests of hand-clapping peculiar to the Bowery—no
> dainty kid-glove business, but electric force and muscle from perhaps 2000
> full-sinew'd men. . . . Such sounds and scenes as here resumed will surely
> afford to many old New Yorkers some fruitful recollections. (1213–14)

A fanatic of city life, Whitman, as literary critic Morris Dickstein aptly puts it,
"assimilates the city to the rhythm of physical activity, not just the movement
of the body but the systole and diastole of its inner pulsations" (187). Nevertheless, his democratic vision was one "taboo'd by 'polite society' in New
York and Boston," though "no such scruples affected the Bowery" (1213).

Somewhat typically, Whitman's plea for cultural tolerance in *Democratic
Vistas* contradicts his earlier 1845 *Brooklyn Star* article "Miserable State of
the Stage," in which he damns the low vulgarity of the Bowery Theater, the
Chatham Theater, and, significantly, Mitchell's Olympic as "nauseating" just
three years before the premier of "New York As It Is." In fact, in 1847, while
editor for the *Brooklyn Daily Eagle*, Whitman wrote a column entitled "Why
Do the Theatres Languish? And How Shall the American Stage be Resuscitated?" Pleading for a reformation of the theater experience, damning the
very culture that he fondly recalls later, he argues for a distinctive American
voice on the dramatic stage, one free from the influences of the Europeans,
but not of convention:

> As to the particular details of the system which should now supplant theatri-
> cals as they now exist, the one who in greatness of purpose conceives the effort
> only can say. . . . That effort must be made by a man or woman of no ordinary
> talent . . . liberal in disposition to provide whatever taste and propriety may
> demand. . . . Until such a person comes forward, and works out such a reform,
> theatricals in this country will continue to languish, and theatres be generally
> more and more deserted by men and women of taste, (rightfully too) as has
> been the case for eight or ten years past. (qtd. in Reynolds, *Walt* 152)

Whitman "once joked," David S. Reynolds reports, "that he considered it
a fall from grace when, in his journalism days during the forties, he got press

passes to sit among more sophisticated types on the parquet, or first level, of the New York theaters" (*Walt* 157); and much later, while conversing with his friend Horace Traubel, "he spent far more of his time . . . talking of the old antebellum performers than of the more stiff, distanced performance scene of the modern day" (*Walt* 563). In 1885, Whitman wrote that "a while after 1840 the character of the Bowery . . . completely changed. Cheap prices and vulgar programmes came in" (1214). In truth, it was not until the 1840s, the years of his disillusionment with the Lower East Side theater experience, that his B'hoys became national figures, no longer restricted to the scope of the Bowery or even Manhattan, no longer a limited urban type. And it was at this time that he wrote: "Of all 'low' places where vulgarity (not only on the stage, but in front of it) is in the ascendant, and bad taste carries the day with hardly a pleasant point to mitigate the coarseness, the New York theatres (except the Park) may be put down (as an Emeralder may say,) as the top of the heap! We don't like to make these sweeping assertions in general—but the habit of such places as the Bowery, the Chatham, and the Olympic theatres is really beyond all toleration" (qtd. in Reynolds, *Walt* 166).

Whitman was, perhaps, sufficiently distanced from the radical historical transformations of the previous half century to reevaluate his perspective on Bowery culture more nostalgically in "Old Bowery Days." Additionally, the "Good Gray Poet" seems to have grown slightly more conservative politically in the years preceding his death in 1892 (certainly more so than his good friend and amanuensis Horace Traubel, who persistently badgered him to declare an affiliation with socialism, which Whitman just as persistently refused to do), while at the same time becoming more open to cultural change. As difficult as it is for literary scholars to locate precisely where Whitman fell on the American political spectrum at the end of his life, by the 1880s, after a debilitating series of strokes, we might say he was far enough into his dotage to encourage more expressive insider cultures in the United States, while at the same time, as Eric Schocket argues of Crane and Jack London (see introduction), employ culture to balance a harder line on the unsettling chaos of class revolution.

Stephen Crane's Maggie *and the Ideology of Victorian Respectability*

As a protective rather than purely egotistical measure on the part of the Victorian middle class, the dissemination of their culture was enforced in all conceivable media. The most powerful aspect of Crane's *Maggie* is the young writer's uncanny ability to recognize this phenomenon of cultural incorporation in urban America, without a historian's benefit of hindsight, and render the insider's point of view—as each of his main characters are, in fact, Bowery insiders—though he himself is an outsider observer. The end result of this inversion is that the more novelistic, less impressionistic qualities of his other long works—above all in *George's Mother,* also a Bowery novel but from the outsider point of view and the subject of the following section—give way to convulsively episodic, irresistibly melodramatic scenes that bring to bear all the "traps and tricks" of the popular stage. Still, the irony in his scenes on Victorian melodrama, both toward the culture that creates it and the culture that buys into it, demonstrates that "if the stage is not 'realism' then by implication the novel *Maggie,* which tells these truths, is realism" (Orvell 129).

In his sketch "An Experiment in Luxury," Crane proffers his take on cultural dissemination. While dining at his wealthy young friend's house, the narrator reflects on the derisive view of the very rich by the Christian middle class and its complementary, condescending view of the very poor:

> Indicated in this light chatter about the dinner table there was an existence that was not at all what the youth had been taught to see. Theologians had for a long time told the poor man that riches did not bring happiness, and they had solemnly repeated this phrase until it had come to mean that misery was commensurate with dollars, that each wealthy man was inwardly a miserable wretch. And when a wail of despair of rage had come from the night of the slums they had *stuffed this epigram down the throat* of he who cried out and told him that he was a lucky fellow. *They did this because they feared.* (173, emphasis mine)

What is taken to task here is the age-old custom of the church's designating the poor as unfortunates and the rich as selfish, unhappy gluttons; "and, in the irritating, brutalizing, enslaving environment of their poverty," Crane insists, the poor "are expected to solace themselves with these assurances" (165). The "youth," as Crane calls his outsider protagonist, is alarmed by how functional and relatively happy the wealthy family actually seems. He further learns that there is no inherent love for the poor in the espoused vision; the espousers are simply terrified of the "other half" confronting their situation on their own terms.

This parable suggests the Victorian fear of a consumer class with access to and control over any and all consumable products. If the epitome of Bowery culture we find in the antebellum years was drummed out of existence because of what Victorians perceived as the threatening nature of subculture, then the subculture of the Gilded Age's nouveau riche is equally condemned. The friend in "An Experiment in Luxury" openly addresses the problem the narrator is grappling with: "'It is impossible for me to believe that these things equalize themselves; that there are burrs under all rich cloaks and benefits in all ragged jackets, and *the preaching of it seems wicked to me*'" (166, emphasis mine). Both the B'hoys and the barons, in other words, had been demonized by the popular media of the age. At bottom, then, the youth's experience with the ultra-rich was a form of reverse slumming.

This cultural posturing and antagonism was a manifestation of the new, broader consumer culture, which Keith Gandal describes as providing "a sort of moral inspiration" (*Virtues* 13) to slummers exploring the Bowery. But for the Bowery population itself, acculturation served as a dampening force rather than a liberating one. In Pete's courtship of Maggie Johnson, for instance, he escorts her through a number of middle-class amusements that accommodated increasingly standardized tastes. These include music halls, dance halls, theaters, dime museum freak shows, the Central Park Menagerie, and the Metropolitan Museum of Art. Pete finds the discomfiture of outsider status at the Met, which though open to the public, meets him with sidelong glares from the security staff. But Crane portrays the theater in particular as offering "an atmosphere of pleasure and prosperity" that "seemed to hang over the throng, born, perhaps, of good clothes and two hours in a place of forgetfulness" (70). Happiness here is equated with distractions and vicarious experience, a historical transformation that might be understood as the inception of the future culture of television, video games, and the internet. As Maggie for the first time blissfully takes in the emollient scenes on stage, "No thoughts of the atmosphere of the collar-and-cuff factory came to her" (33). For Maggie, the stage manifests a form of "personal dissociation" (discussed in the introduction of this book), but without destructively—in reality if not in reputation— indulging in "adultery, perversions, or drink" (Gelfant 33).

Crane presents this continual fall into dreaminess as a manifestation of cultural coercion. Popular melodrama dupes Maggie into idealizing Pete, an actor in life who adheres to a bogus self-image of respectability. When she falls, her neighbors envision her as the Eve-like character that Crane designs her to be, and children "ogle her as if they formed the front row of a theatre" (65).

The standard venue for impressing young ladies on the Bowery was the theater, and the paramount theatrical form in both *Maggie* and the New York it represents was moral-reform drama. Initially developed by Moses Kimball and P. T. Barnum for museum theaters, moral reform dramas were deliberately designed to address the needs of a middle class attentive to Protestant standards of decency (Butsch 383). If the theater had been primarily a working-class space in the opening decades of nineteenth-century New York, by the 1860s it drew a decidedly Victorian audience that determined its content and conduct. These middle-class values, as Henry James reported later, were simultaneously acted out on the stage and absorbed by the audience.

The consequent metamorphosis of theatrical space seems paradoxical in that insider consumption and outsider respectability, previously oppositional paradigms, were now inextricably intertwined. By showing how these oppositions play off of one another, Crane brings his sociological contribution into crystalline clarity. Crane makes the mimetic nature of the "foreign" exchange between buyer and seller remarkably comprehensible. Foolish inconsistency seems to be the fundamental aspect of Crane's *Maggie,* and Joseph X. Brennan identifies the central irony of the novel as the "self-righteous condemnation of a woman who is good by the very society responsible for her downfall" (64). But there remains some question as to why this would be true historically. It is important to expose the origins and nature of this type of cultural dialectic, as causes always inform naturalist fiction far more than symptoms.

Maggie Johnson is, among other things, a control in the Zolaesque experiment of looking at the popular theater as a means of understanding both the issue of class cultural consciousness and the popularized understanding of womanhood. Each time Maggie exits the theater, she "departed with raised spirits. . . . She rejoiced at the way in which the poor and virtuous eventually overcame the wealthy and wicked. The theater made her think. She wondered if the culture and refinement she had seen imitated, perhaps grotesquely, by the heroine on the stage, could be acquired by a girl who lived in a tenement house and worked in a shirt factory" (37).

Crane is being ironic here, perhaps even cruel, in describing the exaltations of his heroine in this way, but his outsider analysis of insider class aspiration nevertheless rings true. Most Bowery insiders complied with the culture of conformity, however unconsciously; they had been nurtured to accept outsider "refinement" as the ultimate state of being. Contemplating her suitor—whose pretensions are most blatantly displayed by the bar where he works, which is adorned with "imitation leather," a "shining bar of counterfeit massiveness," and a "nickel-plated cash register" (46)—Maggie sees him as "extremely gracious and attentive. He displayed the consideration of a cultured gentleman who knew what was his due." In addition, she "perceived that Pete brought forth all of his knowledge of high-class customs for her benefit. Her heart warmed as she reflected upon his condescension" (31). While she dreamily imagines a fantasy constructed by a culture truly at odds with her own, Pete is (in one of the few truly hilarious scenes of the book) chivalrously badgering the wait staff: "'Say, what deh hell? Bring deh lady a big glass! What deh hell use is dat pony?'" (31).

The theater scenes in *Maggie* demonstrate the trend towards what Richard Butsch calls the "taming" of the Bowery theatergoer. In contrast to Whitman's lusty description of early Bowery dramatic performances, in which the insider audience and their players interact to create one large performance that transcends the limits of the play itself, the theatergoers of Maggie's world more complicitly give themselves over to one-way, passive entertainment. Refinement in late Victorian New York had become the status quo in the theater, if it had not yet completely taken hold of the music hall. The mores imposed on Victorian women in the streets of New York—avoid eye contact, dress down so as not to attract attention, maintain emotional self-control, and so forth—were swiftly transferred to the Bowery theater. Emotive expressions such as "call backs," shouting, and laughter were no longer tolerated. The management often established dress codes, and hissing, drinking, eating, arriving late, and leaving early were forbidden at most venues.

Richard Butsch and Ann Douglas have both argued that over the nineteenth century the proliferation of middle-class etiquette effectively "feminized" the popular theater, concurrently making it a feminine space while rejecting audience participation and ardency (Butsch 395). Proprietors increasingly changed the atmosphere of their venues to accommodate this "new cult of middle-class female respectability," and they quickly came to understand that women had supremacy over consumer culture (Douglas, *Feminization* 7). In 1866, a gentleman's magazine the *Spirit of the Times* complained that many men succumbed to the "bore of attending dull or even good performances for the sole purpose of escorting their Mary Janes" (qtd. in Butsch 392–93). And Whitman, in his nostalgic essay "The Old Bowery," poetically, though perhaps too sentimentally, also acknowledges this refinement of the new theater experience: "So much for a Thespian temple of New York fifty years since [1830s and '40s], where 'sceptered tragedy went trailing by' under the gaze of the Dry Dock youth, and both players and auditors were of a character and like we shall never see again" (1216).

In Pete and Maggie's music hall as well, Crane brilliantly introduces his readers to the giving way of insider Bowery tastes to outsider Victorian culture in the later decades of the nineteenth century. The crowd contains, he writes, all of "the nationalities of the Bowery," who "beamed upon the stage from all directions" (30). In the spirit of radical democracy, a singer appeals to the Irish workers in attendance by describing in one of her songs "a vision of Britain annihilated by America, and Ireland bursting her bonds." She then climaxes the performance with "The Star-Spangled Banner," and "instantly a great cheer swelled from the throats of this assemblage of the masses, most of them of foreign birth. There was a heavy rumble of booted feet thumping the floor. Eyes gleamed with sudden fire, and callused hands waved frantically in the air" (32). Crane then juxtaposes this display of old Bowery behavior by smartly introducing a cadre of dancers "attired in some half-dozen skirts," which causes Maggie to wonder "at the splendor of the costume" and lose herself "in calculations of the cost of the silks and laces" (31). At the finale, the prima donna of the dancing troupe "[falls] into some of those grotesque attitudes which were at the time popular among the dancers in the theatres uptown, giving to the Bowery public the diversions of the aristocratic theatre-going public at reduced rates" (31–32).

During all this, little boys with "costumes of French chefs" selling "fancy cakes" attend to the audience under gilded chandeliers, a spectacle substantiating the "vertiginous bridge of American confectionery" Henry James detected at the theater a decade later. Among the performers, a pair of girls, listed as sisters for reasons of propriety, sing a duet that, Crane ironically puts in, "is heard occasionally at concerts given under church auspices" while dancing in a way that "can never be seen at concerts given under church auspices" (32). The continuous and telling juxtapositions of old Bowery and new Victorian culture are served up to his readers, then, just as Crane's boys in French chef hats serve up sweets to the laborers.

Material consumption is not the only proselytizing mode we see in *Maggie*. In one scene, Jimmie Johnson, Stephen Crane's Bowery-style antihero, is strolling past a mission church on the Bowery when he has an epiphany that calls to mind Stephen Dedalus on the strand. The revelation is one that allows him to "clad his soul in iron." Jimmie and a friend stumble upon an evangelical street preacher sermonizing to a Bowery audience. The sermon refers to sinners and is entirely one-directional; the missionary addresses his audience as "you." Crane writes, "Once a philosopher asked this man why he did not say 'we' instead of 'you.'" The missionary replies simply, "'What?'" (20). Language is, of course, restricted by the boundaries of permissible discourse. The outsider sermonizer is a "saved" man and the insider flock "damned" because they have not yet been fully acculturated into what is perceived as the only acceptable cultural paradigm—the Victorian, the

Christian, the respectable. The dialectical nature of the episode is clear to Crane. "A reader of words of wind-demons," he observes in similar terms to James's observation of the subliminal "schooling" that took place in Bowery theaters, "might have been able to see the portions of a dialogue pass to and fro between the exhorter and the hearers" (20). Jimmie the insider stands alone among his own people, a minority oppositional voice.

Maggie, somewhat dislocated in the Bowery world, is a figure under the gaze of her tenement's "philosophers," characters Crane assigns to deliberate over the nature of their condition. The young Maggie's early deferment of Bowery behavior stumps them: "None of the dirt of the Rum Alley seemed to be in her veins," Crane writes. "The philosophers, upstairs, downstairs, and on the same floor, puzzled over it" (24). How is it, they ask themselves, that a girl born and raised in the Bowery can have escaped the then perceived stigma of Bowery existence? In many ways this is the most self-reflexive point in the book. Crane himself directly questions his own motives for making Maggie such an anomaly. The novel, though singled out by many critics as the most artfully crafted Bowery tale ever written because of its combined impressionistic and realistic aspects, makes available, like Jerry McAuley, the ex-convict who had established the Water Street mission, an acceptable insider for mass consumption. Had Crane's heroine been the more G'hal-like Nell, the street-smart, culturally marginal friend of Pete's, no one would have read her death as tragic; in fact, few middle-class outsiders would have picked up the story at all.

The contradictory nature of Whitman's opposing identities—the "low" Bowery perspective and that of Victorian "respectability"—was equally pronounced in the life of Stephen Crane. The son of a Methodist minister, Crane too held contradictory views on the dogma of "respectability." He was especially ambivalent towards prostitution: he had not, for instance, pressed charges on Doris Watts, a prostitute who tried to blackmail him; he testified in court on behalf of Dora Clark, a prostitute who was arrested in his company; and his last companion in life was Cora Stewart, a seasoned Floridian madam. But as Laura Hapke asserts, "Crane never resolved his ambivalence about the unchaste woman, a tension between idealization and condemnation which his work on prostitution embodies" (*Girls* 67). He could not fully accept, nor fully deny that a prostitute could survive society's imposed and enforced judgments.

The overwhelming forces of the sentimental and the respectable unleashed in the novel are not only the product of determining institutions—the church, the family, and the school—but the grotesque imposition of outsider notions of "respectability" onto insiders whose lifestyles prohibit such niceties. No other aspect of the novel is as much a testament to Crane's genius, as he creates for us a transparent portrait of an extremely complicated cultural consciousness caused by the tensions between outsider "respectability" and insider self-esteem and companionship. Each of the primary characters in the novel contributes to Maggie's fall. Each takes the side of popular morality over familial and neighborhood ties. Pete abandons her because the proprietor of the bar where he works "insisted upon respectability of an advanced type" (67). Because he had tarnished her reputation for "pumpkin pie and virtue," as Nell calls it, when he sees her lingering outside the bar, he fears for the "eminent respectability of the place," and goes to her with thoughts of "returning with speed to a position behind the bar and to the atmosphere of respectability upon which the proprietor insisted" (68). He ultimately scares her away with the "anger of a man whose respectability is being threatened." When she asks, Scarlett O'Hara-like, what she should do and where she should go, he tells her "Oh, go teh hell," and turns back "with an air of relief, to his respectability" (69). In one scene, her own brother Jimmie consciously broods over whether or not to forsake his sister to maintain his position in society, which he does in the end: "Of course [he] publicly damned his sister that he might appear on a higher social plane. But, arguing with himself, stumbling about in ways that he knew not, he, once, almost came to a conclusion that his sister would have been more firmly good *had she better known why* [she should be chaste]. However, he felt that he could not hold such a view. He threw it hastily aside" (57, emphasis mine).

In a similarly self-reflexive moment, it "occurred to him vaguely, for an instant, if some of the women of his acquaintance had brothers" (43). Jimmie does not forgive or help his sister, but he is incapable of explaining to himself *why*. This same riddle stumped Jerry McAuley less than a decade earlier:

> You wonder why we don't have more women here [at the mission]. I'll tell you. When a girl has come up, a dozen in her room all her life, what can she know of decency or cleanliness? An' when she's down, she's down, an' no way to get her up, it seems. *I puzzle and puzzle why,* but it's only now an' again you get 'em steady . . . an' what's the reason? Every child that has to begin that way is born in sin an' to sin, an' steeped in nastiness and foulness from the very first day. An' when it comes to hundreds an' thousands of 'em down in these slums, an' good men an' women settin' by with their eyes shut, it tears the heart in you to think of it all. (Campbell, *Problem* 89, emphasis mine)

McAuley's environmental determinism is more conscious than Jimmie's. Jimmie's actions, indeed, run counter to his own constructed Bowery identity. They had both become, along with Pete, marginal men on the Lower East Side. But Jimmie is, unlike McAuley, incapable of the self-reflection necessary to demystify his conflicted, contradictory self. Nevertheless, his Bowery self is clearly weaker than the identity that has been constructed for him by the "well-dressed men . . . of untarnished clothes" he so ardently deplores (21).

Impenetrable Mysteries: The Outsider Perspective in Stephen Crane's "Other Bowery Novel" George's Mother

> Our ancient word of courage, fair 'St. George,'
> Inspire us with the spleen of fiery dragons.
> —William Shakespeare, *Richard III*

William Dean Howells wrote this astonishing praise for Stephen Crane's largely forgotten *George's Mother* in an 1896 *New York World* review:

> The wonder of it is the courage which deals with persons so absolutely average, and the art that graces them with the beauty of the author's compassion for everything that errs and suffers. Without this feeling the effects of his mastery would be impossible, and if it went further or put itself into the pitying phrases it would annul the effects. But it never does this; it is notable that in all respects the author keeps himself well in hand. He is quite honest with the reader. He never shows his characters or his situations in any sort of sentimental glamour; if you will be moved by the sadness of common fates you will feel his intention, but he does not flatter his portraits of people or conditions to take your fancy. ("New York Low Life" 264)

Howells's review "New York Low Life in Fiction" is generally read as a review of *Maggie* (1896 edition) and Abraham Cahan's *Yekl: A Tale of the New York Ghetto* (1896), not *George's Mother*. When Howells's critique is brought up in scholarship on *George's Mother* at all, it is his reworking of the original review for publication as the introduction to the 1896 edition of *Maggie,* which naturally touts the novel in question rather than Crane's other work. Indeed, "New York Low Life" is not included in the *Merrill Studies in* Maggie *and* George's Mother (1970). Instead, there are a series of conventional reviews that debase most any attempts at finding social, psychological, or artistic worth in the novel. We can only surmise from this volume that Crane's contemporary reviewers in 1896 were mostly critical of *George's Mother,* a fact that might explain Crane's reluctance to either discuss or reprint the novel with more verity than the scholar's reasoning that Crane himself disliked it (Colvert 103). An anonymous review from *The Nation* points caustically to Crane's "animalism," what we might call "naturalism," as a source of discomfort for the reader, rather than the "humor, thought, reason, aspiration, affection, morality, and religion" that a conscientious writer weaves into his narrative (qtd. in Wertheim 112); but these are qualities parents extol, rarely youths like Crane. The reviews collected in the *Merrill* volume strike me as written by a cluster of middle-aged Victorians troubled by the onset of youth culture, who reacted to *George's Mother* in ways we might find in 1950s reviews of Jack Kerouac's *On the Road.* In Harry Thurston Peck's scathing *Bookman* review (July 1896), for example, the critic demands to know "who cares about what George said to the bartender, or what the bartender said to George? There is no meaning to any of it" (116). Peck accuses Crane of rhyparography—creating distasteful imagery for its own sake—which is, Peck insists, "the lowest form of art" (116).

Not all reviews were so damning, however (see Weatherford 171–83). One young reviewer named Neith Boyce, the future wife of Hutchins Hapgood (the subject of chapter 4), praised the novel as "a psychological study presented objectively, pictorially. This method is the method of genius" (178). In kind, I would argue that George Kelcey's mother satisfies at least the "affection, morality, and religion" from the anonymous reviewer's criteria, while Kelcey himself is driven by issues altogether more relevant to his youthful position—identity, desire, friendship, wish-fulfillment, and sexuality—topics that stem from the mind of a young man in his early twenties, where Crane's own mind was during the book's composition, topics to which college-level students prodigiously relate. Crane was, as Luc Sante stresses in his new introduction to *Maggie* and *George's Mother,* a "kid," and it is important to keep that fact in mind since "being a kid gave him a number of advantages of stance" (xii). One altogether revolutionary aspect of Crane's career, particularly with regard to *George's Mother,* is that he allowed himself to be a kid and in so doing often circumvented the demands of the established publishing elite. Crane wrote about "low life" on the Bowery, repressed sexuality, hangovers, and jobless indolence with an ambiguousness that appalled genteel critics and fellow authors alike.

Peck assumed that Crane's well-wrought scenes of debauchery in the tenements and taverns of the Bowery are nonsequiturs in the framework of the novel, that "anyone can hang around a bar-room and jot down the conversation and also print it, but this is not realism" (116). In truth, George never speaks to a bartender aside from Pete in the book, as he was too far removed from the pulse of the street; but his outsider partner in crime, Charley Jones, an excitable alcoholic ne'er-do-well, has the ability to cultivate insider acquaintanceships with bartenders, which makes him an almost meta-bartender in the eyes of an inquisitive young greenhorn like Kelcey, a figure of "sublime" proportions. By extension, the saloon and its complementary potations appear to expand the vista of New York knowledge Kelcey seeks: "As he drank more beer Kelcey felt his breast expand with manly feeling. He knew that he was capable of sublime things" (85). Drinking beer does not come naturally to Kelcey, but he conquers his natural revulsion, for the benefits of drunkenness to the youth appear to outweigh the bitterness of the drink: "He understood that drink was an essential to joy, to the coveted position of a man of the world and of the streets. The saloons contained the mystery of a street for him. When he knew its saloons he comprehended the street. *Drink and its surroundings were the eyes of a superb green dragon to him.* He followed a fascinating glitter, and the glitter required no explanation" (110–11, emphasis mine). Crane stylizes the saloon-as-street synecdoche for Kelcey here with repetitive syntax: drink/streets, saloons/street, saloons/street. Furthermore, the chivalric novels that give form to Kelcey's world suggest that the dragon, a mythic monster born of chivalric romance and defeated most famously by Kelcey's canonized namesake, St. George, is conquerable and thus knowable. In fact this dragon metaphor of Crane's, appearing as it does in nearly every chapter, might be read as a symbol for, among other things, the urban sublime, happiness, companionship, alcohol, or insideness itself.

In his study of *George's Mother* and the temperance movement, George Monteiro argues that "echoing the language of 'The Warfare,' George's mother sees herself as a temperance crusader. To fight against George's intemperance is to do the Christian God's work. Her opponent is the dragon of alcoholism that the ironically named (Saint?) George does not have the will to defeat" (15).[5] Joseph X. Brennan shows that from Mrs. Kelcey's outsider point of view, the green dragon is alcohol and the insidious influences of the streets, and thus Crane ironically inverts the old legend wherein the mother sees herself as St. George. Here is the indirect "dragon discourse" from the mother's perspective: "Her mind created many wondrous influences that were swooping like green dragons at him. They were changing him to a morose man who suffered silently. She longed to discover them, that she might go bravely to the rescue of her heroic son. She knew that he, generous in his pain, would keep it from her" (qtd. in Brennan 128).

Kelcey's mother is no less influenced by the material culture of the times than Kelcey, or even Maggie, Pete, or *The Red Badge of Courage*'s antihero, Henry Fleming. Like them, she too deludes herself that romantic fancies come true. Crane, as we know, was a journalist, but he read the newspapers with a novelist's eye. One of the many late nineteenth-century co-optations of the St. George and the dragon legend in both British and American newspapers was single-framed cartoons marking the dragon as intemperance and St. George the temperance movement.[6] Kelcey's mother wishes to slay the dragon of intemperance, while Kelcey's bugaboo is the broader hope to fully comprehend the inner workings of the streets.

Crane was both a product and a producer of the modern ethos. If his only dragon was demon rum, *George's Mother* would be a temperance tract, a genre that, given Crane's actual habits and temperament, is more likely the target of his satire than its weapon. As his close niece Helen R. Crane remembered in 1934, by 1891, two years before Crane began work on *George's Mother*, her uncle, "was in full rebellion against the traditions on which he had been nourished and reared," and he "did marvel always that such an intellectual woman [his mother] . . . could have wrapped herself so completely in the 'vacuous, futile, psalm-singing that passed for worship' in those days" (qtd. in Colvert 107, 108.) However, Kelcey is no more a simple allegory of Crane's youth than "Bartleby, the Scrivener" is of Herman Melville's writing career, but the correspondences that do exist between the novel and its author's life (also the case with Melville's story) cannot be denied; rather, Crane's outsider hero symbolizes the floundering foundations of young men and women breaking away from childhood and experiencing life and its personal dissociations in order to arrive at semblances of meaning. The incomprehensible dragon is, again, more likely "joy," "the world," "the mystery of a street," "the advanced things in life"—simply put, a wholly "vast" knowledge of the city and the cosmopolitan, distinctly modern condition it represents. Henry James adopts the "dragon discourse" in *American Scene* as well, applying the trope to express the inner reactions of the "man of letters" (himself) while exploring the "'seamy' order" of the Lower East Side: "To his mind, quite as old knighthood astride of its caparisoned charger, the dragon most rousing, over the land, the proper spirit of St. George, is just this immensity of the alien presence climbing higher and higher, climbing itself into the very light of publicity" (104, 105). Given his age and origins, Kelcey's naive consciousness naturally tempts him into spinning alcohol and its sensuous accessories into vehicles for conquering the dragon, for becoming an insider in "this city" and thereby understanding the modern complexities it stands for.

Soon after Kelcey's and his mother's arrival in New York, the youth vacillates awkwardly between three social strains in the neighborhood of the Bowery. One is his mother's moralistic devotion to the church and her appeals for her son to attend nightly evangelical prayer meetings; another is a fraternal drinking club of self-aggrandizing men of varying age, lorded over by a former associate of Kelcey's from Handyville, who together sound off Victorian aspirations but are far too dissipated to achieve any public respectability; the last is the alluring but ultra-violent life of the street gang on the corner of his tenement block. Each is presented as a conformist, almost tribal alternative to rural community life, as the perpetual outsider Kelcey guilelessly searches for the sense of social coherence he had left behind. In the case of the evangelical prayer-meeting set, Crane reveals Kelcey's reluctance to join his mother at the local church this way: "In his ears was the sound of a hymn, made by people who tilted their heads at a prescribed angle of devotion. *It would be too apparent that they were all better than he.* When he entered they would turn their heads and regard him with suspicion. This would be an enormous aggravation, since *he was certain that he was as good as they*" (98, emphasis mine). Kelcey's uncertainty on this last point is clear in the unconscious slip of the second sentence. He is unconvinced by his moral standing with the objects of his own criticism, just as Jimmie Johnson in *Maggie* is unwilling to ask himself why his sister might have "gone teh deh devil" or whether his own defiled sexual partners had brothers (36).

Crane perpetuates this pseudo-ironic tone throughout *George's Mother* by repeatedly concluding chapters with glib insights into Kelcey's small-town naiveté, an iterative rhetorical schema that produces conflicting reader responses. The final sentences of each chapter read like punch lines meant to expose Kelcey's bumpkin-style outsider haplessness. On his social dissociation in the late hours of a drunken house party at his drinking companion Bleeker's tenement flat: "[Kelcey], the brilliant, the good, the sympathetic had been thrust fiendishly from the party. They had had the comprehension of red lobsters. It was unspeakable barbarism. Tears welled piteously from his eyes. He planned long diabolical explanations!" (103).

On his lackluster experience at a prayer meeting with his mother: "At last the young clergyman spoke at some length. Kelcey was amazed, because, from the young man's appearance, he would not have suspected him of being so glib; but the speech had no effect on Kelcey, excepting to prove to him again that he was damned" (110).

On his mother's imploring him to stay home, do well at work, and not be carousing at all hours: "He listened to her harangue with a curled lip. In defense he merely made a gesture of supreme exasperation. She never understood the advanced things in life. He felt the hopelessness of ever making her comprehend. His mother was not modern" (117).

The darkly playful irony in these passages produces less hilarity than serious insights into Crane's ambivalence toward the moral and social lessons of modern times, along with his relationship to his own mother. Kelcey apprehends that in the modern world sensuality appears to triumph over Christian morality in ways that Crane's Methodist parents, like Kelcey's mother, adumbrated and publicly spoke out against. Kelcey's moniker among the local street gang is "Kel,'" and Kell, after all, is a form of pottage, which calls to mind the biblical "mess of pottage" Esau substituted for his birthright, and subsequently God's (or a pious mother's) good will.

The most revealing instance of this conflict between Crane's ironic tone and Kelcey's earnestness is the final paragraph of chapter 6, in which Crane emphasizes the powerful hold the city had on Kelcey, elaborates on the disruptive influences of urban mystification and personal dissociation, and, again pseudo-ironically, encapsulates the mysteries of the city in the figure of the Bowery bartender. George later experiences the same revelation connecting his friend Charley Jones's familiarity of bartenders with the depth of Jones's insider status:

> He had begun to look at the great world evolving near to his nose. He had a vast curiosity concerning this city in whose complexities he was buried. It was an impenetrable mystery, this city. It was a blend of enticing colors. He longed to comprehend it completely, that he might walk understandingly in its greatest marvels, its mightiest march of life, its sin. He dreamed of a comprehension whose pay was the admirable attitude of a man of knowledge. He remembered Jones. He could not help but admire a man who knew so many bartenders. (92)

Jones appears to have the two things Kelcey wants most: knowledge of the city and moral certainty. As Paul Orlov has shown, the indirect discourse Crane employs betrays and mocks the "general tendency of city dwellers to see themselves and their lives in an unrealistic, romanticized light" (218). When Kelcey bumps into Jones in the opening chapter, he notices that "there was something very worldly and wise about him. Life did not seem to confuse him. Evidently he understood its complications. His hand thrust into his trousers pocket, where he jingled keys, and his hat perched back on his head expressed a young man of vast knowledge. His extensive acquaintance with bartenders aided him materially in this habitual expression of wisdom" (71).

The qualified tone of the passage, signaled by the words and phrases "there was something," "did not seem," "evidently," "expressed," and "materially" demonstrates that the characterization, drawn from Kelcey's glance at Jones through the mirror behind the bar, reflects an obscured reality, one that "probably" does not exist at all, in spite of Howells's sanguine confidence in Crane's "unerring mastery of absolute knowledge," but if it does exist, it does so in the figure of the insider Bowery bartender rather than the outsider poseur Charley Jones.

Kelcey's conclusion about bartenders in the indirect discourse of Crane's narrative does not entirely lack authorial empathy and, indeed, conviction. Kelcey's "vast curiosity" about the city and the sublimely enticing prospect of striving toward its complete comprehension, a goal Crane implies is a delusion of the uninitiated, speaks to recent studies of literary naturalism's harboring "pseudo-totalizing vitalistic rhetorics" like the sublime, specifically in Christophe Den Tandt's *The Urban Sublime in American Literary Naturalism*. Den Tandt argues that "the function of the rhetoric of sublimity is, first, to give utterance to the writer's doubts about the very possibility of portraying the city as a totality comprehensible in human terms; simultaneously, in an act of rhetorical substitution, the sublime fills the epistemological and existential void of the city's fragmentation by producing its pseudo-synthesis of the urban field . . . the totalizing representation thus created is a metaphorical token for the unrepresentable object" (39). What urban type, we ask ourselves, is more likely in the "detached milieu" of Bowery life to "comprehend it completely," one who symbolizes the "metaphorical token for the unrepresentable object," the city itself, than the Bowery bartender? The saloon keeper on the Bowery after all, as Benedict Giamo suggests in *On the Bowery: Confronting Homelessness in American Society*,[7] is the personification of the Bowery scene: "The saloon keeper fulfilled as many roles as his establishment, shifting from banker to business advisor, employment agent, political contact, publicity director, and messenger. In all, he was a social force in the community, an agent who made the subculture cohere and made his presence known to both insiders and outsiders" (22–23). Even Maggie Johnson is enthralled by Pete's vocation, though unlike George she was born and raised in the Bowery district: "[His] elegant occupation brought him, no doubt, into contact with people who had money and manners" (*Maggie* 23).

If the church, the family, and the school still hold sway as the great triumvirate of small-town American influence, the bartender is the supreme insider of urban communities, as the minister is of the church, the mother of the family, and the teacher of the school. In a trade city like New York, the social literacy of a successful bartender would necessarily be infinitely more complex; the language of the broker, the street walker, the Irish tough must all be naturally absorbed and applied at the workplace. He must be, as Shakespeare's Prince Hal in *Henry IV, Part I,* "so good a proficient in one quarter of an hour/ [he] can drink with any tinker in his own language" (2.4.15–18). Regardless of Kelcey's adoration of Charley Jones, Jones remains an outsider like Kelcey in the purview of the Bowery, both having emigrated to the big city from Handyville; as such, Jones might represent Kelcey's future on the Bowery after the death of his living conscience, his mother, at the end of the novel.

The consummate insider Pete, the pretentious bartender from *Maggie* and Maggie Johnson's corruptor, complicates the disingenuousness of Crane's ironic pose. Like Maggie, Kelcey is utterly star struck when he encounters Pete for the first time in the hallway of his and Maggie's tenement: "[He] had felt a sudden quiver of his heart. The grandeur of [Pete's] clothes, the fine worldly air, the experience, the self-reliance, the courage that shone in the countenance of this other young man made him suddenly sink to the depths of woe" (94–95). He fears that if Maggie were to observe him abreast of a "real" man like Pete, the apex of Bowery masculinity and style, "she might have felt sorry for him" (95). Like Pete, Kelcey aspires to be both Bowery tough and chivalric gentleman. And like Maggie, he apprehends his beloved only through the lens of popular culture. Kelcey derives his imaginings from "scenes which he took mainly from pictures, this vision conducted a courtship, strutting, posing, and lying through a drama which was magnificent from a glow of purple" (92) and, more significantly, in "some books" that he had read while still at Handyville (93).

The final scene of *George's Mother* is more ideologically open-ended than the bowdlerized 1896 D. Appleton edition of *Maggie* Crane's critics would have read. Out of a job and penniless, Kelcey asks his barroom cronies, Jones, Bleeker, O'Connor, and other members of their social club, if he could have a loan, but he swiftly discovers that "he was below them in social position. . . . In them all he saw that something had been reversed. They remained silent upon many occasions, when they might have grunted in sympathy for him" (121, 122). On his way home, his self-esteem in shambles, the street gang on his corner goads him into picking a fight with an insider street tough named Blue Billie, Jimmie Johnson's Devil's Row antagonist in the opening scene of *Maggie* and his ally against Pete in a later chapter. Kelcey demurs at first, but then changes his mind with the idea that fighting Billie, no matter the end result, might serve as an antidote for his wounded pride. Just before the altercation comes to blows, a street herald stops the brawl with a message from Kelcey's mother. "She's awful sick! She was hollerin'! Dey been looki' fer yeh over'n hour!" (124–25). Like the bride in Crane's short masterpiece "The Bride Comes to Yellow Sky" (1898), who symbolically wins the final gunfight between Sheriff Potter and Scratchy Wilson by simply observing their altercation, Kelcey's mother ends the battle before it had even begun by calling her son to her deathbed. For a woman without weapons to defeat the dragon of urban influences, death is the only effectual contingency.

To the end, Kelcey is obsessed with the disappointments he suffered outside the home: "When he entered the chamber of death," Crane writes, "he was brooding over the recent encounter and devising extravagant revenges upon Blue Billie and the others" (125). The young clergyman from Mrs. Kelcey's church group is present, bringing all of the influences of the Bowery to bear on George's conscience. A war of words erupts in the hallway outside their flat. A young man refuses to obey his mother's call to go to the store—"In a minnet, I tell yeh!" (127). That one fillip in the hallway completely absorbs Kelcey's thoughts, and it is the clergyman who discovers that George's mother is dead. There is no resolution in this final scene, only more questions.

In *Maggie,* Crane sustains an ironic distance from his characters. Frank Norris picked up on this in his review of the novel, stating that "the author is writing, as it were, *from the outside,* there is a certain lack of sympathy apparent" (qtd. in Cain 563, emphasis mine). For this reason among others, we might consider *George's Mother* a more roundly developed novel than *Maggie* in that it is somewhat more ambiguous morally and ideologically than its prequel; though *Maggie* was highly controversial at the time for its subject matter, *George's Mother* is a more balanced treatment of that material, which made it downright incendiary. But more importantly, Kelcey, like Crane, is an outsider, and in the end Crane's ability to render the contradictory effects on George's consciousness is more believable than Maggie's insider turmoil.

Maggie would perhaps be a better play than novel and the performative moments Crane weaves into *George's Mother* are more subtly conveyed.[8] Since visual performance in theater and film exacts a manner of caricature and episodic pacing to establish a plot in substantially less time than it takes to read a novel, and additionally since in *Maggie* Crane's social agenda is fairly explicit—the economic, social, and cultural prostration of the urban poor within the naturalistic environment of the slums—then *George's Mother* is a more likely novel, and *Maggie* might be a more likely drama. Howells himself notes the "fatal necessity" of *Maggie* as reflective of "Greek tragedy" ("Low Life" 263). Maggie Johnson's romantic idealism comes principally from theatrical melodrama, whereas Kelcey's desire to be the "sublime king of a vague woman's heart" only fully achieves "clearer expression" after some exposure to the uplifting chivalric romances so popular among readers at the end of the nineteenth century (20).

This treatment of the popular romance and its significance to daily life echoes Crane's own evangelical father's 1869 assertion that the "habit of novel-reading creates a morbid love of excitement somewhat akin to the imperious thirst of the inebriate" (qtd. in Brown 32). The influences of romantic novels on Kelcey do appear part and parcel with his enamored view of social drinking, as the romantic portrait of himself as a knight rescuing Maggie from catastrophe (which Crane implies he might have done had she given him the time of day) finally gives way to a more realistic image of the picaresque socializer roving inside the streets and taverns of the Lower East Side, using his fists to settle injustices, living hand-to-mouth with no steady job, and drinking his life away in unholy boarding house orgies, all of which, his mother's death suggests, might be fully realized in time. Thus the correspondences between rhetoric and ideology are so strong in both *Maggie* and *George's Mother* that the former reads scene by scene like the stage dramas Crane's insiders observe, while the latter pits genre against genre in a self-reflexive move of psychological intervention that allows Crane to explore his own outsider contradictions more fully. In this way, Crane's second Bowery novel is a somewhat more mature articulation for establishing, as Bill Brown has phrased it, "the archetypical maneuver of the realist project, the novel distinguishing itself from romance" (32).

Crane makes Maggie's death scene palatable to his audience, the respectable outsider, by recycling the tragic circumstances of a girl who blossoms in a mud puddle but then meets a fateful death. Still, in the 1893 edition Maggie is murdered by her client, a "huge fat man in torn and greasy garments," who "laughed, his brown, disordered teeth gleaming under a gray, grizzled mustache from which beer-drops dripped" (72). The grotesque man follows her until they stand together: "At their feet the river appeared a deathly black hue" (72). In the D. Appleton edition, on the other hand, Maggie commits suicide, a trope of the Victorian melodrama: "She went into the blackness of the final block. . . . At the feet of the tall buildings appeared the deathly black hue of the river" (144). Crane made these changes to appease the marketplace. By having Maggie commit suicide, Crane could both punish her as a fallen woman and allow her to achieve redemption by contrition, thereby allowing the book to end on a sentimental note. Crane submitted to many concessions of this kind throughout his career, as did many writers defer to the moral standard of the Victorian world of publishing.[9] In the end, Crane was a victim of the very genteel process that was the butt of his own irony.

❖ ❖ ❖

In one of the final scenes in *Maggie,* the fallen title character murmurs the enigmatic utterance "Who?" as a man alongside her "saved his respectability by a vigorous sidestep," refusing to "risk it to save a soul" (69). To address that question—Who?—one that remains unanswered in the text, at least on the surface, I will again draw from T. J. Jackson Lears, who writes, "To resort to the concept of cultural hegemony is to take a banal question—'who has power?'—and deepen it at both ends. The 'who' includes parents, preachers, teachers, journalists, literati, 'experts' of all sorts, as well as advertising executives, entertainment promoters, popular musicians, sports figures, and 'celebrities'—all of whom are involved (albeit often unwillingly) in shaping the values and attitudes of society" (572).

For Henry James, this exchange was realized in the popular theater he visited, but not limited to it. James thinks of the "odd scene [at the theater] as still enacted in many places and many ways, the inevitable rough union in discord of the two groups of instincts, the fusion of the two camps by a queer, clumsy, wasteful social chemistry" (199). This "wasteful social chemistry" brewed on the Bowery and elsewhere in New York as a result of the governing society's desire to bridle the effects of rampageous urban dissent. Unlike many European cities, New York in the nineteenth century promoted itself as a city free from rigid economic class distinctions. In some ways I believe this was true and that the more destructive conflict was fought over cultural legitimacy and representation.

Though Victorian and Bowery culture may have coexisted for a time in the mid-nineteenth century, the Victorian would rapidly come to determine the values, sentiments, and prejudices of civil society on the Bowery, as well as throughout the city. If we accept Alfred Kazin's assertion that "the surest thing one can say about Crane is that he cared not a jot which way the world went" (68), along with F. O. Matthiessen's pertinent claim that *Maggie* is an "outsider's job" (91), it is equally true, as Hamlin Garland once acknowledged, that the harsh realism in Crane's novel "grew out of intimate association with the poor" (Manuscript note 2). Describing Jimmie Johnson, Crane cuts a figure not unlike his own: "On the corners he was in life and of life. The world was going on and he was there to perceive it" (20).

The Bowery Crane drew on for *Maggie* exhibited a very real historical process: the modernization of subcultures whose cultural consciousnesses, specifically in regard to Bowery culture as it survived over the decades, conflicted with and were ultimately determined by nineteenth-century American Victorianism. And when Crane ventured briefly into the neighborhood of the Tenderloin, the subject of my next chapter, he reaffirmed the naturalist revelation that "the power that makes the rain, the sunshine, the wind, now recognizes social form as an important element in the curious fashioning of the world" ("In the 'Tenderloin'" 167).

In the next chapter, I will begin with a discussion of another 1890s moral region, the Tenderloin's "black Bohemia." But rather than stress the impact of outsider morality on insiders like Maggie and Jimmie Johnson, I will show instead the extent to which their region impacted outsiders like George Kelcey who availed themselves of its influences. By the turn of the century, authors objectified the lifestyles of marginalized insiders and demonstrated how it was propitious for genteel outsiders to engage these spaces. In the early years of the twentieth century, New York writers began to represent subaltern cultural landscapes as sites of cultural regeneration. Though instead of crossing moral boundaries with the intention of reforming or coercing "the other half" to accept "respectable" codes of behavior, it was the outsiders themselves who sought cultural acquisition. For better or for worse, the cultural channel by the turn of the twentieth century began to flow upwards on the social ladder—from within, out.

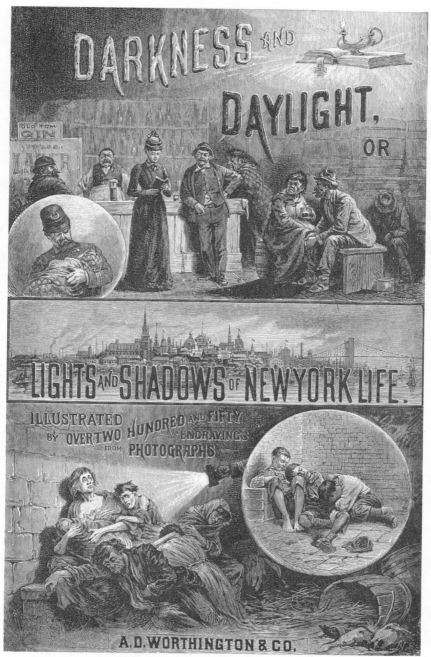

Frontispiece for Helen Campbell's *Darkness and Daylight*, 1895 edition.

The East Side Waterfront, 1897.

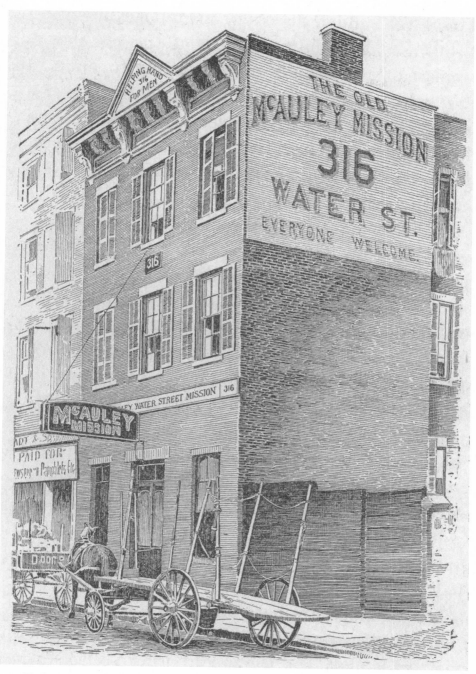

Facing page and above: The Water Street Mission. Library of Congress.

Jerry McAuley.
Frontispiece to *Trans-formed, or, The His-tory of a River Thief: Briefly Told*, 1876.

Helen Campbell,
from *Darkness and Daylight*, 1895 edition.

Ernest Poole. Courtesy of his grandson, David Dixon Porter Poole.

Frank Chanfrau as "Mose, the Fireman." Library of Congress.

Walt Whitman, the "Bowery B'hoy of Literature." Library of Congress.

Stephen Crane. Courtesy of the Photography Collection, Miriam and Ira D. Wallach Division of Art, Prints, and Photographs, the New York Public Library, Astor, Lenox, and Tilden Foundations.

The Bowery. Library of Congress.

A restaurant in the Tenderloin's "black Bohemia," Sixth Avenue and West Twenty-seventh Street (possibly the location of Ike Hines's Club). Brown Brothers: photographer. Courtesy of the Millstein Division of United States History, Local History, and Genealogy, the New York Public Library, Astor, Lenox, and Tilden Foundations.

Paul Laurence Dunbar, from *Progress of a Race,* 1902. Courtesy of the General Research and Reference Division, Schomburg Center for Research in Black Culture, the New York Public Library, Astor, Lenox, and Tilden Foundations.

James Weldon Johnson, 1927. Courtesy of the General Research and Reference Division, Schomburg Center for Research in Black Culture, the New York Public Library, Astor, Lenox, and Tilden Foundations.

Jacob Epstein's drawing *Intensely Serious* in Hutchins Hapgood's book *The Spirit of the Ghetto,* 1902.

Market day on the Lower East Side, 1912. Photographer: Lewis W. Hine. Courtesy of the Photography Collection, Miriam and Ira D. Wallach Division of Art, Prints, and Photographs, the New York Public Library, Astor, Lenox, and Tilden Foundations.

Jacob Riis. Library of Congress.

Abraham Cahan. Library of Congress.

Hutchins Hapgood. Courtesy of the Yale Collection of American Literature, Beinecke Rare Book and Manuscript Library.

Lincoln Steffens. Library of Congress.

William Dean Howells. Courtesy of the Print Collection, Miriam and Ira D. Wallach Division of Art, Prints, and Photographs, the New York Public Library, Astor, Lenox, and Tilden Foundations.

Harlem street scene, "within thirty seconds walk of the 135th Street branch" of the New York Public Library. Courtesy of the Photographs and Prints Collection, Schomburg Center for Research in Black Culture, the New York Public Library, Astor, Lenox, and Tilden Foundations.

W. E. B. Du Bois. Library of Congress.

Cover of the first edition of Claude McKay's *Home to Harlem,* 1928, "a negro's own novel." Courtesy of the General Research Division, the New York Public Library, Astor, Lenox, and Tilden Foundations.

Langston Hughes. Photo by Carl Van Vechten.

Carl Van Vechten. Courtesy of Carl Van Vechten estate.

Claude McKay, from *Negro Poets and Their Poems*, 1923. Courtesy of the General Research and Reference Division, Schomburg Center for Research in Black Culture, the New York Public Library, Astor, Lenox, and Tilden Foundations.

3 Marginal Men in Black Bohemia

PAUL LAURENCE DUNBAR AND
JAMES WELDON JOHNSON
IN THE TENDERLOIN

> "Well, if they don't want to find out things, what do they come to
> N' Yawk for? It ain't nobody's old Sunday-school picnic."
>
> —Character William Thomas in Paul Laurence Dunbar's
> *The Sport of the Gods,* 1902

THE DECADES IMMEDIATELY FOLLOWING the Civil War saw the bulk of New York City's modest African American population shift from Greenwich Village, the center being the corner of Bleeker and Mercer, to the Tenderloin district, located from approximately Twenty-fifth Street to Fifty-fifth and from Fifth Avenue to Seventh. Once the center of white middle-class respectability, by the late 1870s it had turned into a major theater district, and the ensuing army of pleasure-seekers chased its residents uptown. This gave landlords two choices: either turn the brownstones into multiple-family tenements for the crush of immigrant arrivals from southern and eastern Europe, or lease them out to brothel owners and gambling proprietors who could afford higher rents (Gilfoyle 204). Needless to say, they chose the second option, and seemingly overnight the Tenderloin became the most infamous center of gambling and prostitution in New York City history. "Yes, the Tenderloin is more than a place," Stephen Crane wrote in the first of a series of 1896 sketches on the district for the New York *Journal*, "it is an emotion" ("'Tenderloin' as It Really Is" 166).

Within the greater Tenderloin, there was a black section along Sixth Avenue in what is now the Garment District. This region catered to African American musicians, gamblers, stage performers, and prostitutes, as well as white "slummers," and frequenters of the "black and tans" (racially integrated bars that often provided interracial assignations and drew a great deal of public scorn). Through the 1890s, hundreds of African Americans moved to the Tenderloin for its racial tolerance and professional opportunities. Still, what we now call the "Great Migration" of southern blacks escaping the horrors of Jim Crow and the murderous pandemic of public lynchings was just beginning at the turn of the century, but this diaspora did not truly pick up steam until the center of black life in New York moved from the Tenderloin to Harlem.[1] As a result, at the turn of the twentieth century, the black population in New York was largely unknown to its white counterpart. In 1890, Manhattan's total black population was a relatively scattered 25,674 (Osofsky 206n) in a city of 1,441,216 (Jackson 923); in 1910 it was 60,534 (Osofsky 206n) in a borough of 2,331,542 (Jackson 921),[2] and the centers of African American life were located in a small section of the Tenderloin district and San Juan Hill,[3] areas that combined took up no more than ten blocks. Not surprisingly, most literary slummers who explored those areas were black outsiders themselves. One journalist at the *New York Freeman* candidly admitted in 1887 that "the northern white man knows practically nothing of the Negro" (qtd. in Osofsky 41).

The only notable white outsider contribution to our understanding of black Manhattan from this period is Jacob Riis's *How the Other Half Lives* (1890). In the year his book appeared, blacks made up a mere 1.56 percent of Manhattan's total population,[4] and whether consciously or not, Riis overstates the rise over the previous decade. Though he claims that the number of African Americans "quite doubled in number" in New York over the 1880s, there were actually 19,653 in 1880 (Sante, *Low Life* 227n) and 25,674 in 1890 (Osofsky 206), a less than 20 percent increase of an already minuscule number. Like Campbell's *The Problem of the Poor*, *How the Other Half Lives* is in the mode of moral realism, and as such, Riis backs his documentary-style statistics with sensationalistic rhetorical fervor. That he was deliberately invoking terror from his audience (in the way he does with the Jewish population, which will be covered in the following chapter) is doubtful, as he generally regards African Americans as an acceptable group who are viciously discriminated against by avaricious white landlords.

Riis's cursory glance at black Manhattan was the most highly circulated piece of writing on the subject in American history up to that point. And for him it is a fairly even-handed, if still racist and condescending, treatment—what Kevin J. Mumford refers to as "a kind of late Victorian benevolent racial liberalism" (137). It was certainly more even-handed than the one sketch on the subject Stephen Crane wrote for the Philadelphia *Press*, entitled "Stephen Crane in Minetta Lane, One of Gotham's Most Notorious Thoroughfares"

(1896), in which he described the old black section in Greenwich Village as representing "the very worst elements of their race" (179). At a time when "the Italians have begun to dispute possession" of the district around Minetta, MacDougal, and Mulberry, Crane concludes the story, "it is the original negro element that makes the trouble when there is trouble" (184). What is glaringly absent in Riis is any real mention of the Tenderloin district (well on its way to becoming the center of black life in New York by 1890), except to say that "the amount of 'style' displayed on fine Sundays on Sixth and Seventh Avenues by colored holiday-makers would turn a pessimist black with wrath" (Riis 117). Most of his chapter focuses on Mulberry, Thompson, and Sullivan Streets, which were swiftly becoming old news to black insiders (and Riis alludes to this).

Significantly titled "The Color Line in New York," the chapter opens with a social Darwinist perspective on African Americans in New York: "Natural selection will have more or less to do beyond a doubt in every age with dividing the races; only so, it may be, can they work out together their highest destiny" (112). He regards African Americans as "clean" (115) and finds the landlords that reward these upstanding tenants with higher rents than whites to be despotic and shameless (116). Culturally speaking, the cakewalk dances (where cakes were won in dance competitions) "are comic mixtures of elaborate ceremonial and the joyous abandon of the natural man" (118), and he adds that African Americans' "intellectual status is distinctly improving," and they often as not attend church (118). The foulest activities in New York, according to him, were consigned to the black-and-tan saloons, most of which could be found in and about Sullivan and Thompson Streets. Of mixed-race sex in these places, he feels that "there can be no greater abomination" (119).[5] On the whole, however, Riis concludes that "with all [the Negro's] ludicrous incongruities, his sensuality and his lack of moral accountability, his superstition and other faults that are the effect of temperament and of centuries of slavery, he has eminently good points . . . [and] may be seen to have advanced much farther and faster than before suspected, and to promise, after all, with fair treatment, quite as well as the rest of us, his white-skinned fellow-citizens, had any right to expect" (118, 119).

Nevertheless, Carrie Tirado Bramen has noted that in the period's new aesthetics of the urban picturesque that "perambulators rarely ventured into the black neighborhoods of the Tenderloin to comment on the 'quaint' atmosphere or the 'charming' visages. Blackness signaled the representational limit of the picturesque" (448). Bramen makes it clear that if immigrants were "colorful" at the turn of the twentieth century, African Americans were just "colored" (470). Even the new bohemian culture brewing in the somewhat artificial realm of Greenwich Village rejected African American participants (Stansell 67); these "modern" bohemians, mostly from privileged Anglo-Saxon backgrounds, actively sought interethnic experiences in Irish, Italian, and Jewish enclaves, but for the most part avoided interracial contact. Bramen correctly cites white supremacy for this exclusion, but we must also take into account the minuscule black population in the North at that time, an admittedly banal demographic fact that in part explains why canonical realists—Stephen Crane, Henry James, Edith Wharton—almost never included black characters in their urban fiction. African Americans, with or without an intellectual stripe, were simply not as numerous as their immigrant counterparts.

Aside from Riis's short, uncharacteristically sympathetic chapter, blacks in fin de siècle New York do not appear in the white imagination as either much cause for concern or suitable for outsider investigation. In a 1931 essay entitled "Post-Bellum—Pre-Harlem," the mulatto fiction writer Charles W. Chesnutt points to only three novels, all written by *Atlantic Monthly* editors, about African Americans in the 1890s—William Dean Howells's *An Imperative Duty* (1892), Bliss Perry's *The Plated City* (1895), and Walter Hines Page's *The Southerner: A Novel: Being the Autobiography of Nicholas Worth* (1909); but basically the African American through the period Chesnutt coined "post-bellum—pre-Harlem," was both a "social outcast" and a "small frog in a large pond" (Chesnutt, "Post-Bellum" 908).

The writers Chesnutt mentions, along with others like Joel Chandler Harris, Ignatius Donnelly, and Albion Tourgee, were, however well-intentioned, attempting the impossible as racial outsiders, perhaps with the unspoken understanding that African Americans were not their target audience. The southern black essayist and activist Anna Julia Cooper contests as an insider in the preface of her seminal 1892 protest volume, *A Voice from the South: By a Black Woman of the South,* that the "'other side' has not been represented by one who 'lives there.' And not many can more sensibly realize and more accurately tell the weight and fret of the 'long dull pain' than the open-eyed but hitherto voiceless Black Woman of America" (ii). In a chapter devoted to outsider fiction about black American life entitled "One Phase of American Literature," Cooper openly attacks Howells's pretension of realizing the single "true" picture of blacks in his novel *An Imperative Duty,* since "in this single department at least, Mr. Howells does not know what he is talking about" (201). "Our grievance is not that we are not painted as angels of light or as goody-goody Sunday-school developments," she explains, "but we do claim that a man whose acquaintanceship is so slight that he cannot even discern diversities of individuality, has no right or authority to hawk 'the only true and authentic' pictures of a race of human beings" (206). Cooper does not, however, lay the blame entirely on Howells for "hawking" the lives of people he does not understand; rather, "one feels his blunders to be wholly unintentional and due to the fact that *he has studied his subject merely from the outside. . . .* It is my opinion that the canvas awaits the brush of the colored man himself" (209, 223, emphasis mine).

The New York chapters of both Paul Laurence Dunbar's Tenderloin novel *The Sport of the Gods* (1901 in *Lippincott's;* 1902 in book form) and James Weldon Johnson's only novel, *The Autobiography of an Ex-Colored Man* (1912), consciously revolve around African American drinking and gambling habits, cross-racial assignations, and the many other "immoral" activities offered New Yorkers in what Johnson more than once referred to as the Tenderloin's "black Bohemia" of the 1890s (82; *Black Manhattan* 73). But as Dunbar's novel charts the naturalistic slippery slope of a guileless country boy who evolves from well-meaning son and brother in the South to gambling addict, violent drunk, and murderer, Johnson's catenates the steps of a talented vagabond who stumbles into Tenderloin life, is able to take something productive from his experience—the ability to play ragtime piano, for example—and move on.

The Tenderloin harbored a "bohemia" as Christine Stansell defines it, "a coherent milieu with . . . gentlemen at odds with their class, women at odds with their roles, and immigrants [southern black migrants here] seeking conversations outside the ghetto" (14). But rather than a deliberate neighborhood project, Johnson's "black Bohemia" is an organic culture, one that formed spontaneously out of social currents whose white, middle-class architects abhorred the area's moral message.

In his indispensable history *Black Manhattan* (1930), Johnson reflects on the Tenderloin in his discussion of the African American's place in boxing, horse-racing, and baseball: "The New York of the upper twenties and lower thirties . . . was the business and social centre of most of the colored men engaged in these professional sports, as it was also of the genuine black-face minstrels, the forerunners of the later colored performers; wherever their work might take them, they homed to New York. And because these men earned and spent large sums of money, there grew up in New York a flourishing black Bohemia" (73).[6]

In *Black Manhattan* Johnson refuses to engage the subject of gambling and prostitution, historically the district's most notorious pastimes. He prefers instead to address the "artistic effort" that emerged from the area's population and revise, understandably, the outsider image of a black Sodom to the insider image of a black bohemia. "It is in the growth of this artistic effort that we are interested," he writes. "The rest of the manifestations were commonplaces. . . . The gambling clubs need not be explained" (74). This revisionist tactic is consistent with the whole of Johnson's life, which he openly dedicated to elevating the status of African American culture. The "flourishing black Bohemia" Johnson describes in *Black Manhattan* was a later interpretation of the area, more defensible in 1930 after the enormously popular reception of Harlem's cultural renaissance.

Critics often mistakenly assume that since Dunbar's and Johnson's novels pertain to black life, their New York chapters must take place in Harlem,[7] but Harlem was a German Jewish and Irish neighborhood at the turn of the twentieth century. Still, the introduction to the 1970 Collier edition of *The Sport of the Gods* informs us that "Dunbar does not identify the section of New York in which the characters settle" (Nilon 8). These oversights are partially explainable given the low profile of black New Yorkers in the 1890s. Dunbar specifies, in fact, that the Hamiltons boarded on Twenty-seventh Street, well within the confines of the Tenderloin (Dunbar, *Sport* 48); and it was, significantly, the street on which one of the most famous Tenderloin cabarets, Ike Hines's, was located. Though Dunbar indicates no cross avenue, Twenty-seventh was best-known at the time for its migrant African American population (and, incidentally, its ragtime music). An even greater oversight occurs when scholars label Johnson's *Autobiography of an Ex-Colored Man* a Harlem novel, though Johnson frequently slips out of his narrative in order to provide documentary descriptions of the Tenderloin. The Tenderloin's "black Bohemia," after all, had all but disappeared by the time Johnson published the *Autobiography* in 1912.

Dunbar's and Johnson's protagonists take up residence in a well-established neighborhood that harbored a society marginalized by the rest of the city; and both novels confer upon present-day readers a unique understanding of New York life in the 1890s—the mosaic of cultures it contained, the transgressions of popular morality it actualized, the literary watersheds it signaled. *The Sport of the Gods* is a treatise on the pitfalls that a mythologized New York contains for the southern black migrant. The city itself becomes a fiction in this novel, and thus Dunbar provides us with an illusion within an illusion that will render southerners helpless in the face of rampant immorality. Johnson's in contrast, was written a decade later and shows an increased sense of relativism concerning moral regions in New York. Remarkably, the novel includes only a handful of New York chapters. But by only dipping into Tenderloin culture, the narrator, the author, and the readers are all consigned to an outsider status that illuminates the effect of New York City on the nation at large.

Johnson's novel clearly pivots on these chapters, which outline a familiar psycho-cultural literary pattern we also see in *The Sport of the Gods:* an outsider enters an alien cultural context and experiences a cathartic release, followed by, in this order, a loss of control over repressed desire, a redirection resulting from newfound cultural blueprints, and finally, a substantial personal transformation. But while Dunbar's ultimate claim seems to have been that "there is no defense to be made for it" (*Sport* 95), Johnson's estimation is more ambivalent. He acknowledges the dissipating effects the region has on his characters, who drink, gamble, and play ragtime as vehemently as Dunbar's, but like his white counterparts in the Village, the ghetto experience provides his ex-colored man with an enlightened understanding of American citizenship. Rather than defending the parochialism of smaller communities as Dunbar does, Johnson demonstrates how "low-life" experiences cannot be reduced to good or bad for outsiders, they add to our cultural identities in simultaneously jarring and stimulating ways.

"Nobody's Old Sunday-School Picnic": Pre-Harlem Migration in Paul Laurence Dunbar's The Sport of the Gods

The New York chapters of Paul Laurence Dunbar's naturalistic novel *The Sport of the Gods* were inspired by the time he collaborated on a number of lucrative musicals and vaudeville shows in Manhattan.[8] Set in New York's Tenderloin, just southwest of the Broadway theater district, *The Sport of the Gods* appeared in 1902, and the outsider imagination, both black and white, finally had access to black Manhattan. In one glowing review of the novel, a critic importantly asks, "Do we ever think of how such people live? It is a . . . whole stratum of society of which all of us are densely ignorant and of whose very existence most of us are wholly unaware" (qtd. in Osofsky 41). In the same vein, Dunbar's enormously popular collection *Lyrics of Lowly Life* (1896) opens with an introduction by William Dean Howells. A kind individual but one who could make or break an author's reputation, Howells praised the black poet's deviation from the Anglo-Saxon norm by candidly admitting that before Dunbar, "I permitted myself the imaginative prophecy that the hostilities and the prejudices which had so long constrained [the Negro] race were destined to vanish in the arts; that these were to be the final proof that

God had made of one blood all nations of men. . . . Yet it appeared to me then, and it appears to me now, that there is a precious difference of temperament between the races which it would be a great pity ever to lose" (xvii).

It is difficult to overstate Howells's efforts to advance the stature of "small frogs" from various races and nationalities, regardless of the long-held critical consideration of his "famous prescriptions for realists, grounded as they are in white, middle-class ideas" (Ammons 103). W. E. B. Du Bois himself attributed Dunbar's fame specifically to Howells's sponsorship: "It was Howells . . . that discovered Dunbar. We have had a score of artists and poets in black America, but few critics dared call them so. . . . Howells dared take Dunbar by the hand and say to the world not simply here is a black artist, but here is an artist who happens to be black" ("Howells and Black Folk" 1147–48). Du Bois takes this point a bit too far, perhaps, as Howells did identify Dunbar as an insider who provided white readers with an "authentic" view of black consciousness as Chesnutt did for mulattoes. With this in mind, it is striking that Dunbar was not nearly as generous as Jacob Riis in assessing the future of black Manhattan.

In 1898, Dunbar published his Tenderloin manifesto in the Columbus (Ohio) *Dispatch,* entitled "The Negroes of the Tenderloin." Like Helen Campbell, Dunbar reviled the ghetto as a "poison" to both the migrants themselves and to "respectable" New York, which traditional mission work did little to prevent. But unlike Campbell, he perceived no political threat: "[Black migrants] are not Anarchists; they never will be. Socialism has no meaning for them; and yet in these seemingly careless, guffawing crowds lies a terrible menace to our institutions. Everything in their environment tends to the blotting of the moral sense, everything to the engendering of crime. Here and there sits a weak, ineffectual little mission, doing its little best for the people around it, but altogether as inadequate as a gauze fan in the furnace heats of hell" (264). And like Charles Loring Brace, Dunbar targets children as the most vulnerable and thereby most dangerous group in the city. "I pity the children because they are being cheated out of their birthright. . . . Many of them are from the small towns of the South. They have been deceived by the glare and glitter of the city streets" (265). This essay, when read as a precursor to *The Sport of the Gods,* reveals the extent to which Dunbar, unlike his friend and colleague James Weldon Johnson, saw virtually no benefits to southern black migration to northern cities.

Not an uplifting tale, *The Sport of the Gods* is a heart-rending story of a shattered southern black family, the Hamiltons, who try to make a new life for themselves in New York and fail disastrously. The novel begins in an archetypical postbellum southern town. Berry Hamilton is the devoted father of two children, Joe and Kitty, and loving husband to Fannie. For years, they lived happily on their white employer's property until one day Berry is accused of stealing a sum of money, money actually stolen by the employer's gambling brother. Berry is convicted of the crime and sentenced to ten years hard labor. Fannie, Joe, and Kitty, now ostracized by the small community, move to New York's Tenderloin district, a place they know only from folklore. Within weeks of landing in New York, Fannie marries a wife-beater, Joe becomes a dissipated wreck and a murderer, and Kitty finds she has a talent for the stage in the mode of Theodore Dreiser's Carrie Meeber in *Sister Carrie* (1900). Ultimately, Fannie and Berry are reunited, and they journey back to their small-town existence in the South, abandoning their children to the malevolent gods of the northern metropolis.

William L. Andrews suggests that Dunbar's treatment of southern black migration tells us more about the publishing world at that time than African American social realities. *The Sport of the Gods*, Andrews explains, "indicates that Dunbar and his publishers, Dodd Mead of New York, were not willing to take a chance on a novel that dealt in a sober, even grim fashion, with contemporary socioeconomic questions impinging on black Americans" (xv). For Dunbar, New York's cabarets, boarding houses, and side streets are the villains, as opposed to either the people one finds in them or the city's restrictive economic or social impositions.

New Yorkers, both black and white, regarded the handful of southern black migrants in their city as "rovers," "wanderers," "vagrants," "a hoodlum element," "criminals in search of a sporting life" (Osofsky 21). Dunbar shows in *The Sport of the Gods* that this discrimination is largely stipulated by the outsider southerner's tendency to convert themselves in a matter of months into caricatures of insider urbanity and thus reject the positive moral foundation of the rural South—the family, the church, and the school—for that of the fashionable New York sporting set. In *The Sport of the Gods* he classifies these migrant outsiders into two categories: the wise and the foolish. The wise will recognize their love for the great metropolis, but eventually escape: "He will go away, any place—yes, he will even go over to Jersey." The foolish, of course, remain: "They will stay and stay on until the town becomes all in all to him; until the very streets are his chums and certain buildings and corners his best friends. Then he is hopeless, and to live elsewhere would be death. The Bowery will be his romance, Broadway his lyric, and the park his pastoral, the river and the glory of it all his epic, and he will look down pityingly on the rest of humanity" (47).

By identifying New York's most famous tourist attractions with traditional literary genres—the romance, the lyric, the pastoral, and the epic—Dunbar demonstrates how popular conceptions of New York belie its corruption, as poetry and fiction belie the realities they represent. He illustrates its false representation most clearly in the southern black consciousness; the "glare and glitter of the city streets" tantalize the rural migrant and crush the moral will. The implication is not necessarily that mythic images of New York manipulate the facts, but rather that experience itself becomes fictional in his characters' minds. *The Sport of the Gods* was meant to act as a demythologizing agent for innocent outsiders, particularly those who had not yet been irretrievably seduced by the great metropolis.

Dunbar first constructs this fictional consciousness as a kind of revolt against the innocent outsiders' former selves. In the South, the moral atmosphere is under control: they go to church, they go to work, they eat at home, and their only outings are to visit family and friends. Joe Hamilton, Dunbar's palimpsest on which the New York type is set, grew up in an environment that defied most fictional accounts of rural benightedness. The novel begins there, at Joe's family home. The Hamilton household is respectably neat, run with a tempered hand by the parents Berry and Fannie, and the children Joe and Kitty are hardworking and well-dressed. Like New York, the southern countryside is a space imposed upon by fictional representations. Indeed, the novel's first sentence, even its first word, sets this theme in motion: "Fiction has said so much in regret of the old days when there were plantations and overseers and masters and slaves, that it was good to come upon such a household as Berry Hamilton's, if for no other reason than it afforded a relief from the monotony of tiresome iteration" (1).

Dunbar himself seems relieved to shed the belabored anti-southern sentiments of the turn-of-the-twentieth-century cosmopolitan ethos. His post–Reconstruction South appears superior to the northern city, regardless of the injustices dealt by the hands of Jim Crow. "The South has its faults—no one condones them—and its disadvantages," he writes through the eyes of sermonizing New York insiders, "but . . . even what [migrants] suffered from these was better than what awaited them in the great alleys of New York" (122–23). In fact, Dunbar's "The Negroes of the Tenderloin" makes the incredible, barely implicit suggestion that even slavery had been a better state for the black race than northern metropolitan life:

> They are losing the soft mellow voices which even slavery could not ruin.
> . . . It is a pity to see the changes in these, my people, who, with their scant

education, should be like the quaint ante-bellum type of Negro whose praises are still sung at the South. But they are not. . . . It is the duty of the Negro especially to live for his children, to so conduct his life as to destroy in his race the defects, mental, moral and physical, placed upon them by slavery. But these people are not doing it. They are *perpetuating and increasing* all of these deformities, both of mind and body. (265, emphasis mine)

To the Hamiltons, New York is a mythical place, as Dunbar ironically makes clear: "They had heard of New York as a place vague and far away, a city that, like heaven, to them had existed by faith alone. All the days of their lives they had heard of it, and it seemed to them the centre of all the glory, all the wealth, and all the freedom of the world. New York. It had an alluring sound" (43–44). Joe Hamilton in particular is susceptible to this myth of the city, and as a result, he is the first to accept its superficial veil. Back in the South, Joe had contacts among the southern aristocracy and "came to imbibe some of their ideas." "Too early in life," Dunbar writes, Joe "bid fair to be a dandy" (3). This disposition places Joe in Dunbar's second category of outsiders in New York—the fools that stay. Obsessed with the idea of New York, Joe is "wild with enthusiasm and with a desire to be a part of all that the metropolis meant." Like Crane's George Kelcey, he searches for this meaning on the New York streets; and like George, Joe embodies the hordes of migrants who "are selling their birthright for a mess of pottage" (Dunbar, "Negroes" 266).

On his first day in New York, Joe gazes in revelatory wonder at the "manners" of the young men on the street. They are going places other than church or family visiting. Less baffled by their motivations than by his own provincialism, Joe comprehends "that his horizon had been very narrow. . . . Why should those fellows be different from him? Why should they walk the streets so knowingly, so independently, when he knew not whither to turn his steps?" He resolves to shed his southern roots in toto and dreams of becoming an insider, hoping that "some day some greenhorn from the South should stand at a window and look out envying at him, as he passed, red-cravated, patent-leathered, intent on some goal" (49). Dunbar shows this process of assimilation from hick to sport in Faustian terms: "The first sign of the demoralisation of the provincial who comes to New York is his pride at his insensibility to certain impressions which used to influence him at home. First he begins to scoff, and there is no truth in his views nor depth in his laugh. But by and by, from mere pretending, it becomes real. He grows callous. After that he goes to the devil very cheerfully" (50).

James Weldon Johnson later mimics this trope of the anti-urban form in his picaresque novel *The Autobiography of an Ex-Colored Man*. (Though as we will see, his version of the sporting life was far more optimistic than Dunbar's.) Johnson writes that "New York City is the most fatally fascinating thing in America. She sits like a great witch at the gate of the country, showing her alluring white face and hiding her crooked hands and feet under the folds of her wide garments—constantly enticing thousands from far within, and tempting those who come from across the sea to go no further. And all these become the victims of her caprice" (65). The Tenderloin, in particular, consists of a toxic "slough from which it takes a herculean effort to leap" (83).

A debate has developed over Gregory Candela's argument that Dunbar's treatment of New York was ironic, that critics take him too seriously (see Candela; Hurd). I agree with Candela only to the extent that Dunbar, like Crane before him, wrote with the fiction of urban myth in mind. Given Johnson's actual fondness for black Manhattan, however, and Dunbar's open disgust of it—along with the artistic possibilities Johnson found in the Tenderloin specifically, and Dunbar's assertion that southern blacks have abandoned cultural roots that charmed whites and fortified blacks—Candela's claim regarding the ironic mask is more germane to Johnson's upbeat irony in *The Autobiography of an Ex-Colored Man* than in the more grimly judgmental sarcasm of Dunbar's novel.

Like Crane's Maggie Johnson and George Kelcey and Abraham Cahan's Jake Podkovnik, who will be discussed in the next chapter, Dunbar's Joe Hamilton is dissatisfied by his cultural roots and seeks to immerse himself to the point of forgetfulness in New York's culture of consumption. In this way Dunbar, again like Crane and Cahan, demonstrates how clothing and manners are romantic fictions, hiding reality in the way fictional representations of society do. Crane and Dunbar deplored romantic fiction, as they, like other naturalists, considered it psychologically and culturally debasing. Because of romantic mythology, Joe rejected willy nilly the moral foundation upon which he stood in the South, one replaced by a false consciousness of urban gentility.

Dunbar, at bottom, finds these marginal, contradictory aspects of southerners in New York repulsive. We find the novel's first substantial treatment of a converted black southerner in the character William Thomas, a crass and arrogant Tenderloin insider who was raised in the South, but had long ago relinquished his outsider, or "greenhorn" status; and we witness Dunbar's disgust through the eyes of Joe's mother, Fannie, who is experienced enough to regard Thomas's contradictory consciousness as transparent in a way that none of Crane's characters were able to do: "Thomas was not the provincial who puts every one on par with himself, nor was he the metropolitan who complacently patronises the whole world. He was trained out of the one and not up to the other. The intermediate only succeeded in being offensive" (55). Throughout Joe's process of marginalization, he becomes in Dunbar's eyes, a "small-souled, warped being." For the author and his audience, he was a pitiful example of "the jest of Fate"—the sport of the gods. His immersion in Tenderloin life "afflicted [him with a] sort of moral and mental astigmatism that made him see everything wrong" (57).

By rendering the social fiction of the Tenderloin's insider lifestyle as a freeing, sporting one, Dunbar's own fiction reveals more "truth" than the realities he represents. The racial message here is rendered in the scenes set at the Banner Club, a "black and tan" club where whites and blacks mingle freely. In the story, the Banner Club attracts crowds of inquisitive outsiders, "the curious who wanted to see something of the other side of life." "White visitors" enjoyed the club's environment as "visitors." They comprise people "who were young enough to be fascinated by the bizarre, and those that were old enough to know that it was all in the game." No positive insider potential exists in the atmosphere of the Banner Club: "The place was a social cesspool, generating a poisonous miasma and reeking with the stench of decayed and rotten moralities." To bring home this point, Dunbar describes the scene in his own voice: "There is no defense to be made for it. But what do you expect when false idealism and fevered ambition come face to face with catering cupidity?" (67).

The fact that "Joe heard things [at the Banner] that had never come within range of his mind before" is not a good thing for young African American men. But for slumming white outsiders and cynical black insiders who understand the fiction, the game of it is relatively innocuous. For a white journalist named Skaggs, for instance, slumming at the Banner is a source of rich material and nothing more. Condescendingly explaining his motivations to Joe and Thomas, Skaggs remarks, "You see a lot o' fellows say to me, 'What do you want to go down to that nigger club for?' That's what they call it, 'nigger club.' But I say to 'em, 'Gentlemen, at that nigger club, as you choose to call it, I get more inspiration than I could get at any of the greater clubs in New York'" (68). Skaggs is the most dangerous character in the book as he promotes New York's mythical facade.[9] Though insiders comprehend Skaggs's artificial pose, Joe sits "wide-eyed with wonder and admiration, and he couldn't understand the amused expression on Thomas's face, nor why he surreptitiously kicked him under the table" (69).

One insider at the Banner, nicknamed Sadness for his permanently forlorn countenance, acts as Dunbar's insider philosopher of the dispossessed. Dunbar introduces the character as one who finds "being respectable is very nice as a diversion, but it's tedious if done steadily" (65). He is sympathetic in that he is honest with himself about having "aspired to the depths without ever being fully able to reach them" (84). Sadness substantiates the fiction of the sporting life to Joe, but he does so with a kind of pseudo-irony: "Oh, it's a fine, rich life, my lad. I know you'll like it. I said you would the first time I saw you. It has plenty of stir in it, and a man never gets lonesome. Only the rich are lonesome. It's only the independent who depend upon others" (85). The life lessons Sadness impresses on the young greenhorn about the depths of Tenderloin life are told straight, but given his general tone of sarcasm, we can never quite take him seriously: "'You see, Hamilton, in this life we are all suffering from fever, and no one edges away from the other because he finds him a little warm. It's dangerous when you're not used to it; but once you go through the parching process, you become inoculated against further contagion'" (84). The reality of Sadness's situation—that he is an alcoholic intellectual with few accomplishments to his name and a tragic family history—strips any humor we may otherwise take from his philosophy. Dunbar lends a touch of dramatic irony to this character, however, clarified by Sadness's "peculiar laugh" and "a look in his terribly bright eyes that made Joe creep." Joe's devotion to the New York myth was too strong to understand sarcasm: "The only effect that the talk of Sadness had upon him was to make him feel wonderfully '*in it*'" (85, emphasis mine). Joe thanks him for helping him "lots," and Sadness yells back at him, "You lie . . . I haven't; I was only fool enough to try" (85). Joe dismisses the outbreak as the babblings of a drunk, for now he sees himself as an insider in the Tenderloin, "he belonged to a peculiar class, one that grows larger and larger in New York and which has imitators in every large city in this country. . . . [it is] a great hulking, fashionably uniformed fraternity of indolence. . . . It was into this set that Sadness had sarcastically invited Joe" (86).

Inevitably, Joe is seduced by a Tenderloin succubus, Hattie Sterling. In one of the final chapters, heavy-handedly entitled "Frankenstein," Joe displaces the blame of his tragic downfall onto her: "'You put me out—you—you, and you made me what I am.' The realisation of what he was, of his foulness and degradation, seemed just to have come to him fully. 'You made me what I am, and then you sent me away. You let me come back, and now you put me out'" (119). Predictably, he kills her, which earns him a life sentence in prison. If Crane depicts his sermonizers as ironically blind to their pernicious influences on the Bowery population, Dunbar can only agree with his own sermonizers' assertions about emigrating north: "Here is another example of the pernicious influence of the city on untrained Negroes. Oh, is there no way to keep these people from rushing away from the small villages and country districts of the South up to the cities, where they cannot battle with the terrible force of a strange and unusual environment? Is there no way to prove to them that woollen-shirted, brown-jeaned simplicity is infinitely better than broad-clothed degradation?" (122).

This tragic perspective dominates the narrative, but there are exceptions—survivors that appear to transcend the wise/foolish dichotomy. For instance, Kitty Hamilton rises to fame and distances herself from her family's tragic demise. In a chapter titled "All the World's a Stage," Kitty falls "desperately in love" with Hattie Sterling, the stage actress whom her brother eventually kills. By the end of the chapter, she adopts that woman's personality, and though she becomes intolerably vain, achieves a measure of success on the popular stage. Meanwhile, Thomas, the rural southerner turned hard and fast New York insider, remarks of her newfound urbanity, "Who'd 'a' thought . . . that the kid had that much nerve? Well, if they don't want to find out things, what do they come to N' Yawk for? It ain't nobody's old Sunday-school picnic. Guess I got out easy, anyhow" (101).

Rather than viewing marginal characters in a process of cultural development, Dunbar favors a pure sense of authenticity over Joe's broadened horizon, a comprehension of the city George Kelcey had also sought. Authenticity and sincerity are seen as moral imperatives in both *The Sport of the Gods* and *George's Mother*. And regardless of whether you instinctually prefer Bowery culture, Victorian culture, southern culture, or sporting culture, Crane and Dunbar represent those outsider instincts as subconsciously absorbed from a variety of textual lies. By this time in New York history, these urban naturalists contended, Melvillean preferences and assumptions are indistinguishable. Whether you revolt or conform in New York, you will be led into the same jumble of insincerities. Ten years later, however, James Weldon Johnson in *The Autobiography of an Ex-Colored Man* would render the "terrible force" of New York's influence less as a textual flim flam that reduces its victims to "broad-clothed degradation" than a state of mind that, contradicting Dunbar and Crane's premise, will often strip its quarry of social pretense. In Johnson, vice and creativity are no longer mutually exclusive; instead, he argues that moral experimentation is a social necessity, the means by which cultural ascendance might be attained. The "black Bohemia" Johnson's ex-colored man encounters in the Tenderloin district provides fragmented glimmerings of a future Negro "Renaissance."

James Weldon Johnson, "Ragging" the Classics, and the Black "Superstructure of Conscious Art"

James Weldon Johnson was raised in Jacksonville, Florida, one of the most progressive towns in the United States at the time. His mother, Helen Louise Johnson, was a school teacher originally from Nassau in the Bahamas, and his father James, a Virginian, was the headwaiter at Jacksonville's St. James Hotel. Helen and James senior, both freeborn blacks, sheltered their son from the complications of racial identity in the United States. One story goes that when James was only nine years old, a preacher asked him what he wished to be when he grew up; to this the ambitious young man confidently replied, "I am going to be governor of Florida" (qtd. in Andrews ix). Not until working three months one summer as a school teacher in the "backwoods of Georgia" did he grasp the divisive nature of American race relations. The segregated region was impossibly poor; one student had never seen a toothbrush before Johnson arrived. He later wrote in *Along This Way: The Autobiography of James Weldon Johnson* (1933) that "In all of my experience it was this period that marked . . . the beginning of my knowledge of my own people as a 'race'" (119). After graduating from Atlanta University, an all-black school, Johnson accepted a position as principal of the Stanton School back in Jacksonville, the first black high school in Florida. In 1898, he passed the Florida state bar exam—the first African American to do so. But rather than practicing law or continuing his administrative position at Stanton, he moved to New York City and began collaborating with his brother Rosamond and a songwriter named Bob Cole. James, Rosamond, and Cole then formed the popular Broadway songwriting team "Cole and the Johnson Brothers."

In 1905, Johnson toured Europe, but after a year traveling there decided to pursue a career in diplomatic service. He received his first post in 1906 as a United States Consul in Puerto Cabello, Venezuela. Three years later he was commissioned to head the United States consulate in Corinto, Nicaragua. While in Nicaragua, he began writing poetry, which he published in *The Century Magazine* and *The Independent*. In 1910, he married Grace Nail, who had grown up in a traditional, middle-class black neighborhood in Brooklyn. Johnson continued to write through this period, and along with poetry, he revisited a book manuscript he had begun years earlier while studying literature with Brander Matthews at Columbia University. Matthews had read the first two chapters of the manuscript and encouraged Johnson to keep writing. In 1912, Johnson anonymously published it under the title

The Autobiography of an Ex-Colored Man. Though poorly received in its first printing, when scant attention was paid to African American novels, today some consider it the finest American novel of the 1910s.

The novel is semi-autobiographical, though there are important differences between the ex-colored man and his creator. Johnson's anonymous narrator is born in Georgia around 1870 to a fair-skinned mulatto woman and a white southern gentleman. He is raised by his mother as a white child in Connecticut, where his father sends them to clear the way for a respectable marriage. In his early years he is unaware of both his illegitimacy and his racial status. Consistent with many first-person narratives by minority authors, the turning point in the young boy's life comes when the truth of his inferior racial status is revealed to him. Upon graduating from high school, he decides to enter a black college, Atlanta University, but is barely there a week before his only money is stolen. Thus begins a series of misadventures that lead him to Jacksonville, New York's Tenderloin district, Europe, and back to Georgia. In Georgia he witnesses a brutal lynching that fills him with such a profound feeling of shame that he renounces his blackness. At the end of the tale, we find him back in New York as, of all things, a prosperous white landlord.

But his earlier experiences in New York's Tenderloin concern us here, a series of chapters that Johnson constructs to question white America's understanding of both the region's worth and the positive contributions of African American culture to the United States. Alfred Knopf republished the novel in 1927, at the height of the New Negro Renaissance, by which time the public was eager for African American writing, and it was an enormous success. Carl Van Vechten, a subject of this book's final chapter, wrote the introduction to this edition, and in it praised Johnson's work for taking the African American literary tradition in a more comprehensive direction:

> Charles W. Chesnutt, in his interesting novel, *The House Behind the Cedars* (1900), contributed to literature perhaps the first authentic study on the subject of "passing," and Paul Laurence Dunbar, in *The Sport of the Gods,* described the plight of a young outsider who comes to the larger New York Negro world to make his fortune, but who falls a victim to the sordid snares of that world, a theme I elaborated on in 1926 to fit a newer and much more intricate social system [see chapter 5]. . . . Mr. Johnson, however, chose an all-embracing scheme. (Introduction 26)

Like Johnson, the ex-colored man grew up through his formative period relatively affluent and, unaware of his blackness, ill-prepared for the realities faced by African Americans at the end of the nineteenth century. Achieving this sense of preparedness seemed to have necessitated a certain level of personal dissipation. For more than a year he negotiates the pitfalls of the Tenderloin that within weeks had subsumed his fictional predecessor Joe Hamilton in *The Sport of the Gods*. Having been trained a cigar manufacturer during a brief stay in Florida, the ex-colored man initially supports himself in New York by the same trade. Over time, however, his rapturous outings in the gambling clubs and cabarets of the Tenderloin take precedence. Inevitably, he revokes his respectable status as a skilled worker: "I at last realized that making cigars for a living and gambling for a living could not be carried on at the same time, and I resolved to give up the cigar making" (82).

During this time, which he calls his "dark period" (83), the ex-colored man's New York consists of ten city blocks: Sixth Avenue from Twenty-third to Thirty-third Street with the blocks crossing one block west (82), a place where "Central Park was a distant forest, and the lower part of the city a foreign land" (82–83). Though one Harlem Renaissance scholar claims that in the 1890s, "the Tenderloin was a vague area" (Eloise Johnson 10), as opposed to its uptown complement San Juan Hill, Johnson marks out a clearly definable site. Outlining concrete physical parameters, he constructs the Tenderloin as a distinctive moral region, a black community within a predominantly white metropolis.

Johnson visited his friend Paul Laurence Dunbar there in 1899. Dunbar was then overseeing the production of his hit Broadway musical *Clorindy; or, the Origin of the Cake-Walk*. Johnson's Tenderloin experience with Dunbar informed the New York chapters of *The Autobiography of an Ex-Colored Man*, and he also includes discussions of it in his history, *Black Manhattan*, and his autobiography *Along This Way*. In *Along This Way*, he explains that for him, the district was a revelation: "Up to this time, outside of polemical essays on the race question, I had not written a single line that had any relation to the Negro. I now began to grope toward a realization of the importance of the American Negro's cultural background and his creative folk-art, and *to speculate on the superstructure of conscious art that might be reared upon them*" (152, emphasis mine).

The Autobiography of an Ex-Colored Man buttresses the African American "superstructure of conscious art" by adjoining it to the emergent metropolitan modernist aesthetic. Although the *Autobiography* is a work of fiction, Johnson toggles between fictional narrative and documentary discourse, and his New York chapters are decidedly written in a self-contained documentary style.

Although the ex-colored man is a mulatto and would later refer to some white outsiders in the Tenderloin as "slummers" (presumably as distinct from himself), it seems as if no one in the Tenderloin really "belongs." Over the course of his "dark period," the ex-colored man acquaints himself with "a score of bright, intelligent young fellows who had come up to the great city with high hopes and ambitions and who had fallen under the spell of this under life, a spell they could never throw off" (83). One Tenderloin habitué is referred to as "the doctor" for having spent two years at Harvard Medical School. " But here he was," the ex-colored man intones, "living this gas-light life, his will and moral sense so enervated and deadened that it was impossible for him to break away" (83). As Harvard Medical School had already begun matriculating black students by 1865 (Randall Kennedy xix–xx), "the doctor" defies racial categorization. Regardless, when the ex-colored man refers to the Tenderloin as a "lower world" later in the narrative, it can be construed as racially motivated condescension (Cataliotti 67), but its dissipating effects actually have equal-opportunity status among its multi-racial insider participants.

The ex-colored man reports that one white type at the "Club" "was made up of variety performers and others who delineated 'darky characters'; they came to get their imitations first hand from the Negro entertainers they saw there" (78). Along with hosting musicians, minstrels, thespians, and athletes, the ex-colored man informs us, the cabaret was also a place where white outsiders could come for a night of "sight-seeing, or slumming" (78). Though the cabaret existed as a refuge from the greater Tenderloin for black insiders, it also "enjoyed a large patronage of white sightseers and slummers and of white theatrical performers on the lookout for 'Negro stuff,' and, moreover, a considerable clientele of white women who had or sought to have colored lovers" (176). But in the novel the presence of outsider participants is not wholly intrusive, which in some ways foreshadows Johnson's later encouragement of Carl Van Vechten's escapades in Harlem, the subject of my final chapter.

Johnson makes a clear distinction between whites with apparent insider status and white outsiders who found the club's milieu alienating and distasteful. Some would only peer in for a minute or two to satisfy a minor curiosity, others would stay all night, including a number of single white women:

> They were all good-looking and well-dressed, and seemed to be women of some education. One of these in particular attracted my attention; she was an exceedingly beautiful woman of about thirty-five; she had glistening

copper-colored hair, very white skin, and eyes very much like Du Maurier's
conception of Trilby's 'twin gray stars.' When I came to know her, I found
that she was a woman of considerable culture; she had traveled in Europe,
spoke French, and played the piano well. She was always dressed elegantly,
but in absolutely good taste. (79)

In short, the race, class, and gender of the woman, whom he later refers to as
"the widow," all combine to illuminate the very limits of those categories of
definition and exemplify the marginality, or mixed insider/outsider status, of
much of the Tenderloin's cultural milieu. But for the ex-colored man (and
needless to say a white middle-class outsider audience) most profoundly
alarming of all is her open, sexually charged relationship with a black man.
He learns that the widow bestowed jewelry on her escort, and she purchased
clothes for him at the most expensive New York tailors. And that man was
not alone; indeed, there were many more like him. Her companion may
have been reduced to a racially motivated object of sexuality, even prostitution, but it is equally true that the white, well-to-do woman was as much
an insider in the vortex of the club's social action as the ex-colored man, if
not even more so.

   Even the scene of her murder makes her "belong" as much in the purview
of the "Club" as the ex-colored man, who by this time was something of a
celebrity there. Her companion shoots her in the throat after he jealously
spies her sharing a bottle of champagne with the ex-colored man. The ex-
colored man had been warned that "the pair had lately quarreled and had
not been together at the 'Club' for some nights," and if he was seen with her,
the escort, "generally known as a 'bad man,'" might fly into a jealous rage
(89). Regarding this as a jealousy killing complicates the escort's motives. If
it was money he was after, why cut off the supply? Or, if he believed that the
ex-colored man may take his place, why not kill *him*?

   Johnson's Tenderloin as well frustrates deterministic class associations.
Tenderloin gamblers, for example, are not themselves insiders associated
intrinsically with ghetto culture. Their standing in the Tenderloin is determined by the turbulent economics of Tenderloin life. Upon first entering
one of the gambling clubs, the ex-colored man recalls "aristocrats of the
place," who posed elegantly at the tables and "seemed to be practicing a sort
of Chesterfieldian politeness towards each other" (67–68). Startled, he soon
observes seedy-looking men in linen dusters begging for fifty cents to get
back in the game; these latter had literally lost the clothes off their backs and
are provided with dusters by the club's management. At first he has trouble

reading this unusual amalgam of urban types, since up to that point he had experienced rigidly delineated boundaries of caste. It soon becomes apparent that those same patrons exhibiting "Chesterfieldian politeness" could, and most likely would, be wearing linen dusters in a night or two. As the ex-colored man explains, "In my gambling experiences I passed through all states and conditions that a gambler is heir to. Some days found me able to peel ten- and twenty-dollar bills from a roll, and others found me clad in a linen duster and carpet slippers" (83). We are invited to witness a powerful act of citizenship here, where urban vice translates as socioeconomic wisdom.

In *Black Manhattan* Johnson distinguishes between "honky-tonks," night clubs with black and white patrons that sold alcohol and provided both professional and amateur entertainment, and "professional clubs," a more lugubrious atmosphere frequented almost solely by professional entertainers and athletes and their "satellites and admirers" (74). Though the difference between the two club types is negligible, it is at a professional club, modeled after Ike Hines's (formerly located at West Twenty-seventh Street), that the narrator of *The Autobiography of an Ex-Colored Man* receives his education in ragtime piano.

The ex-colored man was trained in classical piano early in life, and for the experienced player, the ragtime he hears in the Tenderloin cabaret is a revelation. Robert H. Cataliotti has recently argued that the ex-colored man's appropriation of ragtime was "closer to a white man appropriating the 'novel charm' of some exotic music, than to a black man adopting and exploring a form of expression that connects him to African American culture" (67). Though in the tradition of literary representations of African American musical culture this may be true, by this point in the narrative the ex-colored man has become a racial and regional amalgamation, a truly marginal man. Ragtime piano powerfully adds to his already complex identity; it is his latest payment from a continuous process of cultural annuity, informed by his exposure to varying regional cultures—New England, the South, Europe, and so forth. Exposure and influence, the ex-colored man himself admits, were the well-springs of his talents: "The fact is, nothing great or enduring, especially in music, has ever sprung full-fledged and unprecedented from the brain of any master; the best that he gives to the world he gathers from the hearts of the people, and runs it through the alembic of his genius" (73).

The ex-colored man would make his artistic strides in the Tenderloin's cabarets, or professional clubs, not in its gambling establishments. Johnson's ragtime "Club" officially prohibited both drinking and gambling, but we are told that the ex-colored man could not afford a night at the "Club" without first winning money at the gambling tables. The two institutions, gambling clubs and cabarets, were a part of one culture, but the cabarets were the focus of those "creative efforts" Johnson chose to emphasize in his history. The ex-colored man would, in fact, update his already well-developed musical talents by "ragging" the classics, an innovative pastiche strictly associated with black artists that merges classical music with ragtime. Self-taught over long nights of exploring the Tenderloin, the ex-colored man discovers in "ragging" the classics a highly marketable commodity and thus the apparatus to improve his condition: "I finally caught up another method of earning money, and so did not have to depend entirely upon the caprices of fortune at the gambling table. Through continuously listening to the music at the 'Club,' and through my own previous training, my natural talent and perseverance, I developed into a remarkable player of ragtime; indeed, I had the name at the time of being the best ragtime-player in New York" (83–84).

Ragtime was the most popular musical genre in the United States from the late 1890s to World War I. It combined the European tradition of crafted composition with signature African American syncopated rhythms, often starkly co-opting Mozart or Mendelssohn for irreverent effect. The fictional ex-colored man takes full credit for inventing the hybrid form: "I brought all my knowledge of classical music to bear and, in so doing, achieved some novelties which pleased and even astonished my listeners. It was I who first made ragtime transcriptions of familiar classic selections" (84). Music critics vociferated against the ill-effects of "ragging" the classics, of course. "We have musical unions in many of our cities," Edward Baxter Perry extolled in a 1918 review entitled "Ragging Good Music," "and one of the first rules they should pass is that any member found guilty of what is called 'ragging' a classic should be dismissed from the organization in disgrace, and never again permitted to appear in any reputable organization" (qtd. in Berlin *Ragtime* 70).

Kathleen Pfeiffer has importantly argued powerfully that rather than simply whitening a black form, as others have claimed, the ex-colored man was blackening a white form as well (406). And in his study of ethnic transience, "Human Migration and the Marginal Man" (1928), Robert Park asserts that "it is in the mind of the marginal man that the moral turmoil which new cultural contacts occasion manifests itself in most obvious forms. It is in the mind of the marginal man—where the changes and fusions of culture are going on—that we can best study the processes of civilization and progress" (166). A marginal man's marginality, in other words, is defined by the psychological and cultural complications that follow exposure to transformative environments. The "changes and fusions of culture" Park highlights in the consciousness of the marginal man serve to punctuate recent assertions of Johnson's novel as a "slippery" text that "rejects the ontology of racial catego-ries" and cultural definition (Pfeiffer 406). They also inform and enliven our understanding of the Tenderloin's signature cultural forms—ragtime piano, for example. In Johnson's Tenderloin, then, there are glimmerings of black cultural ascendancy that naturally ignited a white reactionary backlash; so rather than mere pandering to a mainstream white audience, the ex-colored man is engaging in a subversively creative act.

Ragtime piano in the United States was widely considered both musically and morally corrupt. Co-opting classical music is hardly unique in American popular culture, but there can be no doubt that the form was widely con-demned in the mainstream press. As Edward A. Berlin laconically sums up the dispute: "The main lines of the offensive were: (1) ridicule; (2) appeals to racial bias; (3) prophecies of doom; (4) attempts at repression; and (5) suggestions of moral, intellectual, and physical dangers" (*Ragtime* 40). Critics compared ragtime music with malaria, alcohol, and "a dog with rabies" (44).

Associated with the Tenderloin at least as late as 1909, ragtime still reigned in that district when a youthful Eugene O'Neill spent long nights meandering the clubs, gambling dens, restaurants, and bars of the Tenderloin with his bohemian friends Louis Holladay and Ed Keefe. In his sonnet "The Hay-market" (1912), O'Neill describes one scene at the famous Tenderloin dance hall and peep-show theater of the title, located south of Thirtieth on Sixth, and couples ragtime music with the miserable life of the prostitute:

> The music blares into a rag-time tune—
>   The dancers whirl around the polished floor;
> Each powdered face a set expression wore
>   Of dull satiety, and wan smiles swoon
> On rouged lips at sallies opportune
>   Of maudlin youths whose sodden spirits soar
> On drunken wings; while through the opening door
>   A chilly blast sweeps like the breath of doom.
>
> In sleek dress suit an old man sits and leers
>   With vulture mouth and blood-shot, beady eyes
> At the young girl beside him. Drunken tears
>   Fall down her painted face, and choking sighs
> Shake her, as into his familiar ears
>   She sobs her sad, sad history—and lies!
>   (qtd. in Gelb 244–45)

Regardless of the censorial efforts of its critics, as Johnson jokes in *The Book of American Negro Poetry,* "the earliest Ragtime songs, like Topsy, 'jes' grew'" (xi). Though by today's standards the sounds and lyrics of ragtime piano might seem rather tame, there exist strong parallels between it and the current gangsta rap in terms of public reaction. Berlin writes that "whites [disapproved of the music] because they feared the effects of African American music on impressionable white youth, and many African Americans did because they feared that their own youths would be corrupted by a music associated with brothels and cabarets, and because they found the texts of ragtime songs to be racially demeaning" ("Ragtime" 976). Subsequently, there evolved a strong movement to censor piano rags. In New York City, it succeeded in banning ragtime from a free pier concert in the summer of 1902, and by 1914, the music was prohibited in public schools citywide.

Outsiders swarmed into the Tenderloin to hear this tantalizing new sound, and the ex-colored man boasts that "it was no secret that the great increase in slumming visitors was due to my playing" (84). "Among other white 'slummers'" who frequented the cabaret where he played nightly, he befriends a wealthy white man that he calls "my millionaire." His millionaire "bore the indefinable but unmistakable stamp of culture" (84) and provides the ex-colored man with a means to recommence his temporarily stagnated pattern of mobility: "Through [ragtime] I . . . gained a friend who was the means by which I escaped from this lower world. And, finally, I secured a wedge which has opened to me more doors and made me a welcome guest than my playing of Beethoven and Chopin could ever have done" (84). But the workload was severe at times, and it has been argued that this "wedge" was self-serving, rather than a means to uplift the African American community. "Just like the stereotype of the happy darky," says Cataliotti, "driven 'mercilessly to exhaustion' by a white 'tyrant,' the ex-colored man is content with his pay, looks upon his subjugation as a 'familiar and warm relationship,' and finds in that tyrant an assimilationist model" (68). But this cultural interaction between audience and entertainer serves the musical hybrid the ex-colored man invents, just as much as it serves to entertain the millionaire and his upper-crust acquaintances. Indeed, if white forums for "ragging" the classics should be considered tyrannical assimilation, then we would, by disallowing mutually beneficial influence, greatly hinder both black and white cultural production.

True, the ex-colored man cashes in on an older manifestation of radical chic, and his millionaire has access to a seemingly inexhaustible fortune. Because of his money, along with his open-minded curiosity, the millionaire resembles Prince Rodolphe in Eugene Sue's seminal slumming novel *Les Mystéres de Paris* (1842), an aristocratic outsider able to wander freely among struggling insiders and discover a moral region's most entertaining talents. The millionaire propositions the ex-colored man to play at a fashionable New York soiree for the benefit of those who would never get the opportunity to hear ragtime if it remained within the confines of the Tenderloin. Though the guests in this upper-class parlor party are at first glance "all decidedly blasé" (86), the ex-colored man begins his session with one of his "liveliest ragtime pieces" and observes that almost instantaneously "the effect was surprising." All talking, eating, and cynical repartee broke off—the audience was entranced (87). The marginal millionaire had successfully brought the Tenderloin to the Fifth Avenue salon.

This form of salon slumming was not restricted to importing insiders with musical talent from morally marginalized spaces. The very act of reading about the Tenderloin no doubt provoked a sense of cultural "release" for an outsider audience as well. Johnson shows the chic New Yorkers, not unsympathetically, enjoying ragtime in an upscale parlor as one avatar of the readers themselves: "These were people—and they represented a large class—who were expecting to find happiness in novelty, each day restlessly exploring and exhausting every resource of this great city that might possibly furnish a new sensation or awaken a fresh emotion, and who were always grateful to anyone who aided them in their quest" (87). One reason Johnson designed his short novel to reflect the first-person autobiography was because, as Eugene Levy attests, "for whites, reading a black man's autobiography often served as a vicarious substitute for personal contact with blacks" (130). For an outsider, taking up such a narrative supplanted the experience of engaging in the sordid nightlife of the Tenderloin, laboring in the close atmosphere of a cigar factory, or participating, passively or aggressively, in a southern lynching. The millionaire voices his satisfaction, and perhaps Johnson's, when he remarks at the conclusion of the ex-colored man's first parlor performance, "Well, I have given them something they've never had before" (87). So his Fifth Avenue debut was a secondary form of slumming in three important ways: 1) the ex-colored man was once again exposing himself to a significantly alien group of insiders, albeit more prosperous this time; 2) the modish New York socialites got a taste of African American culture without having to actually enter into it; and 3) for outsiders unfamiliar with the Tenderloin, white or black, the experience of reading *The Autobiography of an Ex-Colored Man* served as a form of slumming as well.

Given this fact, compounded by the cultural variety Johnson advocates, we must ask ourselves whether the author wants us to see the Tenderloin as a perilous area that outsiders should avoid or a fruitful venue for cultural production. The ex-colored man, after all, flees the scene of the white woman's murder and in the process abandons the Tenderloin as well: "Just which streets I followed when I got outside I do not know, but I think I must have gone towards Eighth Avenue, then down towards Twenty-third Street and across towards Fifth Avenue. I traveled, not by sight, but instinctively. I felt like one fleeing in a horrible nightmare" (90). Keeping in mind the district's parameters (Twenty-fifth Street to Fifty-fifth Street and from Fifth Avenue to Seventh) and the address of the "Club" (West Twenty-seventh Street), his route is significant: first he runs to the nearest border of the Tenderloin, Twenty-seventh and Eighth Avenue, which is now fashionable Chelsea, but at that time was a neighborhood strongly identified by working-class waterfront culture along the Hudson River. He then runs down to Twenty-third Street, past the bottom line of the Tenderloin and over to Fifth Avenue, where the Tenderloin gives way to New York's most affluent section. There he is found by his millionaire, who secures his safety and sweeps him away on a tour of Europe.

Given that the *Autobiography* is in part a novel about passing—in the end, the ex-colored man passes as a white landlord in New York, at which point he "shunned the old Sixth Avenue district as though it were pest-infected" (141)—and that his history *Black Manhattan* largely actualizes a feeling of cultural uplift and legitimacy for the African American community, Johnson betrays a sense of personal uncertainty regarding the Tenderloin's legacy. A look at Johnson's actual autobiography, *Along This Way*, which Alain Locke reviewed as a book that "could just as well have been the type story of Black Bohemia . . . a story that must some day be written" ("Saving Grace of Realism" 223) helps resolve the seeming contradiction between the ex-colored man's perceptions of the Tenderloin in the *Autobiography* and Johnson's more culturally uplifting Tenderloin in *Black Manhattan.*

In the 1927 Knopf edition of the *Autobiography* Johnson's name appeared prominently on the dust jacket, and he received numerous letters from a confused public inquiring about various periods of his life. "That is, probably," he admits later in *Along This Way,* "one of the reasons why I am writing the present book" (239). By the time Johnson moved to New York to write songs for Broadway with his brother Rosamond and his friend Bob Cole, the Tenderloin of *The Autobiography of an Ex-Colored Man* no longer existed. And by 1930, the year *Black Manhattan* came out, ragtime had gone the way of many popular forms. After the birth of jazz, ragtime dipped into virtual obscurity with few exceptions, notably "'the forgotten' Scott Joplin" and, "inappropriately," Irving Berlin's "Alexander's Ragtime Band" (Berlin, *Ragtime* 173). By this time in the history of New York music, syncopated rhythms were "not such a startling novelty" (*Along This Way* 175). The new audience was a Broadway audience, a general American public not in the habit of "restlessly exploring and exhausting every resource of this great city," but rather of temporarily escaping their quotidian lives.

Johnson's music ensemble, Cole and the Johnson Brothers, lived and worked at the Marshall Club (West Fifty-third Street) from 1901 to 1905, where African Americans enjoyed "a fashionable sort of life that hitherto had not existed." The Marshall boasted "excellent food," "well-dressed colored men," and parlors in which to "lounge and chat" (*Along This Way* 171). Its habitués were hardworking and highly professional musicians, composers, performers, and managers, all there to make a name for themselves on Broadway, which many of them did. "The Marshall came to be one of the great sights of New York. But it was more than a 'sight'; its importance as the radiant point of the forces that cleared the way for the Negro stage cannot be over-estimated" (177). Johnson further points out the "importance" of black artists claiming their own base of operations, writing that "as the Marshall gained popularity, the more noted theatrical stars and the better paid vaudevillians deserted the down-town clubs and made the [Marshall] their professional and social rendezvous" (176). Professionalism is an unremitting theme in Johnson's writing, and the success of Cole and the Johnson Brothers was a by-product of the team's project to raise the "status of the Negro as a writer, composer, and performer in the New York theater and world of music" (172–73). As such, Cole and the Johnson Brothers pandered to a Broadway audience, but in innovative ways, consequently prospering for four lucrative years.

"As the Marshall gained popularity," Johnson observed, "the more noted theatrical stars and the better-paid vaudevillians deserted the down-town clubs and made the hotel their professional and social rendezvous" (176). And, importantly, his description of Ike Hines's in *Along This Way*, the model for the "Club" in *The Autobiography of an Ex-Colored Man*, corresponds with that of the Marshall, though his choice of words is revealing: "It was principally a club for Negroes connected with the theater, but it drew the best elements from the various circles of Bohemia—except the gamblers" (176). Johnson ironically refers to gamblers as being among the "best" of Tenderloin society. As mentioned above, the ex-colored man could only comfortably afford Ike Hines's if he won at gambling, that is, until he began "ragging" the classics.

In the Tenderloin, insider "vices" like gambling, drinking, ragtime piano, and cross-racial sexuality, are solidly associated with cultural production. Johnson points out in *Black Manhattan* that "it was in such places as this that early Negro theatrical talent created for itself a congenial atmosphere, an atmosphere of emulation and guildship. It was also an atmosphere in which artistic ideas were born and developed" (78). In the novel, "such places" exposed the ex-colored man to a sporting life that ultimately cultivated his talent.

A brief meeting between Johnson and H. L. Mencken, as recalled in *Along This Way,* further clarifies our understanding of Johnson's perception of the Tenderloin's legacy. Mencken was a journalist who, Johnson reveals, had "made a sharper impression [on Johnson] than any other American then writing." For nearly forty-five minutes they talked in Mencken's office at the magazine *Smart Set,* where Mencken was an editor: "I had never been so fascinated at hearing anyone talk. He talked about literature, about Negro literature, the Negro problem, and Negro music." He informed Johnson that he felt African American authors were making a mistake "when they indulged in pleas for justice and mercy, when they prayed indulgence for shortcomings, when they based their protests against unjust treatment on the Christian moral or ethical code, when they argued to prove that they were as good as anybody else." Instead, Mencken argued, "'What they should do . . . is to single out the strong points of the race and emphasize them over and over and over; asserting, at least on these points, that they are better than anybody else.'" Johnson's response to this advice brings together all of the ambiguous threads: "I called his attention that I had attempted something of that sort in *The Autobiography of an Ex-Colored Man*" (305).

For an early twentieth-century black American writer, Johnson's insider status would afford him a grand opportunity for making his mark on American literary history. The racist image of the Negro in American literature as "a happy-go-lucky, laughing, shuffling, banjo-picking being" (*Autobiography* 123)—a mythical "happy darky" that the ex-colored man regards as "better known in American literature than any other single picture in our national life" (122)—"constitutes the opportunity of the future Negro novelist and poet to give the country something new and unknown, in depicting the life, the ambitions, the struggles and the passions of those of their race who are striving to break the narrow limits of traditions. A beginning has already been made in that remarkable book by Dr. Du Bois, *The Souls of Black Folk*" (123).

❖ ❖ ❖

By the 1920s, the Tenderloin's "black Bohemia" existed as a dated precursor to modern Harlem for young New York blacks, but it remained a fond memory to older activists like Johnson. Its legacy was a usable past upon which to build a legitimized future. In the struggle to construct a usable African American past, filling in the gaps of the cultural continuum between slave narratives and New Negro modernism, we must retrieve the Tenderloin's "black Bohemia" and the marginal men and women who inhabited it from its obscured position in the African American tradition.[10] We know Harlem with its far greater numbers after the Great Migration of the 1910s and '20s was enormously important for black and white cultural production. But those ten short blocks in the Tenderloin enabled African American artists to invent new reasons, again, "to grope toward a realization of the importance of the American Negro's cultural background and his creative folk-art, and to speculate on the superstructure of conscious art that might be reared upon them" (Johnson, *Along This Way* 152).

The 1920s, of course, were the glory days of the Harlem Renaissance, what was then called the New Negro Renaissance, when the ethnically cohesive society that was established there could claim true insiders. During that time, which will be covered in chapter 5, Johnson took a pragmatic look back in African American history to find art forms that might bolster the authority and legitimacy of black artists in his own time. His findings are collected in two anthologies: *The Book of American Negro Poetry* (1922) and *The Book of American Negro Spirituals* (1925, 1926). He also produced his book of poems inspired by Negro preachers he had heard over the years, *God's Trombones: Seven Negro Sermons in Verse* (1927). Johnson's preface to his later anthology *The Book of American Negro Poetry* is foremost a pronouncement that African American poetry and music are "the only things artistic that have yet sprung from American soil and been universally acknowledged as distinctive American products" (qtd. in Andrews xiv), arguing, then, that black culture amounted to the only singularly American culture uncompromised by European influences. Globally speaking, it was the only national insider art for the United States to export.

Hence Johnson was not afraid to blend southern black culture with modern cosmopolitan forms, and he rejected Dunbar's notion that the city quashed their ability "to play their simple melodies on the banjo, and strum out 'rags' on the piano" ("Negroes" 266). On the contrary, Johnson's preface to *The Book of American Negro Poetry* charts the course of African American cultural history, citing dance steps such as the "cakewalk" and the "shimmy"; music like spirituals, ragtime, and the blues; and poetry, from the slave poet Phillis Wheatley writing in the eighteenth century, to insider authors of his own time, such as Paul Laurence Dunbar, Claude McKay, John W. Holloway, and Jessie Fauset. He emphasized the artistic quality of the work, as "nothing will do more to change that mental attitude [racism] and raise [the Negro's] status than a demonstration of intellectual parity by the Negro through the production of literature and art" (vii). He argued that "dialect" poetry was no longer a viable poetic form; it had, for too long, been associated with weak-minded sentimental tales and racist propaganda generated by outsiders. Charles Scruggs explains that "for Johnson, dialect was the [Bakhtinian] net entangling the Negro poet, just as for Mencken 'genteel' language was the net entangling the American artist. Both nets tied the artist to a sterile past, preventing him from expressing the multi-layered world around him" (186).

"*Traditional* Negro dialect as a form for Aframerican poets," Johnson later wrote, "is absolutely dead" (*God's Trombones* 8). His preface to *The Book of American Negro Poetry* contains a passage that outlines his alternative vision of African American poetry, which can be applied to other insider art production as well:

> What the colored poet in the United States needs to do is something like what Synge did for the Irish; *he needs to find a form that will express the racial spirit by symbols from within rather than by symbols from without*—such as the mere mutilation of English spelling and pronunciation. He needs a form that is freer and larger than dialect, but which will still hold the racial flavor; a form expressing the imagery, the idioms, the peculiar turns of thought and the distinctive humor and pathos, too, of the Negro, but which will also be capable of voicing the deepest and highest emotions and aspirations and allow the widest range of subjects and the widest scope of treatment. (xl–xli, emphasis mine)

Paul Laurence Dunbar himself resented the insistence of white publishers, critics, and consumers that he produce more of his crowd-pleasing dialect poems and less traditional "literary" verse. As Dominika Ferens remarks of race writing at the turn of the twentieth century, "not only have writers of color historically been expected to produce 'insider' accounts of their ethnic communities, preferably in the autobiographical mode, but also the publishing industry made it very difficult for them to publish anything else" (14). Ironically, in *The Sport of the Gods* Dunbar adds a special twist to Johnson's take on dialect writing: Skaggs "impulsively" remarks to Sadness, "I tell you

. . . dancing is the poetry of motion." To which Sadness replies, "Yes . . . and dancing in rag-time is the dialect poetry" (116).

In the following chapter, any equivocation over the enriching possibilities of entering moral regions is properly abandoned. The intimate relationship between Lower East Side insider Abraham Cahan and Illinois-born Victorian outsider Hutchins Hapgood is symbolic of the growing cultural partnership between marginalized urban neighborhoods and the genteel class. As a self-professed "Victorian in a modern world," Hapgood discovers in the Jewish ghetto a culture that convinces him to completely disavow his Victorian roots. In Hapgood's *The Spirit of the Ghetto* (1902), he explicitly reconfigures the outsider view of Jewish New York that Jacob Riis had reaffirmed and popularized twelve years earlier in *How the Other Half Lives*. Riis depicted the Jewish Lower East Side as a wounding influence to American entrepreneurial morality, one that was growing to proportions that threatened to drastically affect New York's social economy. The Lower East Side, he argued, should be contained, perhaps even destroyed, to preserve the integrity of the larger New York society. Like Dunbar, Riis saw mainly the worst in his subject. But unlike Johnson, and leaving Dunbar entirely at the post, Hapgood's book is a fellow outsider's unrelenting counter-attack.

4 Realism in the Ghetto

JACOB RIIS, HUTCHINS HAPGOOD, AND ABRAHAM CAHAN ON THE LOWER EAST SIDE

> I said to myself that it was among such throngs [on the Lower East Side]
> that Christ walked, it was from such people that he chose his Disciples
> and his friends; but I looked in vain for him in Hester Street. Probably
> he was at that moment on Fifth Avenue.
>
> —William Dean Howells, 1896

> How individuals and groups who represent what might be called the
> underdog, when they are endowed with energy and life, exert pressures
> towards modification of our cast-iron habits and lay rich deposits of
> cultural enhancement, if we are able to take advantage of them.
>
> —Hutchins Hapgood, 1910

JACOB RIIS HAS BEEN RECENTLY HERALDED as the spokesman of an
"alternative ethics" (Gandal, *Virtues* 7), a groundbreaking social theorist who
confronted "the willed ignorance of the middle and upper classes, who knew
that there was human misery in [New York] but preferred to believe that
it was deserved, perhaps even chosen, by its victims" (Sante, Introduction,
Other Half x). And some scholars argue that Riis's anti-Semitic stereotyping
and overt racism are a pose to ingratiate a reluctant outsider audience who
would otherwise be suspicious of such subjects, Jews on the Lower East Side,
for example, particularly if seen through the lens of the immigrant other:
"Having known first hand the prejudice directed against the immigrant, Riis
apparently decided that he could best retain the sympathies of middle-class
readers by establishing a fictional bond with them" (Giles 17). To reposition
our understanding of Riis in this way appears to be the only approach that
would allow for further Riis studies. But Riis's ethnic chapters in his remark-

ably successful treatise on New York tenement life *How the Other Half Lives* (1890) are less sympathetic to their subjects than these studies would have us believe. As Ronald Sanders observes of Riis's ethnocentric characterizations of the immigrant other, "the Jews are nervous and inquisitive, the Orientals are sinister, the Italians are unsanitary" (92).

Riis published *How the Other Half Lives* during the early stages of eastern and southern European immigration to the United States, what we now call the "second wave" of American immigration.[1] Over this period, immigrants poured over in alarming numbers—two million eastern European Jews, five million Italians, and millions more from Austria-Hungary, Ukraine, Poland, Greece, Syria, and other Mediterranean-Slavic jumping-off points. Beginning around 1882, the year the Russian government initiated a series of vicious pogroms against Jewish settlements and the U.S. government simultaneously passed the Chinese Exclusion Act, and ending abruptly in the 1920s, the second wave totaled over twenty million, more than a million a year for over two decades. From 1880 to 1910, approximately 1.4 million eastern European Jews alone would make New York their home. They comprised nearly a quarter of the city's population, and the remainder was unaccustomed to cultures hailing from farther east than Berlin.

In the decade Riis wrote *How the Other Half Lives,* the 1880s, three out of four Jews in Manhattan resided on the Lower East Side, about sixty thousand total; by 1920, the numbers rose to over four hundred thousand (Jackson 620). Eastern European Jews found comfort, such as it was, in this neighborhood where individuals and families inhabited block upon block of five-story walk-ups—immigrants who shared a common language, ate the same foods, and practiced, or deliberately did not practice, the same religion. Outsider reformers and insider immigrants alike characterized the Lower East Side in terms that speak to Robert Park's moral regions, his theory of the relationship between space and morality (see introduction). Here is Abraham Cahan, the consummate insider author from that neighborhood, reflecting on the moral implications of such a neighborhood:

> You find there Jews born to plenty, whom the new conditions have delivered up to the clutches of penury; Jews reared in the straits of need, who have here risen to prosperity; good people morally degraded in the struggle for success amid an unwonted environment; moral outcasts lifted from the mire, purified, and imbued with self-respect; educated men and women with their intellectual polish tarnished in the inclement weather of adversity; ignorant sons of toil grown enlightened—in fine, people with all sorts of antecedents, tastes, habits, inclinations, and speaking all sorts of subdialects of the same

jargon, thrown pell-mell into one social caldron—a human hodgepodge
with its component parts changed but not yet fused into one homogeneous
whole. (14)

Given their vast numbers, *shtetl*-like parochialism, cultural isolation, and
predominating devotion to eastern European Orthodoxy, assimilating this
mystifying "hodgepodge" seemed unlikely to the Anglo-German majority
residing outside its borders.

Christine Stansell convincingly argues in *American Moderns* that although
anti-Semitism was certainly on the rise in turn-of-the-century New York, a
new bohemian sensibility that found its origins in genteel society was also
responsible for a growing sense of relativism among the elite. Referring to
this phenomenon as the "philo-Semitic perspective," Stansell submits that
it was not a pure form of relativism, particularly in the work of the New
York-based journalist and author Hutchins Hapgood: "For all Hapgood's
declarations of newfound comradeship, the immigrants do not yet appear to
be compeers so much as characters in the metropolitan theater." "Still," she
continues, "the philo-Semitic perspective, for all its limitations, opened up
that theater to a new idea of a possible America" (25). To answer the call of
the philo-Semites, many Jewish writers—most prominently Abraham Cahan,
Mary Antin, Anzia Yezierska, and Mike Gold—produced a body of fiction
and journalism that would open a cultural channel between insiders from
the Jewish ghetto on the Lower East Side and outsiders from the uptown
gentile population.

In the earliest years of this trend, and in stark contrast to Riis's pander-
ous ethnocentrism, Hutchins Hapgood's study of the Jewish Lower East Side
The Spirit of the Ghetto (1902) offers a truly "alternative ethics" for outsiders
from the genteel classes. *The Spirit of the Ghetto* was the first book-length
treatment of New York's Jewish tenement district (Rischin, Introduction vii),
which makes it one of the most exciting journalistic experiments in American
history. It was also a critical success, due, in part, to the disgust Americans
felt while witnessing the Dreyfus Affair and its exposure of Old World anti-
Semitism. Since Hapgood was writing from an outsider perspective, Stansell
finds his Jewish insiders somewhat tame, lending a certain condescension to
his reportage of them (25). But Hapgood sacrifices emphasis on the political
instrumentality of the Lower East Side in favor of delineating the complex
mechanisms of the insiders' society, mechanisms that might stimulate New
York's cosmopolitan climate. If outsiders considered the social advancement
of the Jewish population dangerous, as Riis clearly argued in *How the Other*

Half Lives, then Hapgood presented a more vigorous cultural threat than it may at first appear. If we compare Riis and Hapgood, though the latter's may seem a classic counter-ethnocentric paradigm, Hapgood's argument for Jewish advancement was precisely what Riis had beseeched his readers to hold in check.

Jacob Riis, Hutchins Hapgood, and the Ethics of (Non)Conformity

Jacob Riis entreated the Christian middle class to wrest the tenement districts from the hands of the immigrant population, as it was both "the Christian thing to do" and morally sound business practice; and he perpetuated this nativist view through the authority of his own immigrant experience. With photographs and illustrations that handled precisely the same subject matter, the problem of the poor, as illustrated reform literature throughout the century had done, he belabored his book with sentimental tales from the ghetto that were already well-grounded in the American mind. At the same time, he astounded readers with his trademark mortality statistics, tenement blueprints, and shocking photographs. Riis was not in the business of convincing his outsider readership to appreciate the cultural contributions of such a population. The chapters devoted to the Jewish ghetto, "Jewtown" and "The Sweaters of Jewtown," do little to warm his audience to the benefits of harboring a domestic Jewish population; instead, he depicts the Jews of the Lower East Side as penurious, deceitful, litigious, argumentative, fanatically religious, and miserly—a familiar-sounding list, even for our own time, and reaffirming for an irritable native population shocked by the crush of new arrivals escaping from their inhospitable homelands.

How the Other Half Lives sold well for a number of reasons. Ted Burrows and Mike Wallace point out in their comprehensive New York history *Gotham* that its publication date could not have been more perfectly timed (1181–82). Ward McAllister's sycophantic nod to New York's wealthiest financiers *Society as I Have Found It* appeared in the same year, but the general reading public found his well-to-do subjects detestable at the height of the Gilded Age. McCallister offered no tangible vision of a better New York, whereas Riis confronted the city's worst problem areas head on. Burrows and Wallace continue that *How the Other Half Lives* is also a paragon of the popular "sunshine-and-shadow," or city-mysteries, tradition, and "Riis's literary strategy came straight from Dickens's *American Notes,* one of his favorite books" (1182). Dickens's *American Notes,* however, as I mention in the introduction, had been notably unpopular in a city that felt its favorite writer had betrayed it. Much like Riis, the great British novelist emphasized the horrors of New York, but Dickens alienated his American audience rather than embracing it. *American Notes,* published in 1842, had simply come too early. The negative imagery of Riis's jeremiad now unified audiences grown weary by urban growth. Privileged New Yorkers were compelled to impede its effects, particularly in regard to immigrant enfranchisement.

Most educated Anglo-Americans by the 1910s shared the Progressive view that their collective history should consolidate the visibly chaotic "nation of nations" into one acceptable, respectable norm. As the imagist poet Amy Lowell wrote in a 1917 critique of Carl Sandburg's distinctive new verse from the Scandinavian Midwest, "some day, America will be a nation; some day, we shall have a national character. Now, our population is a crazy quilt of racial samples. But how strong is that Anglo-Saxon ground-work which holds them all firmly together to its shape, if no longer to its colour!" (202). As such, immigrants were to become "Americanized," a term that implied not only the rejection of an older culture for a newer one, but also the "initiation" of a people into a democratic society increasingly consumer oriented and actuated by industrial growth (Ewen 15).

In the famous 1911 edition of *Encyclopedia Britannica* (advertised as the most comprehensive compendium of human knowledge the world had ever known), the article on "Migration" focuses on the United States and its complex relationship between the "native" Anglo-German majority and the new mass of immigrants from eastern and southern Europe. The authors report that in 1910, over 20 percent of the American labor force was foreign-born, almost 40 percent if you counted the second generation. In terms of the economy, they find these numbers encouraging, since before the Civil War, "an adult slave used to be valued at from $800 to $1000, so that every adult immigrant may be looked upon as worth that sum to the country" (Ingraham and Mayo-Smith 431). But they discard this and other careless approximations after taking into account the "more numerously represented" immigrants who came from the "criminal, defective and dependent classes," not to mention that "element which has made itself obnoxious to the local sentiment," namely eastern European Jews. With consummate self-assurance, however, "Migration" offers this sanguine proclamation regarding the United States and its noble experiment: "Doubtless immigration in the last fifty years of the nineteenth century had a modifying effect on American life; but on the whole the power of a modern civilized community working through individual freedom to assimilate elements not differing from it too radically has been displayed to a remarkable degree" (Ingraham and Mayo-Smith 431).

But as the immigrant population rose, sociologist David Ward observes that "various immigrant groups were presumed to possess different innate or hereditary aptitudes for democracy" (15). And the culture critic Randolph Bourne would later respond to this popular notion of political atavism in his essay "Trans-National America" (1916): "Let us cease to think of ideals of democracy as magical qualities inherent in certain peoples. Let us speak, not of inferior races, but of inferior civilizations. We are all to educate and be educated. These peoples in America are in a common enterprise. It is not what we are now that concerns us, but what this plastic next generation may become in the light of a new cosmopolitan ideal" (95). Ward and Bourne refer to a pseudoscientific theory of culture and politics that proliferated in the United States in moral reform literature like Charles Loring Brace's and Helen Campbell's, and this moral realism reached its zenith in the works of Jacob Riis.

That New York society as a whole had pegged the Jewish ghetto as a turn-of-the-century corollary to Robert Park's later moral regions concept, like the East Side waterfront, the Bowery, and the Tenderloin, is apparent in Hapgood's preface to *The Spirit of the Ghetto*: "The Jewish quarter of New York is generally supposed to be a place of poverty, dirt, ignorance and immorality—the seat of the sweatshop, the tenement house, where 'red lights' sparkle at night, where the people are queer and repulsive. Well-to-do persons visit the 'Ghetto' merely from motives of curiosity or philanthropy; writers treat it 'sociologically,' as of a place in crying need of improvement" (5).

This passage, the opening paragraph of the book, is remarkable in its categorical responsiveness to Riis's work. In Riis, the character of the Lower East Side and its inhabitants is defined by "poverty, dirt, ignorance and immorality" in its spatial relation to the "sweatshop, the tenement." The passage clearly points to Riis and his view of the ghetto's qualities with which he opened his own book:

> The boundary line lies there because, while the forces for good on one side vastly outweigh the bad—it were not well otherwise—*in the tenements all the influences make for evil*; because they are the hot-beds of the epidemics that carry death to rich and poor alike; the nurseries of pauperism and crime that fill our jails and police courts; that throw off a scum of forty thousand human wrecks to the island asylums and workhouses year by year; that turned out in the last eight years a round half million beggars to prey upon our charities; that maintain a standing army of ten thousand tramps with

all that that implies; because, *above all they touch the family life with deadly moral contagion.* This is their worst crime, inseparable from the system. That we have to own it the child of our wrong does not excuse it, even though it gives it claim upon our utmost patience and tenderest charity. (Riis 6, emphasis mine)

The period's trends toward "curiosity," "philanthropy," and the social sciences as a means of ghetto improvement are all intrinsic to Riis's outsider characterization here. In contrast, Hapgood is determined "to report sympathetically" on the value systems and cultural contributions of East Side Jewish insiders. Hapgood's purpose in *The Spirit of the Ghetto* is to outline reasons for crossing physical moral boundaries, as well as explicitly pointing out why "East Canal Street and the Bowery have interested [him] more than Broadway and Fifth Avenue" (5). In other words, his work is a heartening guidebook for genteel outsiders, like Hapgood, to go slumming on the Lower East Side.

As an outsider calling attention to the positive, one might say superior, aspects of the immigrant other, Hapgood left himself open for a thorough drubbing by the moral reform watchdogs of turn-of-the-century New York (along with later academics who like to see their oppressed populations in terminally oppressed postures). "That the Ghetto has an unpleasant aspect," Hapgood wrote in 1902, "is as true as it is trite" (5). He explains in his preface to *The Spirit of the Ghetto* that further delineation of ghetto depravity and destitution is not going to be "the subject of the following sketches" (5). After decades of American journalism drudging up the "lures and snares" of tormented moral regions, most notably on the Lower East Side, Hapgood finds moralizing urban exposé a hackneyed if often well-meaning mode of writing, a form of kitsch he was determined to avoid.

The Spirit of the Ghetto does contain a patronizing tone, as Christine Stansell suggests, but Hapgood was attempting to overstep generations of anti-Semitic stereotyping, and this required some hyperbole and journalistic oversight. In order to sustain that conviction, Hapgood's undergraduate professor at Harvard, George Santayana, informed him that one must impose an absolute identity on all of those engaging in practices abhorrent to your own world view—what Santayana termed the "vital lie."

The "vital lie" is a cynical word-game Santayana plays on the more optimistic philosopher Henri Bergson's notion of *l'élan vital,* or the spark that provides a social, psychological, and even biological "life force" crucial to the evolution of our species. Hapgood grappled with Santayana's concept, at once self-applying it and projecting it outward, as in the case of his friend Clarence Darrow:

> He seemed to feel like so many men who want to change the world, that everything that has happened in relationship with the development of unjust institutions is evil; in that literature, poetry, morality, which has developed side by side with an unjust political and economic order, is there only to give support to this injustice, and therefore merely aids and comforts the devil. I have had many opportunities to observe this tendency. In the heat of the endeavor to bring something new into the world, all intimate values seem to be lost sight of. Perhaps, in the necessity of concentrated conviction, in order to bring something new and desirable, this vital lie, as George Santayana called it, may be a necessity; but how terrific the sacrifice is. (*Victorian* 190)

The "vital lie" is both the driving force of the individual and that which enables social progress. The terrific sacrifice occurs when actions that accompany the lie lead to a willful disregard for the positive aspects of a perceived enemy. Again utilizing the vital lie, Hapgood describes Mary Jenney Howe, one of the founding members of the feminist group Heterodoxy, as harboring the notion of "a conspiracy of men against women," regardless of her "caring for love and affection" (*Victorian* 332). He attributes this apparent personality contradiction to her need for a vital lie in order for women to achieve the vote. Similarly, my own copy of *Victorian* is inscribed by the author to Rachael Kelly, "Who hates all men but likes me. How about it? Am I a man?"

Hapgood's vital lie can be found in scores of vitriolic pronouncements he aimed at late Victorian sexual prudery, prejudice against new immigrant groups, and the troubling effects of middle-class hegemony. Hapgood found his *élan vital,* that imperative that guides our subjects toward actuating social change, in the tenements of Manhattan's Jewish Lower East Side, in Bowery saloons, and in Greenwich Village café culture. His ultimate goal was to strike as many social contact points as possible in one lifetime, a goal that—given the escalation of "distance" education, Internet media, cell phones, mall culture, and suburban life—speaks to our own era's lack of intimate interconnectedness. Hapgood calls the ethos of a society that favors an intimate mode of social relations *Gemütlichkeit,* an expressive personal nature that enlivens and enriches culture, a pleasantly relaxed intellectualism that energizes the spiritual and creative impulses. *Gemütlichkeit* ignites Hapgood's *élan vital;* it is an attitude that, in concert with what they called on the Bowery "de real t'ing" and on the Yiddish stage "realism," would allow the United States to pursue a radically democratic society. His loathing for the burdensome strictures of Victorianism was his vital lie, one he acknowledged late in life when sitting down to write *A Victorian in the Modern World.* In it, he openly confesses his secretive, lifelong dependency on Victorianism—the bugaboo, he had been arguing throughout his career, that had hobbled radical democracy.

In his quest for a more modern realism, Hapgood discovers the most prolific renderings of ghetto life at the Yiddish theater, where, according to him, outsiders will find the finest Jewish social realism accessible to gentiles. By the early twentieth century, the Bowery had transformed even further since Crane's time, and any semblance of a unified and authentic cultural identity was essentially lost. As I discussed in the first two chapters, consumer culture surpassed mission reform by the 1880s and '90s, but by this time alternative voices began to overstep the genteel formulae to which Maggie Johnson availed herself. "In the midst of the frivolous Bowery," Hapgood reports, "devoted to tinsel variety shows, 'dive' music-halls, fake museums, trivial amusement booths of all sorts, cheap lodging-houses, ten-cent shops and Irish-American tough saloons, the theatres of the chosen people alone present the serious as well as the trivial interests of an entire community" (*Spirit* 113).

Stage actors in the middle decades of the nineteenth century had cari-catured native-born stereotypes—frontiersmen, American Indians, firemen, slaves, and dandified freedmen—as either more or less than human, a process that generated mostly offensive myths that paradoxically suffused the United States with a stronger sense of national identity. Although plays involving Irish "buffos" had existed at least since the 1700s, the sheer volume of im-migrant stage performances rose considerably over the century. The Ireland-born dramatists Edward Harrigan and Tony Hart, for example, included in their repertoire some eighty dramatic sketches about the Irish in the 1870s alone, and more in the years that followed about southern black migrants, Italians, Germans, and Chinese (Wittke 193). William Dean Howells (never one to let ethnic representation go without comment) believed that Harrigan and Hart were "unsurpassed in the fidelity and refined perception of their portrayals of American immigrant types, and that their sociological and psy-chological studies construed true American art" (qtd. in Wittke 194; see also Wonham chapter 1 on how nineteenth-century ethnic caricature interloped, however unconsciously, into Howells's "realist" novels and critical essays in what Wonham calls "the Howellsian ethnic two-step" [61]). Comedies of this sort based their jokes on racial physicality, dialect, and foreign customs in ways that continued well into the twentieth century. But as cruel as many of the stereotypes were on the American stage, they depicted the absurdities of immigrant life based on observations from the streets, even if through the eyes of outsider observers.

In contrast to the popular theater scenes in Crane's Bowery tales and Whitman's "Old Bowery Days," the Yiddish theaters were supremely democratic: everyone from a seamstress to an anarchist to a rabbi attended these performances. As a result, popular melodrama commingled with "a simple transcript from life or the theatric presentation of a ghetto problem" (Hapgood, *Spirit* 114). Some of the more intellectual insider playwrights would draw upon East Side life and culture to produce pieces known as "historical plunder," and create a kind of hybrid realism that combined popular gags with stark mimesis. "It is the demand of these fierce realists," Hapgood relates, "that of late years has produced a supply of theatrical productions attempting to present a faithful picture of the actual conditions of life. Permeating all these kinds of plays is the amusement instinct pure and simple. For the benefit of the crowd of ignorant people grotesque humor, popular songs, vaudeville tricks, are inserted everywhere" (*Spirit* 123). What made these performances extraordinary was the fusion of the popular and the real, according to Hapgood, and "the most interesting plays are those in which the realistic spirit predominates, and the best among the actors and playwrights are the realists" (135).

Hapgood was not just sympathetic but enamored with Jewish "Russianness," a state of mind that ultimately manifests in what he calls a "seriousness" that lends itself to the tenets of the realist movement. This "seriousness" of artistic and philosophic purpose is perhaps most redolent at the three most popular Yiddish theaters on the Bowery—the People's, the Thalia, and the Windsor. By 1902, there were seventy to eighty professional Jewish actors, nearly a dozen playwrights, hundreds of completed plays, and "an enormous Russian Jewish colony, which fills the theatres and creates so strong a demand that the stage responds with a distinctive, complete, and interesting popular art" (150). New York in the first years of the twentieth century was arguably the time and place when the Yiddish theater reached its historical climax, having first been invented, according to the actor Jacob Adler, in Rumania by a Russian Jew named Goldfaden in 1876. The Russian state revoked the right of Jews to stage Yiddish dramas following the first pogroms, and as there was no ghetto in London to speak of, the natural destination for Yiddish language dramatists was New York. By 1887, the year Adler moved to the city, two Yiddish companies were already well underway on the Bowery (Hapgood, *Spirit* 165). Hapgood historicizes New York Yiddish theater in order to prove that there is a well-established and historically significant cultural event going on in the Lower East Side, and outsiders hitherto oblivious to this extraordinary neighborhood should make their way downtown.

The most admired proponents of realism on the Yiddish stage were Jacob Adler and the playwright Jacob Gordin, both of whom collaborated in
an (ultimately failed) attempt to provide exclusively realistic dramas. The
effort was doomed by an insider audience that generally demanded melodramatic amusement as well as cultural and political enlightenment (Hapgood, *Spirit* 136). Hapgood discovers that even the artistically self-conscious
Gordin infused his plays with "clownish and operatic intrusions, inserted as
a conscious condition of success." "On the other hand," he qualifies, "even
in the distinctively formless plays, in comic opera and melodrama, there are
striking illustrations of the popular feeling for realism,—bits of dialogue,
happy strokes of characterization of well-known Ghetto types, sordid scenes
faithful to the life of the people" (137). But regardless of the seemingly contradictory elements of "art" and "amusement" that appear in all Yiddish
plays with varying degree, Hapgood encourages outsiders uptown to attend,
since "they are yet refreshing to persons who have been bored by the empty
farce and inane cheerfulness of the uptown theatres" (149).

"The spirit of the ghetto," Hapgood reinforces in his 1917 essay "The
Picturesque Ghetto," "is the spirit of seriousness, of melancholy, of a high
idealism, which, when interpreted by the sympathetic artist, illuminates even
the sweat-shop, the push-cart market, and the ambitious businessman" (qtd.
in Rischin, Introduction xxiii). He declares that on the Lower East Side "the
old and the new come . . . into close contact and throw each other into high
relief" (*Spirit* 9). Hapgood discovered that oftentimes it proves helpful to
determine what your social identity *is not* in order to comprehend what it
is, and ultimately how it might profitably be revised. Improving one's character by entering a moral region is remarkably distinct from Charles Loring
Brace's ideal vision of bringing "the two extremes of society in sympathy,
and carry[ing] the forces of one class down to lift up the other" (136). Rather,
Hapgood sets out to demonstrate how the class ostensibly on top would do
well to consider social uplift from below.

The Anglo-Jewish playwright Israel Zangwill, author of *The Melting Pot,*
praised *The Spirit of the Ghetto* as "a criticism of life, and moreover a criticism tending toward sweetness and light. For it is the work of no prejudiced
Jew but the work of an Outsider of culture, able to interpret what he sees;
to understand its ratios; and finally to define the deep springs of idealism
that transfuse the ghetto with a poetry that the larger American life often
loses" (qtd. in Rischin, "Abraham Cahan" 23). As an "Outsider of culture,"
Hapgood's implicit project was to undo everything Riis had accomplished
twelve years earlier. *The Spirit of the Ghetto* is one self-professed outsider's

study of the Lower East Side in which "a 'Gentile' [reports] sympathetically on the character, lives and pursuits of certain east-side Jews with whom he has been in relations of considerable intimacy" (5); and this outsider found himself, in truth, extremely adept at forming close relations with first-generation Jewish immigrants.

Jacob Riis culled material for his graphically descriptive chapter "Jewtown" with the help of an insider to guide him through the Jewish Lower East Side, specifically the neighborhoods around Ludlow, Hester, Orchard, and Broome streets. His name was Max Fischel, a man Riis later described as "a little old round, happy Jewish boy" (qtd. in Rischin, Abraham Cahan" 18). Riis assures us that Fischel was "one of their own people who knew of and sympathized with my mission." Like Jerry McAuley for Campbell, Fischel's insider status enabled Riis to get nearer to his subjects, adding some indigenous authority to his study. "Without that precaution," Riis implicitly warns us, "my errand would have been fruitless; even with him it was often nearly so" (*Other Half* 96). Hapgood, like Riis, solicited the aid of insiders to authenticate his investigations, Jews familiar with both Hapgood's world—middle- to upper-middle class, Anglo-Saxon, Ivy League—and the world he would observe. But his greatest influence for conceptualizing this forty-five-block space in lower Manhattan was the Jewish author, newspaper editor, and labor leader Abraham Cahan, whom he met while they were both reporting for the infamous muckraker Lincoln Steffens at the New York *Daily Commercial Advertiser.*

New York Stories: Lincoln Steffens, Hutchins Hapgood, and Abraham Cahan at the Daily Commercial Advertiser

Hutchins Hapgood is most notable for his realistic narratives portraying the lower stratum of urban life in the early decades of the twentieth century. Born in Chicago on May 21, 1869, to a progressive and industrious Victorian family, in childhood he exhibited traits of nervousness, sensitivity, and alienation, traits that persisted through adulthood and were later reflected in his work. Hutch, as he was known, attended Harvard University from 1889 to 1892 and was strongly influenced there by the unorthodox moral philosophies of Professors William James and George Santayana. After completing his masters degree in English at Harvard, he continued his graduate studies at the University of Berlin, where he took seminars with the enormously influential German sociologist Georg Simmel, whose theories of "sociability" and "symbolic play" probably informed much of his social philosophy. Hapgood taught English at the University of Chicago for a time, but soon relinquished his academic career in favor of journalism, a vocation that he felt was more suitable to his roaming temperament than the narrow pursuits of academia. In 1897, he eagerly accepted a position as a street reporter under the editorship of Lincoln Steffens at the New York *Daily Commercial Advertiser.*

Steffens urged Hapgood to investigate New York street life at its core and collect interviews from the disenfranchised, "picturesque" inhabitants of the city. Over the next few years, Hapgood poured out a steady stream of articles that singularly portrayed the lives of vaudeville stage performers, Bowery bums, pickpockets, prostitutes, immigrant laborers, and anarchists. Unlike the moral reform and sensationalist writing of the period, however, Hapgood's sketches reveal little condescension or malice. Openly fed up with the well-established genteel culture, Hapgood still regarded himself as a "Victorian in the modern world," a designation he employed years later as the title of his 1939 autobiography. The rationale he offers in *A Victorian in the Modern World* for his forays among the "submerged" is worth quoting at length:

> I preferred for many years the society of outcasts, men and women, and the dramshops of life to the respectable people and their social resorts. I don't know why it was, entirely, but even from the beginning I felt something limited and repressive in morality as it is ordinarily conceived. It seemed to say, "Thou shalt not," but only rarely, "Thou shalt," and then faintheartedly. I felt that the lid shut away from the human social center a large number of the people who also belonged there, whom we call the submerged. . . . I am aware, of course, of my own over-rationalization of my personal inclinations. It is easy of course to live, during the period of youth especially, with loose and lawless bohemians. It is natural to desire the freedom which is generally and sometimes legitimately denied. In other words, I am sure that I had a more than normal desire to be with the dissipated and self-indulgent gang. But why the mental and temperamental excitement that I felt? It was not sensuality only, it was something of the opposite nature. It was a spiritual and esthetic excitement that one feels in the hope of a less boring, more enhancing existence. (325–26)

Modernity to Hapgood implied a cosmopolitan sense of cultural acceptance and adaptation that rejuvenates the "spirit." Multiplicity defines the modern American consciousness, and to reject new additions to the fold, such as the community that was burgeoning on the Lower East Side, is thus distinctly pre-modern. Rather than alienating his subjects further, Hapgood portrayed immigrant New York in the picturesque vein of the "hobo journalist" Josiah Flynt (his friend and mentor), in books like *The Spirit of the Ghetto*

(1902) and *Types from City Streets* (1910). The American press was so strongly influenced by the successful exposé writing of reform writers such as Brace, Campbell, and Riis that few journalists represented the "other half" as a positive, or even tolerable, presence in turn-of-the-century New York. Steffens, on the other hand, encouraged his young staff to explore the streets and alleyways for colorful stories of immigrant and working-class life. Hutchins, his brother Norman Hapgood, and Abraham Cahan, among others on Steffens's staff, viewed the famous ghetto journalist Jacob Riis, by then a star police reporter for the *New York Sun,* as a man of insufferably outdated journalistic methods and an anemic cultural perspective (Rischin, "Abraham Cahan" 14).

Three years under Steffens inspired Hapgood to "unify" New York in his own way by subverting the Anglo-German majority's renunciations of immigrant and working-class culture in lower Manhattan. In his series of sketches, *Types from City Streets,* he acknowledges that it is not his choice of subject that a "respectable" audience might pass judgment on, but rather his affirmation of it:

> Many respectable people think that there is something perverted or immoral merely in paying attention, unless the object for doing so is reform, to the "low" forms of human life. An attempt to tell the genuine interest and importance in the character, say, of a Bowery "bum," in the personality of an east-side truckman, in the obscure life of a little "speiler" girl, in the career of a Jewish pedler or sweat-shop tailor; or in the keenly individualized personality of an habitual "grafter" of the lowlier type; interest in such things for themselves alone, with no sociological or reformatory purpose, is not commonly approved of in our community. (*Types* 13–14)

His way of thinking allows for the fact that "there are certain moral, intellectual, and temperamental qualities in what are generally called 'low' persons which are admirable and attractive; and these qualities are easily experienced by anybody, except reformers and the 'unco' respectable man or woman" (14). He also discusses his relationship to the novelist Theodore Dreiser in terms that make the reader feel as if there was nothing before Hapgood's "attempt to call attention to the value of neglected or despised groups of people and their ways of thinking" (268). At the time of their first meeting, Dreiser had not appreciated this aspect of Hapgood's writing, that aspect that Hapgood himself thought most important. Though Hapgood "had read none of [Dreiser's] books," he felt a kinship with the great naturalist, equating himself with Dreiser as "a passionate propagandist for what might be called realistic writing" (267).

In *A Victorian in the Modern World* Hapgood remarks that it was his experience as a journalist at the *Commercial Advertiser* that made him appreciate "realistic writing" and "the real thing" in urban life: "When my working experience began . . . as a reporter in New York City, I seemed for a long time to need contact with human beings who had no security; they were so near the line that, in association with them, I came up against what is called the real thing" (111–12). And with the aid of insider-informant Abraham Cahan, he would mine the Jewish Lower East Side for cultural material that would form the basis of his book *The Spirit of the Ghetto* and would significantly rejuvenate his artistic sense of purpose. Hapgood argued that New York's Jewish district not only provided virtuous models for updating the stale atmosphere of New York's literary establishment, but also American society at large.

The *Commercial Advertiser* ran stories that possibly for the first time appealed to both the reading public uptown "who wanted to peek across the 'Social Gulf'" and subjects who found affirmation in the fact that their lives were deemed newsworthy (Stansell 25). Lincoln Steffens had entered this "Social Gulf" between insiders and outsiders early on and made innovative strides to form connections between the two from 1897 to 1901 as the city desk editor for the *Commercial Advertiser*. Its positive take on immigrant life and the potential of urban cosmopolitanism was unheard of up to that point, though its grit proved lacking after only a couple of years. Hapgood later accused Steffens of turning stuffy overnight, kowtowing to the editor-in-chief, and sacrificing time on the paper to work on his own material (*Types* 110–11). Whatever the case, Steffens's top writers, still in the mode of urban celebration, continued to seek out New York stories. Hapgood's *The Spirit of the Ghetto,* which originally appeared as essays in various publications between 1898 and 1902, was one of these spin-off projects.

By representing ghetto culture in a realistic manner, rather than sermonizing about moral discrepancies, Hapgood believed it possible to convert genteel society in New York rather than the other way around. As we have seen on Campbell's waterfront and Crane's Bowery, there was little means by which the lower classes could channel their own influences upwards. The Yiddish stage had been the most highly advertised forum for cultural exchange in the final decades of the nineteenth century, but the channel needed to be constructed by gentile outsiders themselves to attract a broader audience. The valve of this channel was first released by Lincoln Steffens in the offices of the *Commercial Advertiser.*

Steffens took the helm at the *Commercial Advertiser*'s city desk immediately after quitting an editorial position at the *Evening Post.* Under his leadership, the paper quickly transformed from an organ of genteel exclusivity to boasting some of the most creative and stylized newspaper reportage in the country. The atmosphere in the newsroom was exceptional in its combination of youthful energy and prodigious intellectuality. Steffens directed his staff to compose feature articles reflecting his sense of the city as "a romance, to be explored with the assiduousness of a scholar examining a hitherto unknown manuscript, and written about with the imaginative fire of a poet" (Sanders 80). Calling to mind the group of so-called New Journalists who held sway in the later decades of the twentieth century—Tom Wolfe, George Plimpton, Joan Didion, Truman Capote, and, most importantly for this, Norman Mailer and Hunter S. Thompson—the typical *Commercial Advertiser* reporter, Ronald Sanders notes, was an "engaged bohemian, ready to linger on in a slum tenement even after the police had made their call, prone to intense conversations with drunks on park benches, not averse even to get involved in saloon brawls—all for the sake of a story" (80).

Rather than choose his staff from the "professional" journalistic class, Steffens preferred instead to solicit articles from aspiring essayists, novelists, and playwrights who found on the New York streets an endless flow of raw material. The main body of *Commercial Advertiser* staffers consisted of "renegades from the genteel academic posts that had been offered them" (Sanders 80). The *Commercial Advertiser*'s reportage, not unlike moral realism, was balanced on a literary threshold; but rather than rely on social science to temper the effects of sentimentalism, the romantic world of the nineteenth-century novelist had been deliberately and successfully conjoined with the everyday grind of urban reporting without the assimilationist cant of a writer like Riis. Goals to reform the immigrant population—to transform them into respectable, plastic, Christian citizens—had given way to a political aesthetic, one in which Steffens's staff effectively demonized the "Americanization" process.

Steffens's autobiography offers a rare sociology of reception for eastern European Jews, a group that Steffens explicitly distinguishes from their German predecessors. He explains that the new immigrants lived in "a queer mixture of comedy, tragedy, orthodoxy, and revelation," and he emphasizes that the mixture "interested our Christian readers" (243). Steffens's support and direction enabled Hapgood and others to tour the dance clubs of Harlem (then a Jewish and German district), the Irish music halls of the Bowery, the restaurants of Chinatown, and the cafes of the Italian quarter, and draw out this "queer mixture" of ethnic urban life. Their stories drew an outsider audience because the immigrant experience triggered "heart-breaking comedies of the tragic conflict between the old and the new, the very old and the very new; in many matters, all at once: religion, class, clothes, manners, customs, language, culture" (Steffens 244).

Steffens hired Abraham Cahan in the first year of his editorship, at which point Cahan found himself a lone Jew in a crowd of privileged gentiles, mostly handpicked recruits from Harvard University. By this time, in his early forties, Cahan had already spent nearly twenty years covering the Jewish Lower East Side as a reporter and editor for the Yiddish papers. Regardless, Moses Rischin contends, Cahan's years at the *Commercial Advertiser* "comprised a seminal period in his journalistic apprenticeship" (10). One of the rewards of this apprenticeship was establishing his friendship with Hutchins Hapgood, who found in Cahan the intellectual intensity and seriousness of purpose that he himself strived to achieve. Cultivating such friendships is a persistent theme in Hapgood's autobiography. When "intimate values" are "lost sight of," Hapgood believed, then the spirit of mankind has gone with them (*Victorian* 190).

According to Hapgood, Cahan had little trouble winning over his new colleagues: "He formed a striking contrast to the young Harvard men; he gave them his point-of-view, and absorbed theirs; he taught them to understand something of the great East Side of New York, of its picturesque human characters and customs" (*Types* 110). Cahan returned the compliment, referring to Hapgood as "the only Gentile who knows and understands the spirit of the ghetto" (qtd. in Rischin, Introduction xxviii); in contrast, he regarded Jacob Riis as an unsympathetic outsider sensationalizing the Jews for profit (Rischin, "Abraham Cahan" 14).

Reciprocally, Cahan perceived in Hapgood, born as he was of seventeenth-century New England stock, an American counterpart to the Russian intellectual class—inquisitive, iconoclastic, and unencumbered by material temptations (Sanders 89). "Devoid of cunning, sincere, somewhat temperamental, and with a genuine and tender love for good books," Rischin writes, "'Hutch,' like a Russian nihilist or a sincere artist from the Montmartre quarter in Paris, hated all cant or ceremony" ("Abraham Cahan" 22). Cahan embodied precisely the attributes Steffens had in mind for his reporters at the *Commercial Advertiser,* and he effectively passed them on to Hapgood.

Hapgood was powerfully influenced by Cahan's uncanny ability to render Jewish life as he himself saw it while slumming in the district, less concerned with the social dysfunction of an area whose every block housed over twenty-five hundred people and more with the relationship between the immigrant insider and the rest of the city. Cahan portrayed newly arrived Jews on the Lower East Side in precisely the same way Hapgood perceived himself—absorbing the influences of the other group, struggling with the language and the marketplaces, and taking in new and exciting forms of entertainment that were not offered back home. Those things that struck outsiders as darkly foreign on the Lower East Side seemed distinctly American to the new immigrant. Home for most New York Jews was, of course, eastern Europe; for Hapgood, it was Hastings-on-Hudson. In short, Cahan's writing provided Hapgood with a model for cultural adaptation and acceptance in a society that, for outsiders at least, seemed to be doing neither.

Abraham Cahan, the "New Star of Realism"

No one Christian reader was more interested in immigrant fiction, as he was in black fiction by insiders, than William Dean Howells. Howells's turn to the political left in 1886 with the tragic Chicago Haymarket Riots compelled him to seek audience with the more colorful labor leaders of the period. In 1891 he arranged a meeting with Abraham Cahan, then working as a journalist for the Yiddish press in New York and as a union "walking delegate" (Richards vi). Howells was doing research for his utopian novel *A Traveler from Altruria* (1894) in Lower East Side cafes when he and Cahan formed a mutually beneficial friendship: Cahan was attempting to break into American literary circles and Howells into the labor scene. Like several writers I cover in this book, Charles Chesnutt, Stephen Crane, and Paul Laurence Dunbar (not to mention those not covered, now towering figures like Theodore Dreiser, Sarah Orne Jewett, Mark Twain, and a host of others), Howells made Cahan's literary reputation soar, and alternately, Cahan and the other realists repaid the "Dean" by largely crediting him for their success.

Cahan freed his Jewish characters from the roles assigned them by the period's thriving caricaturists. His self-professed influences—Tolstoy, Turgenev, Dostoevsky, Hawthorne, and James—were some of the same authors whose art helped drive the realist movement forward in the United States. Much of American realism was Russian-born, like so many of Cahan's subjects in the ghetto, and this fact was not lost on Howells. In his enormously influential 1896 *New York World* review "New York Low Life in Fiction," Howells praised Cahan side by side with Stephen Crane as "a new star of realism" (qtd. in Richards vii) and regarded his Russianness as the wellspring of his talents:

As Mr. Cahan is a Russian, and as romanticism is not considered literature
in Russia, his story is, of course, intensely realistic.... I cannot help thinking
that we have in him a writer of foreign birth who will do honor to American
letters, as [Hjalmar Hjorth] Boyesen did. He is already thoroughly natural-
ized to our point of view; he sees things with American eyes, and he brings
in aid of his vision the far and rich perceptions of the Hebraic race; while
he is strictly of the great and true Russian principle in literary art. ("New
York Low Life")

Reflecting on his interest in the Jewish quarter in an early essay for the *Atlantic Monthly* (June 1900), Hapgood elucidates the appealing qualities of
Russianness, and how it manifests itself right in downtown New York: "The
intellectual impulse of the Ghetto, no matter what its manifestation, is the
spirit of Turgeniev and of Tolstoi, a spirit at once of realism in art and of
revolt in political opinion" ("Realism" 839). The Russian spirit embedded
in Cahan's artistic sensibility, the "far and rich perceptions" of his Jewish-
ness, and his ability to match the expectations of an outsider audience, meld
in Howells's and Hapgood's eyes into a perfect conglomerate of American
artistic potential. In a later review of Cahan's stories, Howells significantly
remarked that "it will be interesting to see whether Mr. Cahan will pass
beyond his present environment out into the larger American world, or will
master our life as he mastered our language. But of a Jew, who is also Russian,
what artistic triumph may not we expect?" (qtd. in Richards vii).

Hutchins Hapgood also had a hand in forming Cahan's reputation. Perhaps the single most important sketch from a literary point of view in *The
Spirit of the Ghetto* is Hapgood's portrait of Cahan entitled "A Novelist." In
it, he provides a model for reading as slumming to his outsider Anglo-Saxon
peers. He begins by arguing that Cahan's most important writing is his work
in English, as most of his work for the Yiddish papers was "exclusively edu-
cational" (230), informative pieces about the political necessities of socialism,
the implications of scientific discoveries, and emergent literary movements.
To Hapgood, Cahan's journalism is "less intrinsically interesting" than his
fiction because it generally lacked the "strange and picturesque information" that his fiction contains, since fiction is experimental and not as firmly
dictated by the caprices of the streets. And when Cahan switched from Yiddish to English, he abandoned the journalistic sketches popular among his
former colleagues in favor of fictional narratives, which were exceptional for
"the sincere way in which they present a life intimately known" (230–31). By
writing in English, this "life intimately known" could then be passed on to
gentile outsiders uptown. And rather than adopting popular melodrama,

"he felt that Americans as a class were hopelessly 'romantic,' 'unreal,' and undeveloped in their literary tastes and standards" (234). Cahan brought to his outsider readership an obsession with "truth" that, according to Hapgood, characterized Jewish culture for modern outsiders: "Love of the truth, indeed, is the quality which seems to a stranger in the Ghetto the great virtue of that section of the city" (235).

This love of the "truth" that resounded in the cafes, vendor lines, and street corners of the Lower East Side was carried forward into the American book market, lending an authentic quality to reports from the immigrant district that American realists had been incapable of rendering up to that point. Hamlin Garland in his call for an "indigenous literature," insider writing that springs straight from a culture produced by its environment, had already endorsed the cultivation of writers "born into it." Having been "born into it," Cahan had an invaluable advantage over the outsider writers discussed up to this point—except when working among the gentiles, he was not slumming. His "truth" was founded on personal experience as well as cultural observation; but he also had an advantage over his colleagues in the Yiddish press, as he had an integral knowledge of his genteel readership as a result of his experience at the *Commercial Advertiser.* He had immersed himself in the Anglo other and was well-poised to convince his outsider acquaintances to accept the insider voice on its own terms.

In *The Spirit of the Ghetto* Hapgood also emphasized Cahan's perspicacious ability to meld insider "perceptions" into narratives that touched his broad readership's common humanity, tales of the ghetto that might move Anglo outsider sensibilities without becoming tawdry:

> If Cahan's work were merely the transcribing in fiction form of a great number of suggestive and curious "points" about the life of the poor Russian Jew in New York, it would not of course have any great interest to even the cultivated Anglo-Saxon reader, who, tho he might find the stories curious and amusing for a time, would recognize nothing in them sufficiently familiar to be of deep importance to him. If, in other words, the stories had lacked the universal element always present in true literature they would have been of very little value to anyone except the student of queer corners. (237)

Hapgood suggests that Cahan's stories inform the reader about the inherent truths of the Jewish quarter while at the same time rendering those truths "sympathetic by the touch of common human nature" (237). In contrast to much of his labor writing, Cahan dedicates the sum total of his fiction to immigrant psychology and the conflicting processes of ethnic cohesion, acculturation, and assimilation, an internal disaccord between what Werner Sollors has importantly labeled cultural "descent" and "consent," themes that speak to the mind-bending performances of urban life in general. Cahan's model of partial acculturation and his devotion to "the real thing" reflected, in Hapgood's estimation, the spirit of American democracy. Hapgood found that by engaging the people and lifestyles of the Lower East Side, he was able to absorb influences that he would both adopt in his writing and his world view; and he implored his gentile audience to join him in experiencing the spiritually and artistically regenerative qualities found only on the vibrant thoroughfares of Manhattan's Lower East Side.

Hapgood separated Cahan's English language work into two categories: "information" and "human nature." Both of these engage in a "struggle for . . . mastery throughout his work" (237). Cahan's best stories, Hapgood argues, foreground human nature through the vehicle of his "special information" (237–38)—the vehicle, in short, of his insideness. The material elements of fiction, the palpable, the experiential, the sensual, do not give way to the generally human qualities so much as propel them along. Cahan treats orthodox religious practices, including marriage arrangements, generational conflicts, rabbis' influences, abeyance of religious holidays, and the education of immigrant women, "more as a background on which are painted in contrasting lights the moral and physical forms resulting from the particular colonial conditions" (238).

Hapgood singles out Cahan's short novel *Yekl: A Tale of the New York Ghetto* (1896),[2] as a work that "gives a great deal of information about what seems to me the most interesting section of foreign New York" (244). Hapgood, like Mencken with Johnson's *The Autobiography of an Ex-Colored Man* (see Introduction), believed that *Yekl* was more social documentary than novel, a belief that creates a kind of textual hall of mirrors. At what point does a fictional narrative give way to social "reality"? When do we trust ourselves to believe in the images presented to us? Hapgood is not concerned with interrogating the veracity of Cahan's vision, at least from a material standpoint. More than anything, he sought out good literature about and, more importantly, from within the ghetto. He wanted fiction, as well as actual experience on the street, to construct an image of the Lower East Side that might complicate his own consciousness along with the consciousnesses of other gentile outsiders, regardless of their fidelity to material context. Thus Hapgood is generally more inclined to emphasize (and idealize) the deep-seated cultural, psychological, and emotional aspects of Jewish culture—their "spirit," as it were—rather than the quotidian details of everyday life. Not a pure realist, then, he calls for a literary model that demonstrates the inherently Jewish "love of truth." It is this love of truth that he promotes to New York's gentile society, that aspect of Jewish culture that drew him to investigate the district in the first place.

Yekl is possibly the first novel in the English language written by a Lower East Side insider and set in that district with fellow insiders as protagonists. In it, Cahan dissects the motives and tendencies of two immigrant Jews in New York whose stories were paradigmatic of the eastern European immigration experience. The protagonist Yekl Podkovnik, who takes on the American-sounding sobriquet "Jake," is a typical Jewish immigrant from a *shtetl* in northwestern Russia who settles in the United States and works to earn enough money to send for his wife and child. After a time in Boston, he lands a job in a Lower East Side sweatshop. Soon after, he strikes up a relationship with Mamie Fein, an "Americanized" young woman whose flamboyant dress and manners, along with her outspoken contempt for "greenhorns," convinces him to reject his traditional past. Nevertheless, he earns enough to both spend on his modern inamorata and honor his promise to finance his family's passage to the New World.

Jake repents his decision immediately upon his wife Gitl's and their boy Yossele's arrival: "His heart had sunk at the sight of his wife's uncouth and un-American appearance" (34). She too is revolted, initially at least, though inversely by the unorthodox lifestyle of American Jews. But she comes to the realization that in order for her and Yossele to survive in the New World, they must shed socially limiting traditions, while at the same time maintaining some Old World values crucial to survival in a foreign land. In the end Jake, having indiscriminately Americanized himself into self-destruction, divorces Gitl, who will marry her lodger Mr. Bernstein, a more cautious immigrant who has conviction in his Semitic teachings and at the same time the ability to adapt to the social expectations of his new homeland.

On the whole, according to Hapgood, outsider audiences regarded stories from the ghetto as "unpleasant"; and this "unpleasantness" in fiction, he continues, could be found in two ways: "the formal theme, the characters, the result—things may come out unhappily, vice triumphant, and the section of life portrayed may be a sordid one" (248), and "the quality of deadness—a lack of sensitiveness to the vital qualities, to the effects of spring, to the joy in mere physical life" (249). In terms of the latter, "the antithesis of this kind of thing," Hapgood defines by contrast, are Walt Whitman's free verse and Cahan's *Yekl*. In short, *Yekl* is guilty of the first offense, for genteel outsiders anyway, which is precisely what makes it a work of originality.

The Jews in *Yekl* are not restricted to the roles assigned them by most outsider renderings of moral disruption, nor are they entirely sympathetic. Instead, they are multidimensional—some likable, some not; some successful, some not. In the first scene of the book, Jake desire a professional boxing match to a group of fellow sweatshop workers. The conspicuously working-class anecdote is secondary to Jake's desire to show off his speedy acquisition of American vernacular. Cahan invites the audience here, along with Jake's colleagues, to register the absurdity of his character's attempt at pure assimilation: "'Why, don't you know? Jimmie Corbett *leaked* him, and Jimmie *leaked* Cholly Meetchel, too. *You can betch you' bootsh!* Johnny could not leak Chollie, *becaush* he is big *bluffer,* Chollie is,' he pursued, his clean-shaven florid face beaming with enthusiasm for his subject, and with pride in the diminutive proper nouns he flaunted. 'But Jimmie *punished* him. *Oh, didn't he knock him out off shight!* He came near making a meat ball of him'" (2). Jake *should* take pride in his language exercises, but his attempts serve more to draw attention to Yiddish linguistic roots than his potential Americanization. The impact of Cahan's commentary makes the dramatic irony of the situation more unnerving than funny, though Jake's dialogue would have met with big laughs on the popular stage.

On the whole, Jake is an unsympathetic character, likable only when he remembers his Russian past in nostalgic terms. For the most part, the reader is invited to laugh at his overblown obsession with baseball, boxing, American slang, and bachelorhood. But behind the humor lies the tragic sense that the United States has suckered him into its consumerist veneer and will promptly divorce him as he has divorced his wife. As with Crane's Jimmie Johnson, he feels vague guilt over his treatment of the woman character, in this case Gitl, in Jimmie's case Maggie, "a martyr paying the penalty of sins, which he failed to recognize as sins, or of which, at any rate, he could not hold himself culpable" (73). His immigration experience is a failure precisely because, now like Dunbar's Joe Hamilton, he was so blinded by American myths that he could no longer see what was likable about his former self.

His divorcee Gitl, on the other hand, emerges as Cahan's immigrant success story. Gitl's transformation resembles the cultural balancing act that takes place in the minds of Crane's Bowery victims and Dunbar's Tenderloin fools. Like Crane and Dunbar, Cahan shows how the passive acceptance of a dominant outsider voice can lead to a tragic and destructive undermining of that which was good in one's own culture. But unlike Crane and Dunbar, Cahan demonstrates how a process of partial acculturation is a healthy way to refresh stale cultural forms. Gitl adopts customs in New York without which she would always be considered a greenhorn, yet she maintains enough of her own culture that she could take pride in her past. This combination will give her the self-confidence that survival in New York demands. We are told that Gitl and Mr. Bernstein will open a grocery store. The Bernsteins, then, not Jake, who disingenuously woos Mamie with the pipe dream of opening a dancing school in Philadelphia, will realize the American dream.

Gitl's middle-ground "acculturation," like Johnson's marginal men in the Tenderloin, corresponds neatly with the kind of cultural compromise Hutchins Hapgood urged Anglo-Saxon New Yorkers to adopt while they experienced life on the Lower East Side. In *The Spirit of the Ghetto*, Hapgood strived for the self-esteem and psychological autonomy one might find in reverse acculturation; in his ghetto writing he thus presents himself as an acculturated immigrant writing home to his people. Cahan does not take a stand, in *Yekl* at least, on orthodox Judaism per se, but he does regard it as too static to survive long in New York's multicultural, materialist, and politically progressive environment. By the end of the novel, Gitl is an insider on the Lower East Side: "The rustic 'greenhornlike' expression was completely gone from her face and manner, and . . . there was noticeable about her a suggestion of that peculiar air of self-confidence with which a few months life in America is sure to stamp the looks and bearing of every immigrant" (83).

Taking his cue from Gitl's successful method of partial adaptation, Hapgood also renders immigrant women as a class notable for their ability to both acculturate and maintain the sensibilities of their home countries. As Hapgood reports of his fictional source, Cahan had dramatized in *Yekl* that even orthodox women were "beginning to pick up some of the ways of the American woman" (72–73). Gitl achieves just enough Americanization to survive in her new surroundings through her mentor Mrs. Kavarsky, an older lady in her tenement who had emigrated to the United States while Jake was still, in her words, "hauling away at the bellows in Povodye" (72). Over the course of the novel, Mrs. Kavarsky slowly breaks the cultural threads that impede Gitl's modernization. She convinces Gitl to stop wearing a wig or a handkerchief to hide her natural hair; and soon after, she gets her to stop depending solely on God's will to save her. Only Gitl can save herself, she insists, and the way to do that, at first, is by keeping her husband: "Go and try to make yourself agreeable to him and the Uppermost will help. In America one must take care not to displease her husband" (57). At the same time, she teaches her greenhorn pupil that acting like a submissive housewife also conflicts with modernity and new womanhood. "When you talk like a man I like you," she remarks, adding that a "husband hates a sniveller for a wife" (65, 66). She concludes that "when one lives in an *edzecate* country, one must live like *edzecate peoples*" (57).

In two chapters of *The Spirit of the Ghetto,* entitled, respectively, "The Modern Type," and "The Orthodox Jewess," Hapgood identifies two distinct "classes" of Jewish immigrant women: the "ignorant orthodox Russian Jewess" and the "educated class of Ghetto women" (72). The first follow Talmudic law to the letter, every act is performed in deference to her husband and rabbi, and she wears colorless clothing and hides her natural hair under a plain brown wig. The second class is highly political, subscribing to a hybrid ideology of socialism and anarchism, the former in response to the conditions under which immigrant women labor, the latter characterized by "convictions about freedom and non-resistance to evil, and all the other idealistic doctrines for which these Anarchists are remarkable" (78). These women pose a threat to the complacent internal obsessions of "their American sister," Hapgood argues, and "are more apt to abound in the sense of something outside themselves" (72).

Hapgood finds in the "educated class of Ghetto women" a model for female modernization and professionalism that Protestant women might do well to adopt. They become doctors, lawyers, and authors; their devotion to feminist causes is focused and effective: "They have in personal character many virtues called masculine, are simple and straightforward and intensely serious, and do not 'bank' in any way on the fact that they are women! ... The passionate feeling at the bottom of most of their 'tendency' beliefs is that woman should stand on the same social scale as man, and should be weighed in the same scales" (77, 85). Intellectually, they possess a seriousness that emanates from the Russian spirit. Hapgood relates one occasion, for instance, in which an educated married couple from New York conversed with two Russian nihilists about Lord Byron's poetry. The Americans "made light" of his romantic verse, and the Russians praised him with "warm enthusiasm." After the two nihilists took their leave, the Americans referred to them as "interesting" and "amusing." An immigrant Russian woman who eavesdropped in on the conversation was openly offended by the outsiders' flippant condescension: "[She] dilated on the frivolity of a race that could not take serious people seriously, but wanted always to be entertained; that cared only what was 'pretty' and 'charming' and 'sensible' and 'practical,' and cared nothing for poetry and beauty and essential humanity" (83).

Regardless of whether Hapgood romanticized ghetto life—and in many cases he did—he offered his audience something different, a vivid portrait of an enriching cultural site that existed right under their noses. And as a writer, he took away from Cahan's ghetto tales "the consciously held and warmly felt principle that literature should be a transcript from life" (235). In contrast to the unreasonable demands for near complete assimilation we find in the works of Brace, Campbell, and Riis, both Cahan and Hapgood informed their readers about a subject that had not yet been fully investigated: the cultural contributions of the Jewish Lower East Side. We can perceive at this moment in history the slow acceptance and even appropriation of the ghetto culture that the Anglo-German majority had historically been so reluctant to accept. It was now possible, thanks in part to the influential atmosphere of the New York *Daily Commercial Advertiser* and its later manifestations like *Yekl* and *The Spirit of the Ghetto,* for the cultural channel to open upwards on the socioeconomic scale as well as downwards. These authors uniquely represented the social impact of "second wave" immigration in a positive light.

❖ ❖ ❖

Obviously anti-Semitism continued to fester in New York society despite the efforts of writers like Cahan, Steffens, and Hapgood. These sentiments culminated in the 1920 and 1924 immigration restriction statutes. Immigrants and other ethnic Americans could hardly rely on the popular stage, the realist movement, or even the sponsorship of people like Steffens, Hapgood, and Howells to gain democratic participation and empathy from the outsider mainstream. Literature alone could never accomplish the equalitarian policies insider authors and their outsider advocates championed. Co-working in the "kingdom of culture," as W. E. B. Du Bois discovered some time after the publication of *The Souls of Black Folk* (1903), meant co-working in the kingdom of the Anglo-Saxon marketplace as well. By 1914, nearly all ethnic realists became political activists in the fiefdoms of public policy instead. As Werner Sollors has shown, when we compare James Weldon Johnson's *The Autobiography of an Ex-Colored Man* (1912) and Abraham Cahan's second novel, *The Rise of David Levinsky* (1917), to their authors' actual biographies, *Along This Way* (1933) and *The Education of Abraham Cahan* (1926), we find that both authors' fictions portray the "external rise [of their narrators] as an internal fall" (*Beyond* 171). But rather than passing, as their fictional narrators do, into an assimilated "American world," in actual life Cahan and Johnson emphasized their ethno-racial status in the interest of political activism.

Cahan's career, as it turns out, was not destined for the "artistic triumph" Howells imagined, of passing from his "present environment out into the larger American world." Indeed, there is no indication he ever planned to.

Cahan understood perhaps earlier than the rest that what W. E. B. Du Bois called the "kingdom of culture" (*Souls* 365) was insufficient to combat the period's racial and ethnic injustices, nor was the country at large ready for substantial modification. Right up until his death in 1951, Cahan upheld his role as a socialist leader and editor of the *Jewish Daily Forward,* the mainstay of the Yiddish language press, and stood by his work as a proponent of immigrant communities and the labor movement. Johnson became the national organizer of the National Association for the Advancement of Colored People (NAACP) in 1916, and within four years he expanded the association from one that employed three full-time staff members and a membership of under 9,000 to one that boasted 44,000 members and 165 branches nationwide. Four years later, Johnson became the first African American to head the NAACP.

At the same time, young liberal-minded intellectual outsiders like Hutchins Hapgood, Lincoln Steffens, and Randolph Bourne railed against the political aspects of total "Americanization." To quote again from Bourne's 1916 essay "Trans-National America," "The Anglo-Saxon element is guilty of just what every dominant race is guilty of in every European country: the imposition of its own culture upon minority peoples. The fact that this imposition has been so mild and, indeed, semi-conscious does not alter its quality" (97). Bourne argued that the farther an ethnic group was positioned from its "central cultural nucleus," its language, literature, history, and so on, the more desperate and threatening it would become. "It is not the Jew who sticks proudly to the faith of his fathers and boasts of that venerable culture of his who is dangerous to America," he insists, "but the Jew who has lost his Jewish fire and become a mere elementary, grasping animal" (99). The cultural nucleus, he goes on to explain, is a centripetal force, one that maintains, enriches, balances itself. The ethnic population marginalized from its roots creates a centrifugal reaction that is fragmenting, unstable, and finally "anarchical" (99).

Hapgood articulated this same concern nearly fifteen years earlier. In one case, he did so by providing an anecdotal hypothesis: A boy from the Lower East Side leaves his tenement home and joins a Bowery gang. Like other characters discussed here—Pete, George, Joe, and Jake—"his talent for caricature is developed often at the expense of his parents, his race, and all 'foreigners'; for he is an American, he is 'the people,' and like his glorious countrymen in general, he is quick to ridicule the stranger" (*Spirit* 27). Hapgood's runaway "is an acquisitive little fellow, and seldom enjoys himself unless he feels that he is adding to his figurative or literal stock" (29). If this process of inculcation were carried to its logical conclusion, American culture would become a perverse caricature of itself whose author would be the popular press. Marginalized insider voices would then be shouted down by one overwhelming bellow, and children would transmit cultural values with little variation.

Bourne spoke of a "spiritual welding" (108) in the United States, visualizing the country as a patchwork of ethnic spaces of which Americans should be proud. But this argument was articulated long before Bourne's famous essay appeared. In similar language, Hapgood had called for a "*spiritual unity* such as, perhaps, will only be the distant result of our present special activities" (*Spirit* 37, emphasis mine). And six years earlier than that, Cahan described the Jewish ghetto as a "social caldron—a human hodgepodge with its component parts changed but not yet fused into one homogeneous whole" (*Yekl* 14). Cahan, Hapgood, and Bourne all proffered an argument that in today's political climate of cultural relativism, in academia at least, may itself be considered kitsch. But in the context of turn-of-the-century ethnicity discourse, it was highly original. The Lower East Side Jews "still appeared to most of their social betters," as Christine Stansell professes, "in the Victorian guise of 'lowlife'" (15). If ethnic neighborhoods were to be cultivated and appreciated by the larger community in New York, they must first be endowed with the cultural "stock"—or cultural "capital"—that a boy on the Bowery would be proud to retain, not forced to reject as in the case of the corrupt, "belligerent, exclusive, inbreeding" European model (Bourne 100).

These remarks, though subversive, did not exist in an epistemological void. At this point in New York's literary history, it became the deliberate project of a small group of artists to inhabit the garrets and brownstones of Greenwich Village for the sole purpose of providing a new complexity to their work and to their own cultural consciousnesses. Though Henry F. May has written of the Village's embryonic years that "the massive walls of nineteenth-century America were still apparently intact" (xi), the Whitmanic work of a small group of avant garde intellectuals, including, along with Hapgood, Steffens, and Bourne, Neith Boyce, John Reed, Emma Goldman, Mabel Dodge, Max Eastman, Van Wyck Brooks, Alfred Stieglitz, Eugene O'Neill, and Edna St. Vincent Millay, would tilt into the newest creative space beyond the threshold of nineteenth-century discourse. In a sense, these thinkers were indicative of both the last gasp of nineteenth-century New York thought and the first glimmerings of the city's twentieth-century cosmopolitan ethos. Greenwich Village in the 1910s was an ethnic working-class enclave, mainly Italian and Jewish, quite disconnected from highbrow intellectual interests. The formation of Greenwich Village was the deliberate establishment of a distinctly disestablishmentarian neighborhood spirit, and from within this slum simulacrum, these "American moderns" sought to redefine American culture with the moral ambiguities of immigrant and working-class life as their model.

But if Greenwich Village had national impact, Harlem changed the Western world. Gilbert Osofsky writes that by the 1920s, "as a by-product of their attack on traditional American middle-class values, which were constantly called 'Puritanical,' literary rebels and others discovered the Negro, America's 'outcast,' and created a semi-mythical dreamland which they came to idealize—'storied Harlem'" (180). This "dreamland" was conceived out of a perception of ethno-racial insider authenticity in contrast to its deliberately contrived counterparts in Greenwich Village and Coney Island.

During the Great Migration of blacks to northern cities following the First World War, a period when tens of thousands of African Americans exiled themselves from the violence and disenfranchisement taking place in the Jim Crow South, white outsiders openly availed themselves of African American life in New York. It seemed as if Harlem might redeem a city, and a nation, which had been held in traditional Anglo-Saxon restraints since the beginning of its existence. The white intellectual elite in New York was not turned off by racial otherness at this time, as they had been at the turn of the century. On the contrary, inquisitive white writers poured en masse into the uptown neighborhood that had become the city's established black enclave.

For the African American population in New York, turn-of-the-century bohemianism was, in Christine Stansell's words, "not . . . so elastic" (25). But in the following chapter, I will discuss how it was, ironically, black insiders in northern Manhattan who successfully, if temporarily, transformed New York's perception of ghetto morality. Though like the Jewish immigrants downtown, blacks from the American South and West Indies poured into Manhattan at an unbelievable rate—a phenomenon traditionally regarded with fear and loathing by genteel New Yorkers—white outsiders swiftly made Harlem the slumming capital of the world. Many of these "literary rebels" enthusiastically endorsed the efforts of the African American founders of what was then called the New Negro Renaissance, and one, the flamboyant novelist and art critic Carl Van Vechten, took it upon himself as a white outsider to write the first novel based in Harlem's New Negro Renaissance—*Nigger Heaven* (1926). By the 1920s, the upward channel was a floodgate flown wide open.

5 "Nigger Heaven"

CARL VAN VECHTEN, CLAUDE MCKAY, AND THE CONSTRUCTION OF MYTHIC HARLEM

> There is a certain snobbishness in terming the less literate and less
> sophisticated, the more simple and more primitive classes of Negroes as
> "lower." At least as literary material, they are higher.
> —James Weldon Johnson, 1929

> Ain't it hell to be a Nordic when you're struggling with Ethiopian
> psychology?
> —Carl Van Vechten, letter to H. L. Mencken, 1925

BY THE 1920S, NEIGHBORHOODS IN WHICH cultural rebels sought "moral vacations" from the realm of "Puritan conscience" gained reputations among outsiders that were largely undeserved, or at least overrated. The legacy of Greenwich Village and the practice of ghetto celebration would have ominous overtones following the First World War and arguably contribute to a ghetto population desperately vulnerable to the ravages of the Great Depression. By the First World War, David Levering Lewis writes, "the African American had indisputably moved to the center of Mainstream imagination . . . a development nurtured in the chrysalis of the Lost Generation" (Introduction xvii). This mythicization of the ghetto, though generated largely by both outsiders with good intentions and insiders trying to achieve some cultural capital for themselves, masked the realities that nineteenth-century reformers had foregrounded decades earlier—overcrowding, sanitation issues, and the proliferation of vice in the forms of drug addiction, prostitution, and gambling. The evangelical diatribes of these outsider reformers had thrown out the proverbial baby with the bath water, however, so that this mode gradually gave way to a more relativistic understanding of the insider voice that existed in New York's ghettoes; following the First World War, an experience that signaled the death knell of Victorian dominance in the United States and Great Britain, the pendulum of culture had swung in the opposite direction.

Unlike the comparatively diminutive black Tenderloin of the 1890s, Harlem occupied a rectangular area of approximately forty-five city blocks: from One Hundred and Thirtieth Street to One Hundred and Forty-fifth south to north and from Fifth Avenue to Eighth east to west. Though the numbers of African American residents uptown were widely scattered, this section was visibly a black city within the much larger, predominantly white one. About two-thirds of New York's African Americans lived within its borders (Osofsky 123). The Great Migration of southern blacks relocating to northern cities, the arrival of tens of thousands of new immigrants from the West Indies (unfettered by the restrictive immigration legislation following the First World War), and the plunging of Harlem real estate values following the recession of 1907, all combined to make Harlem both "a Negro world unto itself" (Osofsky 127) and the largest ghetto in New York history.

Harlem's most vehement advocates drowned out pleas for help from social workers, sanitation officials, and statisticians. Historian Gilbert Osofsky writes that "at the very time Harlem was transformed into the city's worst slum its image for most white Americans, and some Negroes as well, was just the reverse—a gay place inhabited by 'a singing race'" (151). But the region was vastly overcrowded, economically unstable, and intra-racially divided. In the decade of the 1920s alone, 120,000 blacks from downtown, the American South, and the West Indies moved into the area and as many whites retreated (Jackson 114). Harlem's death rate was 42 percent higher than that of the rest of the city, and infant mortality was twice as high. Over ten percent of infants in Harlem between 1923 and 1927 died either at birth or soon thereafter (Osofsky 141). Remarkably, Harlem's real estate values climbed during this period, causing rent prices to appreciate as well. For landlords uptown, there was a "slum boom" (Osofsky 136). Needless to say, the combination of high rents and the surge of new migrants created a glut in the job market and an ominous housing crisis. This was the mise en scène of the so-called New Negro Renaissance. "The ordinary Negroes hadn't heard of the Negro Renaissance," Langston Hughes recalls in his 1945 autobiography *The Big Sea*, "And if they had, it hadn't raised their wages any" (228).

What we now call the Harlem Renaissance was a deliberate enterprise to raise the status of African Americans in the United States. But as David Levering Lewis has shown, very distinct schools of thought emerged to determine what form this movement would take: the "genteel" and "overly literary" on the one hand, and the "demotic" and "bottom-up" school on the other (Introduction xxx, xxxii).[1] A few years after the war, under the leadership of W. E. B. Du Bois, the NAACP along with the National Urban League conceptualized a New Negro Arts Movement as a public relations project guided by the strategy of uplift. This movement included African American civil rights leaders such as Du Bois, Charles Johnson, and Jessie Fauset, and revolved around the offices of the NAACP's political organ *The Crisis* and the National Urban League's journal *Opportunity.* This group, the first wave of 1920s Harlem intellectuals, believed that African Americans would gain equality only after proving themselves a respectable and, more importantly, an educable race to outsiders. As Du Bois famously pronounced, "The Negro race, like all races, is going to be saved by its exceptional men . . . its Talented Tenth" (qtd. in Eloise E. Johnson 14). Many of these intellectuals, particularly Du Bois, felt that representations of African American "low life" in fiction were injurious to the insider image of African Americans nationwide and would deter civil rights efforts. Langston Hughes later reflected on this divide in his autobiography:

> The Negro critics and many of the intellectuals were very sensitive about their race in books. (And still are.) In anything that white people were likely to read, they wanted to put their best foot forward, their politely polished and cultural foot—and only that foot. There was a reason for it, of course. They had seen their race laughed at and caricatured so often . . . when Negroes wrote books they wanted them to be books in which only good Negroes, beautiful and nice and upper class were presented. Jessie Fauset's novels they loved, because they were always about the educated Negro—but my poems, or Claude McKay's *Home to Harlem* they did not like, sincere though we might be. (266–67)

By 1926 a "veritable Ministry of Culture . . . presided over Afro-America," a "Civil Rights Establishment" that the Jamaican American poet and novelist Claude McKay dryly regarded as "that NAACP crowd" (Lewis, Introduction xxix, xxxii). McKay later admitted that after meeting Du Bois for the first time, the leader "seemed possessed of a cold, acid hauteur of spirit" (qtd. in Lewis, *When Harlem* 51). McKay was one of a number of new voices, largely returning home to Harlem from the "universe of the Lost Generation" in Paris (Lewis, *When Harlem* 50). What can be called the second wave of Harlem intellectuals and artists—including McKay, Langston Hughes, Wallace Thurman, and Zora Neale Hurston—defied the model of genteel respectability and encouraged the more open, more "primitive" aspects of their African ancestry. It was with this artistic signature that they wished to cultivate the image of the American Negro, rather than the calculating sociopolitical polemics of the older generation that relied upon outsider models for cultural uplift. Du Bois himself acknowledged this divide in African American thought in his 1926 address to the NAACP in Chicago. On the one hand, he professed, there are the more politically minded African American intellectuals who ask, "What have we who are slaves and black to do with art?" On the other, there is the perhaps more optimistic view that finds relief in the new obsession with African American art forms: "After all it is rather satisfactory after all this talk about rights and fighting to sit and dream of something which leaves a nice taste in the mouth" ("Criteria" 317). Though he admitted that "neither of these groups are right" (317), he held the opinion that African American art without a social agenda was useless for advancing the social and political standing of African Americans in the 1920s. "I do not care a damn," he announced, "for any art that is not used for propaganda" (324).

The work of the flamboyant, hyper-social white art critic and novelist Carl Van Vechten represents a liminal space between these two directives; it is located in the trough between the waves. In 1926, his controversially titled *Nigger Heaven* appeared, an unrelenting critique of "respectable" blackness and white slumming in Harlem, along with the new vogue of "primitivism." It is inarguable that "like so many self-proclaimed modernists writing in the wake of the Great War, [Van Vechten] based his artistic mission on the rejection of middle-class values" (Worth 467). But unlike Hutchins Hapgood and other rebellious Victorians in the modern world, Van Vechten's certainty in Anglo-Americans overcoming their rigid past was equivocal at best.

In *Nigger Heaven* the outsider Van Vechten combined a modernist's contempt for narrow middle-class respectability with an equally modernist ethos of tragic pessimism. Van Vechten had little faith in the ultimate success of marginal groups in urban America. The ignoble underbelly that lurked beneath Harlem's golden facade, he speculated, could, in fact, prevail—and, tragically, from the 1930s until relatively recently, the history of Harlem was to prove him right. As such, the call to "Go inspectin' like Van Vechten" in Andy Razaf's popular song "Go Harlem" was tempered by a realistic understanding of the outsider looking in on a situation he was powerless to affect.

As a white man discovering the other, Van Vechten tried to demonstrate in *Nigger Heaven* how the search for the "primitive" is an alienating principle for both white slummers and first-wave insiders; paradoxically, it was also the most enticing aspect of Harlem life. Rather than seeing the novel as a "message that the Talented Tenth's preoccupation with cultural improvement was a misguided affectation that would cost the race its vitality" (Lewis, Introduction xxxi), it more clearly equivocates over which of the waves might be more practical for the future of Harlem insiders. But two years later, the "low down" Harlem that Du Bois desperately tried to cover up would be most descriptively and lyrically mythologized in Claude McKay's *Home to Harlem* (1928). It was this Harlem—the Harlem of lights, cabarets, and sex, the Harlem that McKay's "Lennox Avenue Noble Savage" (Lewis, Introduction xxxii) Jake in *Home to Harlem*, adores: "'Good old Harlem! Chocolate Harlem! Sweet Harlem! Harlem I've got you' number down'" (14)—that became the most painful signifier of a "dream" that would ultimately be, as Langston Hughes mourned decades later, "deferred."

"*Read it first, then discuss it*": Van Vechten's Nigger Heaven

No one individual did more to contribute to Harlem's popularity for white society during this period than Carl Van Vechten. Ann Douglas, in fact, locates the birth of Harlem's literary renaissance as 1924, "in good part because it was in that year that Van Vechten immersed himself in Harlem life, and he did so [according to Langston Hughes's biographer Arnold Rampersad] . . . more completely than any prominent white man in New York had ever done" (*Terrible Honesty* 287). In 1924, Walter White, the "Negro of pale complexion but dark anger," first made Van Vechten's acquaintance through Alfred Knopf.[2] Within a few weeks he introduced his new friend to every conceivable milieu in the Negro metropolis. In no time, Van Vechten gained the audience and often long-lasting friendship of many insider intellectuals and celebrities, including Langston Hughes, James Weldon Johnson, Jessie Fauset, Paul Robeson, and Wallace Thurman. The speed with which he effected change there was remarkable. After less than three weeks of meeting the locally acclaimed poet Langston Hughes, for example, Van Vechten convinced his publisher Alfred Knopf to offer the twenty-three-year-old Hughes a publishing deal for his first book of poetry, *The Weary Blues* (1926). Van Vechten was boundlessly important for his part in forming such social connections between black insiders and white outsiders. It was precisely his talent for forming associations with the most prominent Harlem insiders that made him, intentionally or not, the inventor of white New York's mythic Harlem, a Harlem that outsiders were led to believe was an innocuous but vital black haven defined by sex, self-expression, and jazz.

Not only did Van Vechten befriend Harlem's cultural elite, but he offered financial advice and public support as well. A natural promoter in the mode of Johnson's fictional millionaire (who also held salon parties at his Fifth Avenue apartment), he hosted and attended many drinking parties designed to unify black notables in an untraditional salon setting, and he later admitted that he was subsequently drunk for most of the 1920s. These parties were singular in their almost surreal blend, for the time at least, of black and white culture. At one Van Vechten soiree in June of 1925, George Gershwin kicked off the evening playing show tunes at the piano, only to have Paul Robeson replace him with Negro spirituals. Later that night, James Weldon Johnson recited "Go Down, Death." Theodore Dreiser, by now considered one of the greatest American novelists ever, most likely sat brooding in a solitary corner of the flat, rocking back and forth while grimly folding his handkerchief into a tiny square; he was legendarily morose at such otherwise cheerful gatherings (Matthiessen 170). Van Vechten's high profile get-togethers entered New York folklore and bring to mind Johnson's reverse slumming sequences in *The Autobiography of an Ex-Colored Man.* One story has it (possibly apocryphal, though probably not) that a black Pullman porter approached a well-heeled matron at Grand Central Station and said, "Good morning, Mrs. Astor," to which she replied, "How do you know my name young man?" "Why, ma'am, I met you last weekend at Carl Van Vechten's."

In only a few years, Van Vechten secured a place in the "Great White" book market for a number of key Renaissance texts, including, among others, a new edition of Johnson's *The Autobiography of an Ex-Colored Man* (1927), for which he wrote the introduction; Nella Larsen's *Quicksand* (1928) and *Passing* (1929); and early books of verse by Langston Hughes and Countee Cullen. Harlem insiders were not entirely averse to his advances. One symbolic fact, telling as much about Van Vechten's habits as it does about Harlemites' reception of him, was that if at any point in his rambles through uptown night spots he lost his valuable silver flask, he would have it back in hand within a day (Douglas, *Terrible Honesty* 287). Born in 1880, he was substantially older than many of the youthful talents he supported, and as a result he took on an avuncular role within their society. Paul Robeson's wife Essie referred to him as "godfather," and the *Herald Tribune* adopted this appellation, reporting in 1925 that Van Vechten was "the beneficent godfather of all sophisticated Harlem" (qtd. in Douglas, *Terrible Honesty* 288). He was, in Ann Douglas's words, "a liaison and PR man extraordinaire between Harlem and white New York" (81).

In 1926, Van Vechten came out with *Nigger Heaven.* Most insiders condemned the book, though many of them overreacted to its inflammatory title rather than its literary worth or social bent. Regardless, this one volume probably sold more copies than all of the books by black writers during the Harlem Renaissance combined (Worth 466). Langston Hughes alludes to this, noting in his *Courier* review that "more Negroes bought it than ever purchased a book by a Negro author" (qtd. in Worth 466). And much later, in 1945, Hughes must have been thinking of Van Vechten when he reflected that during the period when the Negro was in vogue, "white writers wrote about Negroes more successfully (commercially speaking) than Negroes did about themselves" (228). The novel's popularity caught Knopf entirely off guard. It commanded nine printings in its first four months—the original sixteen thousand copies had sold out in a proverbial New York minute—and it was translated into many languages and sold well in Great Britain and across continental Europe.

Nigger Heaven is a social novel that renders Harlem both as a charming addition to New York's cultural landscape and a tragic site of black segregation. The first half focuses on the character Mary Love, a not-so-loosely based portrait of the author, educator, and *Crisis* editor Jessie Fauset; indeed, the fictional Mary owns a signed copy of Fauset's most acclaimed novel, *There is Confusion* (1924). Mary is a well-read librarian who longs to unearth the authentic Negro-cum-savage side of her emotional makeup. Attending a house party at her wealthy friend Adora Boniface's Long Island residence, Mary falls for Byron Kasson, a handsome black college student and would-be writer on vacation from the predominantly white University of Pennsylvania. After the weekend, Byron returns to school and Mary to Harlem. The narrative then follows Mary from intellectual gathering to intellectual gathering, where we hear various positions on the "race question" and the emerging "Negro Renaissance."

Byron eventually migrates to Harlem, and the two fall promptly in love. His father, aware that his son had disregarded his letters of introduction to respectable New York businessmen, revokes Byron's regular allowance, a move that forces his son to take a job as an elevator operator. Byron returns to Harlem despondent after his first day at work, for as an outsider in the ghetto, much like Crane's George Kelcey in his dealings with the Bowery street gang, Byron's insider co-workers look down upon his middle-class "airs." "I forgot to warn you," a Harlem acquaintance remarks, "You ought to speak in dialect. These low-class smokes haven't any use for a fellow that puts on airs. You have to be a mixer" (194). Byron ultimately breaks his relationship with Mary, having been seduced by the infinitely dissolute and highly successful Lasca Sartoris. Van Vechten's biographer Bruce Kellner informs us that Lasca is "a full-blown portrait" of the "glamour girl" Nora Holt, who resided in Paris as Lasca does in the novel. Apparently, Holt never voiced a word of resentment toward Van Vechten for characterizing her in the figure of a dissipated man-eater. In fact, when the book came out she wrote: "The cries of protest from the Harlemites reach me even in Paris. . . . Strange in such a short time you caught the attitude of the Negro toward the Negro and not one in a thousand of them will admit it" (qtd. in Kellner 218). Like Mary, she was "golden-brown, his color" (179), but unlike the respectable librarian, Lasca is a cocaine user, an absinthe drinker, a sexual sadomasochist, and a dabbler in satanic ritual; over time, she introduces Byron to all of New York's vices as Hattie Sterling had done for Joe Hamilton in Dunbar's *The Sport of the Gods.* Though Byron eventually returns to Mary with his tail between his legs, he has adopted the "savagery" that Mary guilelessly covets. But this cult of the primitive, one that feeds the imagination of black Harlem and attracts its white audience, symbolically ends Byron's career.

Regardless of prepublication assistance by Harlem insiders like James Weldon Johnson, Walter White, Rudolph Fisher, and Langston Hughes, all of whom proofread and contributed to the manuscript in one way or another, the novel elicited enormous debate in the black press. The most clearly divisive responses came from W. E. B. Du Bois, who hated it utterly, and James Weldon Johnson, who just as vigorously applauded it. Du Bois's review in the December 1926 issue of *The Crisis* (of which he was the editor) begins with this sentence: "Carl Van Vechten's 'Nigger Heaven' is a blow in the face." "It is an affront," he continues, "to the hospitality of black folk and to the intelligence of the white." The title, as inflammatory as it seems, was not at issue for Du Bois; rather it was the idea of Harlem actually resembling a "Nigger Heaven," in its vernacular meaning. Du Bois argued that the application of the term was both misleading and insulting. He explains that the term "Nigger Heaven" (most commonly applied to the balcony seats where African Americans were consigned in segregated theaters and movie palaces) "does not mean . . . a haven for Negroes—a city of refuge for dark and tired souls," but rather it is a self-effacing idiom in black vernacular that admits a tendency among Negroes to allow whites to force them into "a nasty, sordid corner," which "they in crass ignorance are fools enough to enjoy." A "Nigger Heaven" was associated with Negro foolhardiness, with stupidity and complacency, and, Du Bois writes, "Harlem is no such place as that, and no one knows this better than Carl Van Vechten" ("Van Vechten's" 1216).

Du Bois admits he is indulging in semantic quibbling over this point: "after all, a title is only a title" (1216). So he proceeds by identifying two elements to judge a good piece of writing: its veracity to real life and its artistic merit. Neither of these, he contends, are present in *Nigger Heaven*. The book employs characters that are nothing but caricatures of Harlemites and a plot that is driven solely by one "wildly, barbaric drunken orgy" after another (1217). But significantly, if we consider the rise of Harlem as a mythic space, *Nigger Heaven* "is worse than an untruth because it is a mass of half-truths" (1216). Du Bois makes the distinction, for example, between the Harlem of the cabaret that Van Vechten depicts and the Harlem of the struggling laborer:

> The author counts among his friends numbers of Negroes of all classes. He is an authority on dives and cabarets. But he masses this knowledge without rule or reason and seeks to express all of Harlem life in its cabarets. To him the black cabaret is Harlem; around it all its characters gravitate. Here is their stage of action. Such a theory of Harlem is nonsense. The overwhelming majority of black folk there never go to cabarets. The average colored man in Harlem is an everyday laborer, attending church, lodge and movie and as conservative and as conventional as ordinary working folk everywhere. (1216)

In the end, Du Bois contends, Van Vechten has produced little, aside from some "laboriously stated facts, quotations and expressions," but "cheap melodrama." As a slummer, he is artless, "not the great artist who with remorseless scalpel probes the awful depths of life. To him there are no depths. It is the surface mud he slops in." Du Bois's critique is ultimately an ad hominem character assassination: "Life to [Van Vechten] is just one damned orgy after another, with hate, hurt, gin, and sadism" (1217). He concludes by suggesting that if his readers desire distractions with this kind of sensationalist trash, they should "try the Police Gazette" (1218).[3]

The most glaringly antithetical response to Du Bois's on *Nigger Heaven* by a respected black insider was James Weldon Johnson's *Opportunity* review, "Romance and Tragedy in Harlem." By contrast to Du Bois's acerbic opener, Johnson's first line reads this way: "From its intriguing prologue to its tragic end, here is an absorbing story" (392). Instead of seeing Van Vechten's characters and themes as "caricature," Johnson defends the author's integrity, raising the outsider author to the middle-ground, "marginal" status Abraham Cahan afforded Hutchins Hapgood, and that Cahan himself enjoyed at the *Commercial Advertiser:* "Mr. Van Vechten is the only white novelist I can think of who has not viewed the Negro as a type, who has not treated the race as a unit, either good or bad.... Mr. Van Vechten does not stoop to burlesque or caricature" (392, 393). And contradicting Du Bois's assertion that Van Vechten's novel contains no social or artistic depth, Johnson praises the author's "scope," and his ability to comprehend "nearly every phase of life in the Negro Metropolis. [*Nigger Heaven*] draws on the components of that life from the dregs to the froth" (392). Rather than rely on the "deus ex machina" of white plot structure and character type, Van Vechten has "completely discarded and scrapped the old formula and machinery for a Negro novel" (392). Defending the novel against insider criticism, Johnson protests that there should be no public outcry against the title, as there was in 1910 when Edward Sheldon's play *The Nigger* came out, a bold retort to Thomas Dixon's overtly racist Reconstruction-period novel *The Clansman* (1905; later made into the 1915 silent film *The Birth of a Nation* by D. W. Griffith), since the title *Nigger Heaven*, "is taken from the ironic use of the phrase made by the characters in the book" (393).

For Johnson, the scenes of "wildly barbaric drunken orgy" Du Bois condemned, "set off in sharper relief the decent, cultured, intellectual life of Negro Harlem" (393). Whether in the cabaret or the intellectual salon, "It is all life. It is all reality. . . . Van Vechten the satirist, becomes . . . Van Vechten, the realist" (393, 396). *Nigger Heaven* to Johnson is far from the "cheap melodrama" Du Bois feels it is: "[Van Vechten] does not moralize, he does not over-emphasize, there are no mock heroics; there are no martyrdoms" (396), and he concludes that "NIGGER HEAVEN is . . . bound to be widely read and . . . arouse much diverse discussion" (396). The review's final sentence is an adamant appeal to the readers of *Opportunity* to read the novel before discussing it.

How are we to decipher these reactions, reflecting as a mirror, exact replicas of form, substance, and subject matter, but in direct opposition to one another? Point by point, Du Bois and Johnson discuss the book in the same terms, with the same organizational strategy: its artistic merit; its place in the tradition of white outsider representations of the Negro race; its depictions of Harlem; its literary worth in regard to character development, realism, melodrama, the ending; and finally, the concluding recommendation—"drop it gently in a grate" (Du Bois) / "read it first, then discuss it" (Johnson). The easy answer is probably the best here: each read what they wanted to read. For one thing, Johnson knew that Van Vechten considered Johnson's *Autobiography of an Ex-Colored Man* to be, while writing *Nigger Heaven*, "an invaluable source-book for the study of Negro psychology" (Introduction 26). But Du Bois, the political activist, saw in Van Vechten the epitome of a dangerous trend for Harlem and Harlemites—that the New Negro Metropolis would come to dictate the image of African Americans nationwide, an outsider's image more inclined towards fun than fury. Johnson, on the other hand, had dedicated his life to uplifting the status of blacks in the United States by promoting their positive cultural contributions to the larger society, rather than its political puissance, and Van Vechten's tale has enormous cachet as an outsider text appealing to his "Nordic" peers.

Later on, the mulatto fiction writer Charles W. Chesnutt, whose reflections on 1920's Harlem are covered in the final section of this chapter, and Langston Hughes, in his chapter on the New Negro vogue in his autobiography *The Big Sea*, ultimately sided with Johnson's estimation of Van Vechten's work. "One of the first of the New York writers to appreciate the possibilities of Harlem for literary purposes was Carl Van Vechten," Chesnutt wrote, "whose novel *Nigger Heaven* was rather severely criticized by some of the colored intellectuals as libel on the race, while others of them praised it highly. I was prejudiced in its favor for reasons which those who have read the book will understand. I found it a vivid and interesting story which presented some new and better types of Negroes and treated them sympathetically" ("Post-Bellum" 911). Along with Chesnutt, Langston Hughes admitted that "all of us know that the gay and sparkling life of the so-called Negro Renaissance of the '20's was not so gay and sparkling beneath the surface as it looked. Carl Van Vechten, in the character of Byron in *Nigger Heaven,* captured some of the bitterness and frustration of literary Harlem that Wallace Thurman [six years later] so effectively poured into his *Infants of the Spring*" (227).

Hughes devoted an entire section of his concise 1945 autobiography *The Big Sea* to Van Vechten's novel and the "phenomenon of that violent outburst of rage" by black critics in the press that lasted "for months" (268). Along with "the strange inability on the part of many of the Negro critics to understand irony, or satire," Hughes simply explains that "the word *nigger* to colored people of high and low degree is like a red rag to a bull. Used rightly or wrongly, ironically or seriously, of necessity for the sake of realism, or impishly for the sake of comedy, it doesn't matter. Negroes do not like it in any book or play whatsoever, be the book or play ever so sympathetic in its treatment of the basic problems of the race. Even though the book or play is written by a Negro, they still do not like it" (268–69). Understandably, the word's racist power, "like the word *Jew* in Hitler's Germany," overwhelms whatever well-meaning sentiments the book might convey (269). He goes on to say that had Van Vechten's critics read his novel *The Tattooed Countess* (1924), which treats Van Vechten's own home town in a far more critical way than Harlem in *Nigger Heaven,* "they could not then have written so stupidly about *Nigger Heaven*" (270). He concludes that "to say that Carl Van Vechten has harmed Negro creative activities [as Du Bois did] is sheer poppycock. The bad Negro writers were bad long before *Nigger Heaven* appeared on the scene. And would have been bad anyway, had Mr. Van Vechten never been born" (272).

In an odd way, this split echoes the earlier discourse between Riis and Hapgood on the Lower East Side. Though Du Bois was obviously an activist for racial justice, as opposed to the anti-Semitic Riis, the contradictions and ambiguities inherent in a definable moral region are unraveled in both and each takes away their own strands of truth; one determined by socioeconomics, the other by cultural impact. But the truth, of course, is elusive and can only be taken as a whole. *Nigger Heaven* is a great American novel if for nothing else than that it authenticated its complexity by soliciting such polar opposite reactions by two intellectuals of Johnson's and Du Bois's caliber. But as with Crane's *Maggie*, it is possible to reconcile the paradox by admitting that there is more than one truth present, that responses will vary according to the audience's agenda.

If there exists any consensus about Carl Van Vechten, it is that he was not a racist. His biggest transgression was that he betrayed, as Emily Bernard writes, "a combination of naiveté and arrogance [that] led him to believe he was unique, a white man who had transcended his whiteness" (xix). In fact, his early experiences with African Americans may have made him even more sympathetic to them than any sizable group deserves. His father, in particular, was one of the founders of the Piney Woods School for African Americans in Cedar Rapids, Iowa (where Carl grew up), and he counseled his son to treat black laborers in the same manner he would treat any adult (Bernard xviii). His father passed away seven months before the novel was completed but was still one of the many critics of the title. In a letter to his son he wrote, "Your 'Nigger Heaven' is a title I don't like. . . . I have myself never spoken of a colored man as a 'nigger.' If you are trying to help the race, as I am assured you are, I think every word you write should be a respectable one towards the black" (qtd. in Kellner 210–11).

While attending the University of Chicago as a young man, Van Vechten spent a great deal of time in black neighborhoods—the churches at daytime, the clubs at night. During this period, he seemed to have adopted an ideal image of African American life. At the age of seventy-six, Van Vechten explained in a letter to Chester Himes that his youthful prejudices, benign as they may have been, disappeared after a revelation that not all African Americans were angels: "You see, like everybody else who goes into this New World, at first I had a Messiannic complex (My God, how DO you spell it). But one day I came home shouting, 'I HATE a Negro! I HATE a Negro!' It was my salvation and since then I've had no trouble at all. From that point on I understood that they were like everybody else, that is they were thieves and cut-throats, generous and pious, witty and wise, dumb and foolish, et., etc." (*Letters* 259).

This realization must have come before his Harlem experiences in the 1920s, a time in which he confessed an "addiction" to African American culture (Bernard xviii), but belied the notion that African Americans should be treated as exceptional to the general standards of cultural influence. In a 1925 letter to Countee Cullen, we can glean his racial views immediately preceding his writing of *Nigger Heaven:*

> I think, perhaps, it is a little excessive to make such an arcanum of the Negro mind. I believe all races to be more or less human, and susceptible to what are known as human reactions—I am speaking quite generally and include the Japanese and the Malays. In each case, however, these human reactions are modified by conditions (from within or without) which produce superficial differences in reactions. Thus conditions have created certain subtle differences in reactions between white Americans and American Negroes. . . . I may be wrong; I often am, but I cannot help feeling that the distinction between white and colored psychology has been overstressed. (*Letters* 86)

This early treatise on social construction reveals a great deal about Van Vechten's authorial intent in *Nigger Heaven.* It was meant to be a humanizing social novel, neither knee-jerk sycophancy nor traditional typecasting. Van Vechten understood that African Americans exist all along the spectrum of human morality, and Harlem must be portrayed as one rendition of that spectrum. The idea of a perceptible moral region to be marginalized in the public eye was anachronistic to Van Vechten, a formula for moralizing outsiders that had outlived their heyday. Nevertheless, black critics were so stung by the title that, as Langston Hughes tells it, at a meeting at the Harlem Public Library there was an aged white gentleman whose hoary locks resembled Van Vechten's signature shock of white hair; the congregants assaulted him verbally until the stranger comprehended the misunderstanding and spluttered, "Why, I'm not Carl Van Vechten" (270).

Like Stephen Crane, Van Vechten applies color as an impressionistic stylistic device and "associates it with his characters," combining their "hopes and fears with aspects of the environment he creates" (Simoneaux 222). "Primitivism" appears in *Nigger Heaven* as a co-optation of African art forms. Those forms are then superimposed onto Harlem's cabaret lifestyle, which is rendered as sexually tempestuous, sublimely colorful, and inherently violent. In the first cabaret scene with the Scarlet Creeper (Van Vechten's own "Lennox Avenue Noble Savage") and Ruby Silver (an obvious name for someone obsessed with material possessions but who, unable to suit her needs, loads herself down with artificial accouterments), Van Vechten utilizes Crane-like impressionism to create a dizzyingly electric visual montage. The cabaret is called the Black Venus,[4] a place where "bodies in picturesque costumes rocked, black bodies, brown bodies, high yellows, a kaleidoscope of colour transfigured by the amber searchlight. Scarves of bottle green, cerise, amethyst, vermilion, lemon" (14). Outward appearances are altered while at the same time exalted and glorified. The participants, like those of Crane's dance hall scenes, bivouac themselves in the Black Venus from the quotidian realities of their compeers outside—commuting to their downtown jobs in the early hours of the morning—what Van Vechten, through his male protagonist Byron's eyes, refers to as the "symbolic procession, the procession of an oppressed people."

Both insider and outsider authors employed skin color in Harlem Renaissance texts to evoke behavioral and ideological difference as well as racial mixture. In *Nigger Heaven,* all of the myriad of racial combinations are present at the Black Venus, and skin tone provides the texture of the setting. The Scarlet Creeper observes there "Blues, smokes, dinges, charcoals, chocolate browns, shines, and jigs" (13). Mary Love witnesses at a charity ball "the variations in colour in the faces of men, the shoulders of women: black shoulders, brown shoulders, tan shoulders, ivory shoulders"; she was "fascinated" by this display (153). In the minds of Van Vechten's characters, color is analogous to the diverse nature of the population, contrasting bluntly to the standardized "pinks" downtown. This obsession with color is, of course, tied to race in a way that it never was in Crane,[5] but the cabaret experience is also imagined as a kind of museum in which the flamboyant use of color is observed as a painting might be in a museum: "On the floor a scrawny yellow girl in pink silk, embroidered with bronze sequins in floral designs began to sing. . . . The Creeper sipped his gin meditatively" (16). If the use of color illuminates the ideology and themes in Crane's *Maggie,* his "deterministic, fatalistic philosophy" (Simoneaux 222), then Van Vechten's color-laden sequences generally belie a sense of hope, celebration, contribution, and progress. Langston Hughes wrote that in *Nigger Heaven* Van Vechten wrought out "a whole rainbow of life above 110th Street that had never before been put into the color of words" (qtd. in Lueders 90).

In addition to the stylistic use of color in *Nigger Heaven,* animal metaphors, again evincing Crane's work, substantially contribute to the pathos of Van Vechten's cabaret scenes. The jazz bands that perform at the Black

Venus act bestial and generate an audience response in kind: "The drummer in complete abandon tossed his sticks in the air while he shook his head like a wild animal" (14); "The band snored and snorted and whistled and laughed like a hyena" (14); "The jazz band vomited, neighed, barked, and snorted and the barbaric ceremony began" (212); "The saxophone cooed like a turtle dove" (245), and even Ruby, in the way Crane's Maggie had gazed at Pete in naive adoration, swoons over the Creeper's "great brown eyes, like a doe's" (15). But it is a far cry from the Bowery children "howling" and "circling" and "writhing" we find in Crane's opening sequence of *Maggie* (7). Instead of demonstrating environmental dehumanization, Van Vechten offers up a newer, perhaps less condescending, form of primitivism that his character Mary Love consciously wishes to emulate. It is related to the primitivism hailed by Alain Locke in his introduction to his *The New Negro* (1925), a seminal collection of modernist writings by black authors, and to the African sculpture that Mary has been collecting for a show at her library in Harlem.

Mary Love is enamored by the new primitivism on display in Harlem's cabarets, editorial offices, libraries, and progressive museums. The newest artists black and white all became unbound by their authentic, at best unconscious, revisiting of a primitive past. In one of the most quoted passages of the book, Mary sums up her artistic goals:

> Savages! Savages at heart! And she had lost or forfeited her birthright, this primitive birthright which is so valuable and important an asset, a birthright that all the civilized races were struggling to get back to—this fact explained the art of a Picasso or a Stravinsky. To be sure, she, too, felt this African beat—it completely aroused her emotionally—but she was conscious of feeling it. This love of drums, of exciting rhythms, this naive delight in glowing colour—the colour that exists only in cloudless, tropical climes—this warm, sexual emotion, all these were hers only through a mental understanding. (89–90)

The rejection of civilized behavior and estheticism was too conscious an act for Mary, who wished to engage art on its most visceral level. She found that deep down she had more in common with her respectable foils than with her more "savage" neighbors. "We are all savages," she remarks of Harlemites, "all apparently, but me!" She resents this lackluster aspect of her character: "If she could only let herself go, revel in colour and noise and rhythm and physical emotion, throw herself into the ring with the others . . . how had she, during the centuries, lost this vital instinct?" (90, 91–92).

Like Mary, the character Byron Kasson finds his middle-class self-restraint limiting. His aloof mien of respectability, acquired from a middle-class upbringing and experiences among white Ivy Leaguers at Pennsylvania, stops him from engaging Harlem and its insiders' working-class society on its own level. During his stint as an elevator operator, his colleagues think little of him: "posin' an' signifyin', high-toned mustard-seed, arnchy yaller boy, sheik from Striver's Row" (192).[6] The feeling was mutual: "You want to be a writer, he adjured himself, and this is probably first class material" (192); but "nevertheless, his immediate pendant thought was that he could never write about this life, that he could never feel anything but repugnance for these people, because they were black. I can't bear to think of myself as a part of this, he sighed" (192). Byron's demure response to working-class Harlem was counterproductive for a black writer in the midst of the New Negro Renaissance, at least commercially. Though first-wave African American leaders such as Du Bois staunchly opposed "low down" representations of Harlem life, the demand for such texts grew over the decade of the 1920s and would culminate in Claude McKay's operatic frenzy, *Home to Harlem.*

The white publishing world's demand for realistic narratives of the black underworld from both radical and conservative circles was overwhelming; in contrast, there was tepid interest in its middle-class, or even Harlem's relationship to white New York.[7] Bringing Jimmie Johnson's reaction to Maggie and Pete's affair to mind, as he wonders whether the girls of his acquaintance have brothers, Byron conceptualizes a story in which a white boy has a love affair with a black girl. The white boy's sister then meets a black boy and they fall in love too. The story ends with the white boy killing his sister's lover. Byron's white character resembles Crane's Jimmie in their restrictive and destructive double standards—that they can have such relations but not their sisters. But this is a played-out story by the 1920s (as it probably was even by Crane's time), and Mary feels that the plot is in danger of "becoming melodramatic, cheap even" (204). Like the criticisms aimed at the outsider Van Vechten's portrayal of Harlem insiders, Mary does not believe that Byron is capable of thoroughly understanding the psychology behind his white characters' "motives" (204).

Nevertheless, Byron submits the piece to a number of white literary journals with Mary's half-hearted approval. In one of the most arresting scenes in the book, because Van Vechten was writing about a world he knew better than any other, Russett Durwood, the fictional editor of *American Mars* magazine, summons Byron for a meeting to discuss his submission. *American Mars* is obviously a play on the magazine *American Mercury,* which makes Durwood

H. L. Mencken, a close friend of Van Vechten's. Like Mencken's, his hair is "parted in the middle" (221), and the meeting remarkably resembles that which Van Vechten's friend and editor James Weldon Johnson had conducted with Mencken years before. It turns out Mary was right about the story from the start. Durwood explains that he has visited Harlem quite often and is familiar with many of its intellectuals and its cabarets. "The whole place, contrary to the general impression, is overrun with fresh, unused material." And like Mencken, Durwood is an arbiter of white literary fashion. Ethnographic material from an insider's point of view is scarce at this time in American literary history, he informs Byron, and as the editor of a modern journal he is obligated to fill the void: "Nobody has yet written a good gambling story; nobody has touched the outskirts of cabaret life; nobody has gone into the curious subject of the divers tribes of the region. Why, there are West Indians and Abyssinian Jews, religious Negroes, pagan Negroes, and Negro intellectuals, all living together more or less amicably in the same community, each group with its own opinions and atmosphere and manner of living; each individual with his own opinions and atmosphere and manner of living" (222).

This position echoes Mencken's own essay "Gropings in Literary Darkness" (1920), in which he argues that "the thing we need is a realistic picture of the inner life of the negro by one who sees race *from within*—a self-portrait as vivid and accurate as Dostoevsky's portrait of the Russian or Thackeray's of the Englishman. . . . He will force the understanding that now seems so hopeless. He will blow up nine-tenths of the current poppycock" (qtd. in Scruggs 176, emphasis mine). Just as he was finishing up work on *Nigger Heaven*, Van Vechten himself published a piece entitled "Moanin' Wid a Sword in Mah Han'" in *Vanity Fair* (February 1926), sounding very much like Durwood/Mencken:

> Until recently, in fact, the Negro writer has made a free gift of his exceptionally good copy—one should except Paul Laurence Dunbar and Charles W. Chesnutt from this indictment—to the white author. Lately, however, a new school of colored writers, of which the best known and the most gifted are probably Rudolph Fisher, Jean Toomer, and Langston Hughes—the talents of Countee Cullen, Walter White, and Jessie Fauset have been exercised in other directions—have perceived the advantage of writing about squalid Negro life *from the inside*. In the carrying out of this laudable ambition, it may be added, they have not met with much encouragement from the Negro public. . . . When the white author, who reasonably enough makes use of any good material he discovers, attempts to deal with this milieu, he is more than frowned upon. (57)

"Nordic" writers prove useless for capturing the full vitality of such a diversified space, Van Vechten ironically enough has Durwood explain. From what he has seen, now echoing Hamlin Garland, Negroes disappointingly "continue to employ the old clichés and formulas that have been worried to death by Nordic blonds who, after all, never did know anything about the subject from the inside" (223). Byron's story of interracial love gone awry is one such cliché "worried to death by Nordic blondes."

One of the "Nordics," or whites, Van Vechten may be referring to is Eugene O'Neill, whose incendiary play *All God's Chillun Got Wings* (1923) is a domestic drama that most likely takes place at the intersection of Bleeker, Hudson, and Eighth Avenue and treats the social and psychological complexities of interracial marriage. The plot charts the course of the relationship between a black man, Jim Harris, and a white woman, Ella Downey, from their preadolescent days as childhood sweethearts to their tumultuous marriage. This interracial union, divisive for both black and white audiences, ultimately destroys Jim's professional ambitions and sends Ella spiraling into violent psychopathology. In his 1922 work diary, O'Neill significantly jotted down the seed of the idea in this way: "Play of Johnny T.—negro who married white woman—base play on his experiences *as I have seen it intimately*—but no reproduction, see it only as man's" (in Floyd 53, emphasis mine).

Langston Hughes later rebuffed the Durwood/Mencken line on white writers, or at least qualified it, claiming that though "Negroes have writer-racketeers, as has any other race . . . most of the good ones have tried to be honest, write honestly, and express their world as they saw it" (*Big Sea* 227). Durwood warns Byron that these same Nordic types will dominate the Harlem scene too if African American writers like him do not take advantage of their unique insider positions. He alludes to many possible subjects: Marcus Garvey, black servant girls, the "fast set." Stop thinking in academic terms, is his final enigmatic piece of advice, just "pray and get drunk" (223).

Byron takes it personally, storming away from the meeting feeling humiliated and patronized. But from the professional publishing point of view, the talk was a practical one, as the later hubbub over *Nigger Heaven* would attest: Byron must defeat his own blindness to the rich subject matter the Harlem "low-down" lifestyle provides if he is to advance his writing career. Van Vechten himself again wrote candidly about whites co-opting the African American subject for themselves. In 1926, the same year as *Nigger Heaven*'s publication—when the uptown Renaissance's second wave was just beginning to proliferate its more primitive envisioning—Van Vechten self-reflexively wrote in *The Crisis*, "Are Negro writers going to write about this exotic material while it's still fresh or will they continue to make a free gift of it to white authors who will exploit it until not a drop of vitality remains?" (qtd. in Worth 470). Eugene O'Neill counseled black insiders in a similar vein while serving as a judge for black playwriting contests sponsored by *The Crisis* and *Opportunity,* "Be yourselves. . . . Don't reach out for our stuff which we call good!" (qtd. in Pfister 121).

Indeed, in *Nigger Heaven* Van Vechten poises outsider "Nordic blonds" from midtown to mine Harlem for all it had. In one of the final scenes, scenes that perpetuate the tragic circumstances that prove Durwood right and annihilate Byron's mental stability, Byron meets his friend Dick, who is chaperoning a couple of white literati from downtown at the Black Venus. Dick is an ex-colored man—a light-skinned mulatto who has successfully "passed" in the white world. He returns to Harlem only to impress his new colleagues as a white man who knows something about Harlem nightlife. When Byron asks what Dick is doing there, he laconically retorts, "Slumming" (208). One of the outsiders Dick chaperones, a novelist and columnist, is delirious with effusive appreciation for the scene at the Black Venus. He condescends, like Skaggs in *The Sport of the Gods,* but with a lick of competitive danger. He would love nothing more than to write about Harlem's cabaret scene, and he threatens to move uptown: "Well, it's wonderful up here. . . . I had no idea it would be like this. It's as wild as a jungle. Look at that waiter dancing the Charleston up the floor. . . . I think you are a wonderful people! Such verve and vivacity! Such dancing! Such singing! And I've always thought colored people were lazy! I suppose, he added reflectively, that it's because you're all so happy . . . oh, but this place is great! I could live up here. Is all Harlem like this?" (209, 210, 215).

African American social realists from the first wave would have answered that question with a resounding "no!" if they had even remained at the table; and perhaps a second-wave intellectual would have responded with a swift under-the-table boot to Byron's shin, like Thomas's to Joe Hamilton while Skaggs pronounced similarly patronizing reflections in *The Sport of the Gods.* But Byron, like Joe, was largely unfamiliar with the region and finds the question puzzling; he sees "too much, too much and too little." "The question awakened a swarm of perverse, dancing images in [his] brain. They crowded about each other, all the incongruities, the savage inconsistencies, the peculiar discrepancies, of this cruel, segregated life. . . . Yes, he replied, I suppose it is" (215).

To revisit Van Vechten's use of the term "Nigger Heaven" is perhaps the best place to conclude an analysis of the goals and methods of this ambiguous novel. Lightheartedly complaining about the inevitable controversy over the title in a letter to James Weldon Johnson, Van Vechten was bemused by the fact that the *New York News,* a black-run daily, charged that "any one who could call a book *Nigger Heaven* would call a Negro Nigger" (89). "Harlem," he reports to Johnson, who was out of town at the time, "is seething with controversy. Langston [Hughes], the other night in Craig's [a popular Harlem restaurant], suggested to a few of the knockers that they might read the book before expressing their opinion, but this advice seems to be regarded as supererogatory" (90). Twenty-five years later, in a letter to Charles S. Byrne responding to Byrne's request that the 1951 Avon books paperback be published under a different title, Van Vechten held fast: "Concerning the title there was certainly some objection when the book first appeared, particularly from people who had not read the novel, and it is likely that there may be now. That is not the important fact which is that the book is called *Nigger Heaven* (a tragic and ironic title as any fool who reads the book may see) and no other title would do. That is what is for sale. If you offered them Black Beauty,[8] for instance they wouldn't know anything about the contents and wouldn't buy the book" (*Letters* 241). The Avon edition was, incidentally, removed from the shelves after its publication in February of 1951 "because of complaints over the title" (*Letters* 241n).

There are only two direct references to Harlem as a "Nigger Heaven" in the novel. The first appears in the opening sequence during an assignation between "the Scarlet Creeper," a man about Harlem known for his ability to attract women, and his latest conquest, Ruby Silver. Ruby takes credit for the appellation "Nigger Heaven" as it pertains to Harlem specifically, remarking to the Creeper, "Ah calls [Harlem], specherly tonight, Ah calls et Nigger Heaven! I jes' nacherly think dis heah is Nigger Heaven!" (15). But even in an ironic sense this is not Van Vechten's voice. The Scarlet Creeper and Ruby Silver are the designated caricatures of the novel, dramatis personae that a white outsider could have contrived a priori without the slightest exposure to Harlem life.[9] Van Vechten himself admitted in a letter to Langston Hughes that had he not spent so much time in Harlem, the novel would have been much easier to write: "It would have been comparatively easy for me to write it before I knew as much as I know now, enough to know that I am thoroughly ignorant!" (*Letters* 82). In fact, that same self-effacing use of the term "Nigger Heaven" that Du Bois asserts might be quite properly applied in this context, even by an insider. Here is Langston Hughes's commentary on the controversial title:

A great many colored people never did discover that the title was an ironi-
cal title, applying to segregated, poverty-stricken Harlem the words used to
designate in many American cities the upper gallery in a theater, which is
usually the only place where Negroes may buy tickets to see the show—the
nigger heaven. To Mr. Van Vechten, Harlem was like that, a segregated gallery
in the theater, the only place where Negroes could see or stage their own show,
and not a very satisfactory place at that, for in his novel Mr. Van Vechten
presents many of the problems of the Negroes of Harlem, and he writes of
the people of culture as well as the people of the nightclubs. (270–71)

Another character who applies the term directly is Byron Kasson, an
outsider from Harlem regardless of his black status[10] who finds white New
York to be too confident in its assessment of Harlem as a "Nigger Heaven"
with all of its Du Boisean connotations. Once again, Van Vechten follows the
pattern of most slumming narratives discussed in this study in that Byron
consciously enhances what William Dean Howells called the "knowledge
of the lines." But this time it is through the eyes of a racial insider who is
cognitively mapping out his new environment: "They walked up Seventh
Avenue in silence. . . . As they approached One hundred and Twenty-fifth
Street, the blacks began to predominate. Almost immediately after they had
passed that thoroughfare they met only Negroes. *They had crossed the line*"
(148–49, emphasis mine). The discovery of the line is just as disturbing to
Byron as it was for Helen Campbell and William Dean Howells nearly a half
century before. But it is the outsider perception of the region as immoral
and yet innocuous that Byron finds most unnerving:

Nigger Heaven! . . . Nigger Heaven! That's what Harlem is. We sit in our
places in the gallery of this New York theatre and watch the white world sitting down below in the good seats in the orchestra. Occasionally they turn
their faces up towards us, their hard, cruel faces, to laugh or sneer, but they
never beckon. It never seems to occur to them that Nigger Heaven is crowded,
that there isn't another seat, that something has to be done. It doesn't seem
to occur to them either . . . that we sit above them, that we can swoop down
from this Nigger Heaven and take their seats. No, they have no fear of that!
Harlem! The Mecca of the New Negro! My God! (149)[11]

In a strong effort to parallel the outsider view of Harlemites (the Scarlet
Creeper) with the reality of Harlem's destructive potential for well-meaning
youths with high aspirations (Byron), Van Vechten shows in the end that the
benighted view of Harlem as a "Nigger Heaven" may prevail over the enlight-

ened insider view of Harlem as a powerful agent for social transformation. This may have been what rankled Du Bois most—the prediction, even more than the application. Robert F. Worth suggests that Byron's "tirade . . . might have been all right coming from a black author. From a white, it was probably all the more stinging for its fidelity to black sentiments" (465). Indeed, one "respectable" black character from Brooklyn in Claude McKay's novel *Home to Harlem,* the subject of the next section, joins the debate by saying, "I should think the nigger heaven of a theatre downtown is better than anything in this heah Harlem. . . . When we feels like going out, it's better we enjoy ourse'f in te li'l' corner the white folks 'low us, and then shuffle along back home. It's good and quiet ovah in Brooklyn. . . . This here Harlem is a stinking sink of iniquity. Nigger hell! That's what it is" (98, 99).

But Byron is as much a victim of his exposure to the "lures and snares" of Harlem as he is of outsider misjudgment. The climax of the story, when seen in this light, is far from being the "utterly senseless murder which appears without preparation or reason from the clouds" that Du Bois took it for. In a deft narrative slight of hand, Van Vechten portrays the morally corrupt influences of Harlem as corruptive for respectable young Talented Tenthers like Byron, as he has taken primitivism beyond its intended mark. He will most certainly be wrongly accused of killing a wealthy "bolito king," Randolph Pettijohn, though the Scarlet Creeper, like Johnson's black consort in *The Autobiography,* actually murders him in a jealous rage for appearing at the Black Venus with Ruby Silver. But we also know that Byron did plan to seek revenge against Pettijohn for having relations with his seducer, Lasca Sartoris. Van Vechten implies that if the Scarlet Creeper had not killed him, Byron probably would have. Byron even fires a couple of shots into his writhing body after Pettijohn collapses to the floor. Harlem's most superficially alluring aspects—embodied in the flamboyant and ultimately despicable Lasca—draw out a hidden nature of ferocious instinct that may in fact cause the seemingly prosperous district to self-destruct. In this sense, Van Vechten's novel plays more to Du Bois's antagonism toward second-wave "low down" behavior than Du Bois ever imagined, if he ever even read the book.

Du Bois was correct in his assessment of the perfidious possibilities of white outsiders publicizing a mythic Harlem. He is less accurate, taking into account the literary history covered in this study, when he contends in "Criteria of Negro Art" that "the only chance [a white writer] has to tell the truth of pitiful human degradation was to tell it of colored people" (324). Regardless of the sincerity of Van Vechten's purpose, or the relativism of his imagination, *Nigger Heaven* ultimately fell into the genre that had been, in the character Russett Durwood's words, "worried to death by Nordic blonds." As Worth has noted, "white reconnaissance missions into the black world, no matter how careful or conscientious, would always smell of sensationalism" (464). Byron's plight is one we see over and over in New York writing, one that smacks of city-mysteries prodigality. Byron's father in a letter to his son sounds suspiciously like a Helen Campbell, Paul Laurence Dunbar, or even back as far as 1850s city-mysteries authors like George Foster or Ned Buntline: "Harlem is a great Negro city, the greatest Negro city in the world, and it is as surely as full of pitfalls for young men as all great cities are. Unavoidably you will encounter your share of temptations. You are to an unfortunate extent, as we know to our cost, a slave to your appetites" (171). And Van Vechten in a special note to the short-lived Avon edition wrote that *Nigger Heaven* is "one of the oldest stories in the world, the story of the Prodigal Son, without the happy ending of that biblical history. In my book a boy from a small town is bewitched, bothered, and bewildered by a big time Lady of Pleasure and is unable to meet the demands made on his character by life in a big city" (qtd. in Lueders 89).

One's fate in New York relies on a person's ability to strike a healthy balance between Dionysian life-lust and Apollonian moral stamina and self-restraint, an ability Van Vechten has never been accused of practicing in his own life. This lack of self-restraint, the "personal dissociation" demonstrated by Harlemites, regardless of Van Vechten's appetites, is not a recommended remedy for middle-class claustrophobia. Byron's resentful acquisition of savage African American inspiration became his tragic undoing, as it might have been for Mary had she successfully adopted it. Though Mary equivocates throughout the novel, her frustrations ultimately seem out of character, as she maintains a mien of respectability that does not invite images of her grinding to jazz in a vermilion dress. Additionally, Van Vechten based Mary on the first-wave literary editor of *The Crisis,* Jessie Fauset, and Fauset was *not* a woman as consumed by African primitivism as her later successors would be. Durwood made a critical mistake when he urged Byron to write about Harlem, as Byron was in fact more a product of the Ivy League club than the cabaret. Just like Maggie and Pete on the Bowery, Joe in the Tenderloin, and Jake on the Lower East Side, Byron was ill-equipped to resolve the "savage inconsistencies, the peculiar discrepancies" of his neighborhood. Racially, he may have been an insider, but the moral foundations on which indigenous Harlemites stood were inaccessible to him. The only difference between Byron and the slumming whites on a "moral vacation" is that the whites knew they were slumming and could always—as Helen Campbell, Paul Laurence Dunbar's Skaggs, Hutchins Hapgood, James Weldon Johnson's millionaire, and other slumming figures could do—retreat back to their genteel lives.

The "Negro Emergent": Claude McKay's Home to Harlem

The white publishing world's call for black insiders to supply authorial representations of Harlem's "exotic material" was answered in the middle to late 1920s mainly by second-wave writers like Rudolph Fisher, Langston Hughes, Countee Cullen, Wallace Thurman, and Zora Neale Hurston. But the culminating insider mythologization of Harlem came in 1928 with Claude McKay's *Home to Harlem*. As early as 1923, McKay wrote to H. L. Mencken from France promising to "do a series of prose sketches of my contacts in America, using the most significant things, yet, leaving no subject, however degraded, untouched" (qtd. in Cooper, Foreword xv). Rejecting the view that "Negro art . . . must be dignified and respectable like the Anglo-Saxon's," McKay rejoiced in the "Return to the Primitive": "Happily the Negro retains his joy of living in the teeth of such criticism; and in Harlem . . . expresses himself with a zest that is yet to be depicted by a true artist" (qtd. in Cooper, Foreword xii); and after a time working a series of menial jobs, McKay importantly distinguished himself from white writers of New York "low life" by submitting that "when I came to write about the low-down Negro, I did not have to compose him from an outside view. Nor did I have to write a pseudoromantic account, as do bourgeois persons who become working-class for a while and work in shops and factories, whose inner lives are closed to them (qtd. in Pfister 263n).

The modernist writer Jean Toomer remarked on the imposed "images" of whiteness and blackness—whiteness signifying freedom and intellectual superiority and blackness as "inherently inferior . . . a slave by nature" (87)—by noting that the natural reaction for blacks who faced this outsider image was to try to become white. But whiteness was not a full enough design for Negroes. Instead they began to emerge on the basis of their own strengths:

> For Negroes had a special cause for their submission and desires: the white man claimed that the Negro was mentally inferior. Here was a chance to disprove that statement. The Negro would cram his brain with theories, dates, the Greek alphabet, and become equally civilized. He has done so; he is beginning to question the profit of his efforts. For now he seeks a balanced

life, based upon capacity, wherein *all* faculties are given the necessary usage. He is beginning to discard the image for reality. (88–89)

As a mixed-race member of this new avant garde, Jean Toomer reflected on his station in a letter to the *Liberator* editors Max Eastman and Claude McKay, stating that his "growing need for artistic expression has pulled me deeper and deeper into the Negro group" (qtd. in Sollors, "Jean" 33).

On what does Toomer base his claim for the emergent Negro? Why then and not earlier? His rationale is that African Americans had a special relationship with the spirit of the modern age: "The chaos and strain . . . the lack of functioning religion, religious pretense and charlatanism, the reaction from these to materialism, industrialism, the ideal of material success, a devitalizing puritanism, herd psychology, the premium placed on individuality, the stupidities, lies, and superstitions that Mr. Mencken has warred on, and so on" (89). (Alain Locke in 1926 also singled out the general "revolt against Puritanism" as the grounds for which "something almost amounting to infatuation has invested the Negro subject with interest and fascination" ["American Literary Tradition" 438]). Taken as a whole, Toomer submits that all of these modern influences come from without—are external and environmental, not internal and biological. As such, the Negro is emergent due to his close relationship with the nation's new order, an order that is "opposed to essential nature" (90) and, most importantly, an openness to individual and cultural "discovery." Furthermore, through this process of discovery he is "assured that in proportion as he discovers what is real within him, he will create, and by that act at once create himself and contribute his value to America" (93). With Toomer's statements in mind, we can see that textual interactions with life on the margins up to this point have been initiated mainly from outside the region's milieu. And if they had been present, as in the case of Cahan, they had not been entirely celebratory. Cahan attempted to render the Lower East Side at its most realistic, while it was Hapgood who did the promotional work. With Van Vechten and McKay, we see this paradigm in reverse. McKay constructed his mythic image from within.

McKay's *Home to Harlem* stands as the most deliberate attempt to render Harlem at its most strikingly and poetically primitive. James De Jongh cogently argues that the distinction between *Nigger Heaven* and *Home to Harlem* is that the district is treated novelistically in Van Vechten and lyrically in McKay (26–27)—again, an inversion of Cahan's and Hapgood's textual interactions. This literary distinction can be most clearly understood if we compare the outsider Byron's acerbic complaints about "Nigger Heaven" above and McKay's insider protagonist Jake's rhapsody of Harlem's intense sensuality: "Oh, to be in Harlem again after two years away. The deep-dyed color, the thickness, the closeness of it. The noises of Harlem. The sugared laughter. The honey-talk on its streets. And all night long, ragtime and 'blues' playing somewhere! Oh, the contagious fever of Harlem. Burning everywhere in dark-eyed Harlem. . . . Burning now in Jake's sweet blood" (15).

But as we have seen, Van Vechten did apply impressionistic stylistic devices in *Nigger Heaven*, albeit comparatively less than McKay. Those elements of Crane's impressionistic language that we find in Van Vechten are short-lived in his novel. His Harlem is mostly plot-driven and intellectualized, a book rather than a canvas. Strangely, the only redeeming feature of *Nigger Heaven* for Du Bois, contradicting his invectives against "low down" Harlem writing, was the opening chapter, an intensely colorful piece that renders Harlem cabaret life through the eyes of the Scarlet Creeper. Van Vechten actually bracketed his novel by employing dialect, rhythm, and color in the opening and concluding chapters, each with the Scarlet Creeper in the foreground. McKay's novel, on the other hand, sustains the "low down" speech patterns, attitudes, and atmospheric delights of Harlem street life throughout its entire length. If Van Vechten's work exists in the trough between the two initial waves of the Harlem Renaissance's chronology, McKay's rides on the crest of the second—in *Home to Harlem*, "primitivism" overwhelms "respectable," highly educated social uplift.

McKay is far more open than Van Vechten to the use of skin color as a technique to demonstrate ideological purpose. "Yallers," or light-skinned blacks, for example, become more "black" with sustained exposure to the Harlem cabaret. They absorb the primitive influences of the "black fellows" who let instinct dictate their music and dancing styles. In one cabaret scene, light-skinned blacks in the audience become even more "abandoned" than the "black" dancers upon hearing song lyrics describing the triumph of dark skin over yellow: "Yaller gal sure wants mah pa-pa, / But mah chocolate turns her down, / 'Cause he knows there ain't no loving / Sweeter than his loving brown" (297). McKay speculates that "the yellow in the music must have stood out in their imagination like a challenge, conveying a sense of that primitive, ancient, eternal, inexplicable antagonism in the color taboo of sex and society" (297). They are competing for cool in the land of primitive tastes. Harlem's touch is infectious in McKay, and any individual from whatever background, he implies, would come away with the same affectation of primitive blackness: "'White,' 'green,' or 'red' in place of 'yaller' might have likewise touched the same deep-sounding, primitive chord" (297). Rather than seeing this as a demonstration of intra-racial divide, however, McKay sees in the Harlem cabaret a collection of "New World Africans" whose variations in color add to the splendor of the atmosphere: "It was a scene of blazing color. Soft, barbaric, burning, savage, clashing, planless, colors—all rioting together in wonderful harmony. There is no human sight so rich as an assembly of Negroes ranging from lacquer black through brown to cream, decked out in their ceremonial finery. Negroes are like trees. They wear all colors naturally" (320).

McKay does not entirely abandon Harlem's intellectual side, however. Like Van Vechten, he represents the dilemma of Dionysian instinct and Apollonian reason in imagining the Harlem of the 1920s. But in the consciousnesses of McKay's characters, rather than competing impulses, instinct and intellect are perfectly compatible. His two main characters are Jake and Ray, Jake symbolizing instinct, Ray intellect. Like Cahan's success stories in *Yekl,* the two pick and choose which of the other's characteristics they might adopt. In Cahan, Gitl's is a successful immigration experience because she maintains a balance between Jewish tradition and cultural acquisition. Cahan's Jake, on the other hand, shares with Van Vechten's Byron an ill-fated totality of cultural adaptation—Yekl as the caricatured "Yankee," Byron the murderous savage. Jake and Ray are totalities in and of themselves, but when they interact, each is eager to learn from the other. From the moment they first meet as waiters on a Pullman train (a job McKay himself once held), they demonstrate the most unshakable form of friendship, the kind in which judgment is surpassed by understanding.

At first Ray, a Haitian exile, is overwhelmed with homesickness. Chased out of Haiti by political upheavals, Ray stumbles into "the quivering heart of a naked world whose reality was hitherto unimaginable. It was what they called in print and polite conversation 'the underworld'" (224). Jake takes issue with this term, as it implies that Harlem itself has an underworld. He grasps in a backhanded way that New Yorkers understood their "underworld" to be a region as a whole, rather than a hidden domain beneath the visible city: "The compound word baffled him, as some English words did sometimes. Why under-world he could never understand. It was very much upon the surface as were the other divisions of human life. Having its heights and middle and depths and secret places even as they. And the people of this world, waiters, cooks, chauffeurs, sailors, porters, guides, ushers, hod-carriers, factory hands—all touched in a thousand ways the people of other divisions. They worked over there and slept over here, divided by a street" (225). Ray's observations of Harlem here would have struck the reformers of the late nineteenth century as precisely the reason such "underworlds" should be eradicated. They bleed their influences outward and affect the whole of New York society. But in McKay's imagination, Harlem's influence on "polite society" is infinitely necessary—how working-class culture should function in a democracy. Harlem's most primitive aspects are precisely what genteel New York requires to overcome the kind of phariseean insincerity we see in Edith Wharton's New York novels. As such, rather than strictly exposing their foibles, as Edith Wharton had been doing, he offers genteel outsiders an alternative. In one of the final passages of the novel, McKay insists that in Harlem there are

> none of the well-patterned, well-made emotions of the respectable world. A laugh might finish in a sob. A moan end in hilarity. That gorilla type wriggling there with his hands so strangely hugging his mate, may strangle her tonight. But he has no thought of that now. He loves the warm wriggle and is lost in it. Simple, raw emotions and real. They may frighten and repel refined souls, because they are too intensely real, just as a simple savage stands dismayed before nice emotions that he instantly perceives as false. (337–38)

In spite of Ray's initial shame at being ghettoized in what outsiders perceived as an "underworld," his experiences with Jake teach him that this kind of authenticity in act and emotion reveals the path to psycho-cultural salvation. "Can't a Negro have fine feelings about life?" Ray's uninitiated friend Grant asks him. "Yes," Ray replies, "but not the old false-fine feelings that used to be monopolized by educated and cultivated people. You should educate yourself away from that sort of thing" (242).

In this contest of representation, *Home to Harlem* follows through with the theme of McKay's 1921 poem "Baptism." In it, he boasts that he will enter regions in which "The yawning oven spits forth fiery spears" and "come out, back to your world of tears, / A stronger soul within a finer frame" (*Passion* 125). *Home to Harlem* represents black Manhattan as a formidable region with an effectual culture—in some ways like Ishmael Reed's postmodern revision of the Harlem Renaissance in his novel *Mumbo Jumbo* (1972)—against which the "desperate, frightened, blanch-faced, the ancient sepulchral Respectability" futilely fortified itself (300). *Home to Harlem* comes from an insider's point of view, and rather than steering his audience away from the lures of a moral region or speaking didactically to fellow insiders with an outsider audience in mind, McKay explicitly argues that standards of outsider morality themselves must be redefined.

The novel was destined, of course, to receive the same treatment as *Nigger Heaven* from first-wave critics. Du Bois responded just as one might guess: "It looks as though McKay has set out to cater to that prurient demand on the part of white folk for a portrayal in Negroes of that utter licentiousness which convention holds white folk back from enjoying" (qtd. in De Jongh 31). In fact, if Du Bois made an accurate assessment of either of these best-selling novels, this was it. McKay's Harlem became the Harlem of popular imagination—within a decade after its publication, in the area of twenty Harlem novels by insider writers followed suit (De Jongh 33). In 1931, the mulatto realist Charles W. Chesnutt, who was critical, on the whole, of modernist texts that took place in "low down" Harlem, wrote of the many novels that poured from the New Negro Renaissance in the 1920s (though tellingly, he never mentioned his own Harlem novel *The Quarry* [1928], for which he could not find a publisher in his lifetime),

> I have lived to see, after twenty years or more, a marked change in the attitude of publishers and the reading public in regard to Negro fiction. The development of Harlem, with its large colored population in all shades, from ivory to ebony, of all degrees of culture, from doctors of philosophy to the lowest grade of illiteracy; in its various origins, North American, South American, West Indian and African; its morals ranging from the highest to the most debased; with the vivid life of its cabarets, dance halls, and theatres; with its ambitious business and professional men, its actors, singers, novelists and poets, its aspirations and demands for equality—without which any people would merit only contempt—presented a new field for literary exploration which of recent years has been cultivated assiduously. . . . *Negro writers no longer have any difficulty in finding publishers. Their race is no longer a detriment but a good selling point, and publishers are seeking their books, sometimes, I am inclined to think, with less regard for quality than in the case of white writers.* (911, 912, emphasis mine)

❖ ❖ ❖

Tragically, the lion's share of Harlem's black population was like Van Vechten's Byron Kasson, go-getting outsiders who moved to the "Mecca of the New Negro" in order to make a name for themselves and thrive economically. Many were escaping Jim Crow and lynching in the South, many pouring into what was advertised as the ultimate land of Negro opportunity. In a sense, these migrants would symbolically share Byron's fate. As Langston Hughes wrote retrospectively, "non-theatrical, non-intellectual Harlem was an unwilling victim of its own vogue" (*The Big Sea* 229). Like the Hamiltons in *The Sport of the Gods,* migrants to Harlem would be drawn in by the myth and live with the reality. Though southern black migration persisted well into the 1930s, mythic Harlem disappeared once slummers, white and black, no longer found a moral region worth exploring. "The '20's are gone," wrote Hughes, "and lots of fine things in Harlem night life have disappeared like snow in the sun . . . it became utterly commercial, planned for the downtown tourist trade, and therefore dull" (226).

As Daniel Boone escaped from civilization while at the same time para- doxically expanding it, white slummers searched out new moral regions to plumb for cultural regeneration. In a 1926 letter to Louis Bromfield, Van Vechten even threatened to take his business to Chinatown, a threat he never carried out: "Now that I thoroughly explored Harlem, I think I shall take up the Chinese" (*Letters* 88). Additionally, the Great Depression relieved most New Yorkers of their disposable incomes; a number of African American cultural leaders were dead by the 1930s—Wallace Thurman, A'Lelia Walker, Rudolph Fisher, and Charles S. Gilpin, to name a few; the original Cot- ton Club and the Lafayette Theatre were closed down; and every black-run literary journal collapsed under the weight of the region's poverty. McKay himself died, utterly broke, in a Chicago hospital bed in 1948. Harlem's "procession of the oppressed," of course, would remain. The Harlem that existed all along overwhelmed its 1920s persona—the Harlem of the social worker, the high mortality rate, the unromantic alcoholism, the drug abuse, and the bread line—and this revised image would remain until the turn of our present century, at which time many Harlemites are at last enjoying the fruits of outsized Manhattan real estate prices.

The contradictory trends of ghetto celebration and social reality in the 1920s combined to form the myth of the ghetto, a myth that was utilized to act as a reconciling agent for an irreconcilable paradox—in the case of Har- lem, the disjunction between its socioeconomic reality and its simultaneous appeal to ambitious black insiders and slumming white outsiders. On the application of myth-as-reconciler for Harlem's intrinsic ability to compel a white audience, Gilbert Osofsky asseverates that "it would be difficult to find a better example of the confusions, distortions, half-truths and quarter- truths that are the foundations of racial and ethnic stereotypes than the white world's image of Harlem in the 1920's" (180). In hindsight, we comprehend the injurious implications of mythic Harlem. Though droves of white outsid- ers took full advantage of the sensual, modern releases offered by the New Negro Renaissance, doing so distracted them from facing the social realities of the insiders who lived there. Mythic Harlem provided a reconciling element to the very social injustices of racial prejudice and economic despair that quite blinded outsiders and insiders to a critical situation.

The construction of a mythic ghetto space—one in which social reality deferred to the philosophy of a more atavistic sense of personal freedom—masked brutal environmental realities that demanded immediate attention, and both blacks and whites perpetuated this process. It was in Harlem, more than any other neighborhood covered in this study, that insiders from the "other half" responded most vocally to outsider representations of them and made substantial contributions to the discourse. In the interest of non-conformity, white, middle-class slummers and African American culture advocates alike constructed, in the words of Alain Locke, "cruelly deceptive mirages" (qtd. in Osofsky 187) among the famously dilapidated brownstones of black Harlem. In the end, however, I would again like to borrow from Langston Hughes, who, in his impassioned rejoinder to George Schuyler's proto-postethnic attack on the existence of "insider" art as "hokum," finally concludes that "the present vogue in things Negro," though sometimes harmfully distracting from social realities, "has at least done this: it has brought him forcibly to the attention of his own people among whom for so long, unless the other race had noticed him beforehand, he was a prophet with little honor" ("Negro Artist" 93).

Epilogue

THE CITY TURNED INSIDE OUT

NEW YORK'S CHANNEL OF MORALITY AND MANNERS descended down-ward over the course of the nineteenth century in favor of "respectability" over "low life," but by 1900—from outside in to inside out—it began its upward ascent. Textual interactions with New York life on the margins first emphasized fundamental spatial distinctions, then concrete sites within the city, then the cultural distinctions of those sites, and finally how those cultures affected individual consciousness. Logically enough, the next step was modernism, with its refined emphasis on the psychology of the self. The practice of literary slumming in New York from 1880 to 1930 both depended on and informed New Yorkers' understanding of morality and its relationship to physical space. These slumming narratives naturally corresponded with one another, and their interactions, between themselves and the city in which they were written, all contributed to the discourse of marginality. Though these texts served a variety of social functions—popular entertainment, reform efforts, high literary aspirations, and journalistic exposé—each was dependent on the others to order and reorder their cosmopolitan city and the moral landscape it generated.

Such a volatile history is appropriately imbued with a broiling sense of progression through which social and textual changes occur. But it is a progression characterized by perpetual movement, if often two steps forward and one step back. Looking at a substantial stretch of time, from the 1880s to the 1920s, a discernible pattern does come into focus. For one thing, New York culture on the margins went from evoking images of "Babylon" to achieving a "Renaissance." But a number of broader and more familiar changes transpired over this period: it was a time and place in which the pastoral sensibility was replaced by a modern obsession with the inner workings of the urban arena; "primary" social relations became more "secondary"; regionalism and race gave way to ethnic identity; the United States transformed from a producer economy to a consumer economy; and the previous emphasis on local communities was relinquished, as Carrie Tirado Bramen has recently argued, in favor of a nationalization of urban aesthetics (446). The significance of New York slumming narratives is that the discourse they cultivate, the discourse of marginality, incorporates all of these trends.

Starting with Helen Campbell and her dealings with Jerry McAuley, the insider is clearly rendered, but he is necessarily complicit in transforming the waterfront to reflect her vision of a model "city on the hill"—Jerry McAuley is an insider with a decidedly outsider Protestant look. Ernest Poole, on the other hand, although he sets his novel only a decade or so later than Campbell, begins to show the strong influence of waterfront morality on inquisitive urban youths. Stephen Crane and Henry James form a critical turning point in representations of the "other" in American literary history. In many ways they saw their Bowery dwellers as they truly were—victims of progressive standards of morality (such as Campbell's and Riis's) that did not practically translate in their world. James Weldon Johnson tempers Paul Laurence Dunbar's assumptions about the effect of urban spaces on the minds of emigrant Negroes in New York. In Johnson, respect for and trepidation of "black Bohemia" go hand in hand. Hutchins Hapgood and the determined efforts of his Villager cohorts turn popular morality on its ear by demonstrating the extent to which the immigrant population was appealing in its freshness and rejuvenating effect on the dominant moral order. Abraham Cahan is his case in point. Cahan is the shining light from below, one that anticipates what might have been all along, what would later emerge in the writings of immigrants and working-class authors in the decades to come. Like Crane, Carl Van Vechten voiced the contradictions in the consciousnesses of his insiders, but unlike Crane, he was writing about a culture that was largely accepted for what it was, at least so long as it remained in vogue.

Insider fiction from immigrant and black communities exploded during the 1920s, '30s, and early '40s, when ethnic contention in the form of anti-immigration legislation and institutionalized segregation heightened the need for intra-ethnic solidarity. The Norwegian American novelist Ole Edvart Rölvaag; Jewish American authors, Anzia Yezierska, Mike Gold, and Henry Roth; contributors to Harlem's New Negro Renaissance, Langston Hughes, Jean Toomer, Claude McKay, and Zora Neale Hurston; and later Italian American novelists John Fante, Mari Tomasi, and Pietro DiDonato, all rose up between the world wars and employed ethnic difference, in part, as a political tool to defend their groups' legitimate place in a democratic society.

Each of these insiders depict candid, even practical versions of their milieus, suggesting that cycles of urban alienation and prostration can only be broken by educating fellow insiders and achieving empathy from the outsider mainstream. Robert Morss Lovett has reflected on the Joycean quality of the Irish American naturalist James T. Farrell's work set in the predominantly Irish section of Chicago (connecting Washington Park and Wabash Avenue) by observing that Farrell's novel *A World I Never Made* (1936) tells of a "segment of society which the author knows from the inside," and it also reflects Proust's artistic logic in that it delineates the processes of the "'individual human being in interaction with other human beings in society'" (xx). Farrell was known to vituperate his contemporaries for following the spurious literary coda of the upcoming formalists—the imaginatively blind followers of T. S. Eliot. "When form and structure become predominant values in literature," he argued, "the material from life on which literature draws is falsified" (xxxvi). He believed that the "revolt in American literature" stemming from realism and naturalism was most uniquely carried out by insider ethnic voices spurred on by realism's precept of inclusion by way of documentary-style sociological writing. Farrell is the United States' finest articulator of the burgeoning insider voice in American fiction, and as such he is worth quoting at length. Looking backward on the rise of multi-ethnic American literature, Farrell writes that

> in early years, there was the literature of the American immigrant, of first-generation groups, written in an unreal and patronizing vein. The melting pot was a typical literary theme. The treatment in such works was without vitality, conventional, intended to be humorous. *The stories contained little truth and were written from the outside.* Writers played on variations of such themes as that of the stage Irishman who was manufactured by some nineteenth-century Irish novelists for English consumption. In a vulgar and insulting manner, such fiction sentimentalized Jewish characters. It was a literature of the Cohens and the Kellys, of Abie's Irish Roses, Uncle Remus, a literature of the upper classes and of good old Star-Spangled-Banner patronage. With [the] so-called revolt in American literature, several generations of writers arose and began articulating the experience of groups in America, of phases in American life that had hitherto received false and patronizing treatment, or no attention at all. Immigrant groups, the working class, the poorer elements in general began to receive some degree of realistic representation

in American fiction. This tendency has now reached a point where, viewed sociologically, American writing treats of an infinite variety of types, racial and economic groups, and localities that go toward making up the totality of American life. . . . The revolt in American literature . . . [has] been, to a certain degree, victorious. (xlii, xliii, emphasis mine)

Thus, paradoxically, while outsiders refined and reconfigured their portrayals of insiders over the fifty years covered in this book—eventually giving way to the emergence of the insider voice itself—by 1930, the "truth" becomes reserved for insiders alone. By the mid-twentieth century, "the Outsider," Robert K. Merton affirms, "no matter how careful and talented, is excluded in principle from gaining access to the social and cultural truth" (330). The "Insider doctrine," as he calls it, that "one must not only be one to understand one; one must be one in order to understand what is most worth understanding" (332), has triumphed in the American literary imagination and marketplace. Rölvaag's *Giants in the Earth* (1927), Gold's *Jews Without Money* (1930), Roth's *Call It Sleep* (1934), Hurston's *Their Eyes Were Watching God* (1937), and DiDonato's *Christ in Concrete* (1939), have rightfully taken their place as near classics of American literature. Representations of American ghettoes and ethnic groups since the 1930s, in short, have been turned inside out.

Hamlin Garland's call in the 1880s for a literary realism that only indigenous voices can bestow was not fully accepted until the 1920s, and at the turn of the twenty-first century, it is the rule rather than the exception. McKay and Cahan are more widely read now than Van Vechten and Hapgood will probably ever be. This dominance of the native insider informant over the genteel outsider investigator, however, still does not complete the narrative development of New York's insider voice. How does one explain the uncanny proliferation of latter-day historical novels of Old New York?

The last ten years seem to have produced as many novels about the sepia-soaked New York "underworld" of the nineteenth century as the nineteenth century itself: *The Alienist* by Caleb Carr (1995) and its sequel *The Angel of Darkness* (1997), *The Waterworks* by E. L. Doctorow (1997), *Dreamland* (2000) by Kevin Baker, and *Metropolis* by Elizabeth Gaffney (2005), just to name a few, all take place before and around the turn of the twentieth century. They go back even earlier in New York history with Peter Quinn's *The Banished Children of Eve* (1994) and Kevin Baker's *Paradise Alley* (2002) about the Draft Riots of 1863, and a couple of city mysteries involving Herman Melville and Edgar Allan Poe as reluctant detectives: for Melville, *The Night Inspector* by

Frederick Busch (1999); for Poe, *On Night's Shore* by Randall Silvis (2001). Additionally, studies of nineteenth-century New York "low life" in literature, history, sociology, musicology, and art history have enjoyed a remarkable rebirth. I would argue that when we can just as readily turn straight to the source, literary outsiders are a justifiable redundancy, a thing of the past, barely viable in a publishing world where the insider is an accessible, highly regarded authority.

Interpretations with the widest audience, of course, dictate the level of cultural capital they will enjoy. With the waning influence of Victorianism on contemporary images of nineteenth-century New York, we are discovering that the urban literature of the nineteenth century presented the city as the ultimate proving ground for the success or attrition of the United States. Cultural historians like Sean Wilentz, Christine Stansell, David S. Reynolds, Timothy J. Gilfoyle, Keith Gandal, and George Mariani have deconstructed the myth of nineteenth-century Victorian totality over the last fifteen years or so, opening new doors of perception for scholars and students alike, though most contemporary scholarship on American literary realism continues to reinforce the dominion of late nineteenth- and early twentieth-century canonical writing.

On the popular level, director Martin Scorsese, whose film based on Wharton's *The Age of Innocence* (1993) reflected more conventional images of Old New York (and viewers might have assumed the director of *Mean Streets* [1973] and *Good Fellas* [1990] had been groping for older representations of his city and could only find Wharton's genteel Fifth Avenue), has produced a long overdue film version of Herbert Asbury's popular 1927 history of New York "low life" *The Gangs of New York* (the latest edition advertises the book's stature as a modern classic by opening with a foreword by Jorge Luis Borges). As the audience for contemporary slumming texts narrows, New York outsiders investigating the margins have now found it necessary to return to the spot in New York history where they "belong." After being stripped of any meaningful authority on what may be considered the moral regions of today, outsider intellectuals fascinated with the "tastes and temperaments" of marginalized urban neighborhoods are for better or worse returning to a time in New York history when their voices had power, when their voices defined what was good and bad about both the New York they observed and the New York they helped to create.

NOTES

Introduction

1. See my essay "Ethnic Realism" in *The Blackwell Companion to American Fiction, 1865–1914*, eds. Robert Paul Lamb and G. R. Thompson (Oxford: Blackwell Publishers, 2005), and Laura Hapke's *Labor's Text*.

2. This definition of "ghetto" comes from the sociologist David Ward's usage of the term—"the residential segregation of ethnically defined migrants in the inner-city slums" (Ward 2). His study *Poverty, Ethnicity, and the American City, 1840–1925*, remains the finest source for understanding the causes of this urban transition from slum to ghetto.

3. See my essay, "On Eugene O'Neill's 'Philosophical Anarchism.'" *Eugene O'Neill Review* (Spring 2007).

Chapter 1: "Under the Bridge and Beyond"

1. Helen Campbell wrote approximately one-third of this enormous volume. The other contributors were Colonel Thomas Knox, a journalist; and Superintendent Thomas Byrnes, head of the New York Detective Bureau.

2. This dichotomous format was conceived of by Miller and Miller (93).

3. The translation of McAuley's dialect into standard English is not restricted to the nineteenth century. Duane V. Maxey of the Repairer Publishing Company in Atlanta, Georgia, after discovering a damaged tract-booklet, *Life Story of Jerry McAuley* by McAuley himself (n.d.), introduces the text, prepared for the Holiness Data Ministry in 2000, with a note entitled "Conversion of McAuley's Irish Dialect into Proper English." In it, he writes:

> In the printed booklet, McAuley used such dialectic-English as (me father) instead of (my father), (an') instead of (and), (livin') instead of (living), etc., etc. I converted such words into correct English, and this editing also involved the changing of entire phrases

and portions of text, such as the following: "But I was tall o' me years an' strong, an' had no fear . . ."—changed into—"But I was tall for my years and strong, and had no fear . . ." I made these changes in the text as a matter of personal preference, and also I felt that these changes might tend to make the message of the book more readily and more easily understood by most readers. (n.p.)

The thirty-two-page narrative is a condensed, recycled version of *Transformed*. For missionary reminiscences of McAuley soon after his death, see Offord.

Chapter 2: A Culture of Contradictions

Portions of chapter 2 appeared in a different form in *Twisted from the Ordinary: Essays on American Literary Naturalism*, Tennessee Studies in Literature, vol. 40, edited by Mary E. Papke. Copyright 2003 by the University of Tennessee Press and in *Stephen Crane Studies* (2007).

1. I admit that "Victorian" is a highly unstable category, but I do not want the argument here to be obfuscated by semantics. I am using the term "Victorian" to identify the culture of middle- to upper-middle-class American Protestant moralism that manifested itself in a cult of "respectability" from the middle to the late nineteenth century and into the early twentieth.

2. "Mercheen" is Bowery dialect for a fire engine.

3. The "oiled bang" and "red scarf" constituted a fashion statement remarkably similar to the B'hoys' "soaplocks," long locks of hair that hung in front of their ears and were slicked down with bear grease or soap, and their penchant for wearing red shirts and scarves. All references to Crane's *Maggie* refer to the Library of America edition, unless otherwise noted in the citation.

4. The B'hoy character in folklore who was Mose's trusted companion.

5. In a footnote, Monteiro calls our attention to Crane's *Publisher's Circular* obituary (72, June 9, 1900; p. 629), which lists *St. George's Mother* as one of his books and further that "curiously" there exists a 1907 book entitled *St. George and the Dragon: England and the Drink Traffic*, by Rev. J. Johns (16n).

6. The legend of George and the dragon was also popularly adopted as a symbol of the United States defeating Spain in the Spanish-American War and of white supremacy. Thanks to Professor Faye Ringel of the U.S. Coast Guard Academy for her tutelage on the legend of St. George.

7. *On the Bowery* is a penetrating study, with a somewhat misleading subtitle, that treats the turn in urban representation from the "sensational mystification" of the middle decades of the nineteenth century to the "critical realism" of Crane and Dreiser.

8. The dramatization of the novel, *Maggie, Girl of the Streets*, by Arthur Reel, premiered in a Drama Committee Repertory Theater production on January 17, 1976, in New York City. It was revived by the Drama Committee at the Sanford Meisner Theatre in May 2003.

9. Significantly, the graphically violent, sexual, politically dissident, and wildly popular novels of the so-called city-mysteries group of the 1840s and '50s, led by George Lippard, Net Buntline, John Vose, and George Thompson, among many others, have no substantial corollaries in the 1890s.

Chapter 3: Marginal Men in Black Bohemia

Portions of chapter 3 appeared in a different form in *Post-bellum, Pre-Harlem: African American Literature and Culture, 1877–1919*, edited by Caroline Gebhard and Barbara McCaskill. New York: New York University Press, 2006.

1. The Great Migration and the settlement of blacks in Harlem will be discussed in more detail in chapter 5.

2. The highest recorded population in Manhattan's history through the present.

3. Located from Sixtieth Street and Sixty-fourth between Tenth Avenue and Eleventh. It was named "San Juan Hill" with the Spanish-American War in mind; the analogy was made between that war and the race riots that regularly took place in the New York neighborhood.

4. This figure does include the relatively rural South Bronx that was a part of New York City before the consolidation of the boroughs in 1898.

5. For more information on the negative reception of black/white sexual relations in urban districts and the role of sex in slumming narratives, see Kevin J. Mumford's comprehensive study *Interzones*.

6. "Black Bohemia" signifies the sporting lifestyle of the Tenderloin's black section, located along Sixth Avenue from Twenty-third to Thirty-third Streets (82; *Black Manhattan* 73).

7. See Hurd 94; implied in the title of Morgan ["city of refuge" refers to Harlem]; Nilon 8; Den Tandt *Urban Sublime* 232, and "American Literary Naturalism" 113.

8. In regard to this section title, I understand that the word "picnic" is an offensive shibboleth for many African Americans, particularly among the older generations, that calls to mind the white picnic parties that ghoulishly accompanied lynchings in the South. I sincerely apologize to any reader if they find the usage disagreeable. It must be understood, however, that Paul Laurence Dunbar does use the term in a different context in *The Sport of the Gods* to make a telling point about the southern black migrant experience.

9. This is true, regardless of the fact that he is the one man who proves capable of freeing Berry Hamilton from jail. He exposes Berry's former employer's brother as the culprit, but does so strictly to increase his newspaper's sales and to add to its spurious reputation as a voice for the disenfranchised (Dunbar, *Sport* 131).

10. See Caroline Gebhard and Barbara McCaskill, eds., *Post-Bellum, Pre-Harlem*. The second section of this chapter is based on my essay in that anthology, "A Marginal Man in Black Bohemia: James Weldon Johnson in the New York Tenderloin" (289–319).

Chapter 4: Realism in the Ghetto

Portions of chapter 4 appeared in a different form in *The Blackwell Companion to American Fiction, 1865–1914*, edited by Robert Paul Lamb and G. R. Thompson. Oxford: Blackwell Publishers, 2005.

1. The first wave of nineteenth-century immigration consisted of over a million Irish exiles escaping the horrors of a potato blight that decimated Ireland's popula-

tion after 1845. A million or so Germans, or "forty-niners," also arrived during this period, many of whom chose emigration over the violent backlash enacted by central European monarchies after the failed worker revolutions of 1848. The second wave or "new" immigration, significantly imbricated with the first, transplanted more unfamiliar Old World traits to the New World, since they emigrated from the more "foreign" nations of southern and eastern Europe.

2. The film *Hester Street* (1974) is based on this novel.

Chapter 5: "Nigger Heaven"

1. Lewis actually discusses the Harlem Renaissance in terms of three "phases": "The first phase ending in 1923. . . . The second from 1924 to mid-1926. . . . The last phase from mid-1926 to the Harlem Riot of March 1935" (Introduction xv). Only the second two phases will directly concern us here.

2. Knopf had published White's *The Fire in the Flint* in 1924.

3. *The Police Gazette* was a tawdry, sensational newspaper that featured crime stories, mild pornography, and scandalous exposés.

4. Probably modeled after Small's, a basement-level cabaret on Fifth Avenue that Van Vechten made his headquarters in Harlem. In a later scene, when Byron is discussing Harlem with white slummers, we see waiters doing the Charleston down the aisles—a common sight in Small's. In addition, it was here that Van Vechten preferred to take his white guests as an introduction to Harlem's nighttime offerings (Kellner 198–99).

5. Crane's lack of African American characters in most of his New York writing seems to be at issue lately. It must be remembered that New York's African American population in the 1890s—as I discuss in chapter 3—was extremely small.

6. A well-to-do street in Harlem that boasts a row of townhouses designed by the famed New York architect Stanford White.

7. Jessie Fauset's novel *There Is Confusion* (1924) took place in a middle-class African American setting in Philadelphia.

8. Van Vechten refers here to a late 1920s composition by Duke Ellington.

9. Du Bois felt that the Creeper, otherwise known as Anatole Longfellow, was the only "promising figure" in the book. Van Vechten defines "creeper" in his glossary as "a man who invades another's marital rights."

10. In *Interzones,* Kevin J. Mumford discusses Byron's interview with Durwood by showing the irony of Durwood the outsider lecturing Byron the insider on "how to create 'authentic' representations of African-American culture" (155). I argue here and farther down, however, that Byron may be black, but he is no insider in Harlem. Like Joe Hamilton in Dunbar's novel, Byron is too eager and at the same time too unaware of the district's realities to withstand the powerful temptations of personal dissociation Harlem life had to offer.

11. It must be noted, to avoid any confusion, that Du Bois incorrectly identifies this passage in his review for *The Crisis* as appearing on page 199, as opposed to 149.

BIBLIOGRAPHY

Abell, Aaron Ignatius. *The Urban Impact on American Protestantism, 1865–1900.* Cambridge, Mass.: Harvard University Press, 1943.

Alexander, Doris. "O'Neill as Social Critic." *O'Neill and His Plays: Four Decades of Criticism.* Eds. Oscar Cargill, N. Bryllion Fagin, and William J. Fisher. New York: New York University Press, 1961.

Allen, Gay Wilson. *Solitary Singer: A Critical Biography of Walt Whitman.* New York: Macmillan Co., 1955.

Ammons, Elizabeth. "Expanding the Canon of American Realism." *Cambridge Companion to American Realism and Naturalism.* Ed. Donald Pizer. 1995. Cambridge, U.K.: Cambridge University Press, 1999. 95–116.

Andrews, William L. Introduction. *The Autobiography of an Ex-Colored Man.* By James Weldon Johnson. 1912. New York: Penguin Books, 1990.

Anonymous. Rev. of *George's Mother* by Stephen Crane. 1896. Wertheim 111–12.

Beer, Thomas. *Stephen Crane: A Study in American Letters.* Introduction by Joseph Conrad. New York: Alfred A. Knopf, 1923.

Bell, Bernard W. *The Afro-American Novel and Its Tradition.* 1987. Amherst: University of Massachusetts Press, 1989.

Benfey, Christopher. *The Double Life of Stephen Crane: A Biography.* New York: Alfred A. Knopf, 1992.

Berlin, Edward A. "Ragtime." Ed. Kenneth T. Jackson. New Haven, Conn.: Yale University Press, 1995. 926.

———. *Ragtime: A Musical and Cultural History.* Berkeley: University of California Press, 1980.

Bernard, Emily. Introduction. *Remember Me to Harlem: The Letters of Langston Hughes and Carl Van Vechten, 1925–1964.* Ed. Emily Bernard. New York: Alfred A. Knopf, 2001.

Blumin, Stuart. Introduction. 1856. *New York by Gas-Light and Other Urban Sketches.* 1856. Edited by Stuart Blumin. Berkeley: University of California Press, 1991. 1–61.

Bonner, Arthur. *Jerry McAuley and His Mission*. Neptune, N.J.: Loizeaux Brothers, 1967.

Bourne, Randolph. "Trans-National America." *Theories of Ethnicity: A Classical Reader*. Ed. Werner Sollors. 93–108.

Boyce, Neith. Review [of *George's Mother*]. *Lotus* (Sept. 1896). Ed. Richard M. Weatherford. London: Routledge and Kegan Paul, 1973. 178.

Brace, Charles Loring. *The Dangerous Classes of New York, and Twenty Years among Them*. 1872. Washington, D.C.: National Association of Social Workers Classic Series, 1973.

Bramen, Carrie Tirado. "The Urban Picturesque and the Spectacle of Americanization." *American Quarterly* 52.3 (Sept. 2000): 444–77.

Brennan, Joseph X. "Ironic and Symbolic Structure in Crane's *Maggie*." Stephen Crane. *Maggie: A Girl of the Streets*. 1893. Ed. Thomas A. Gullason. New York: W. W. Norton, 1979. 173–84.

Brown, Allston T. *A History of the New York Stage: From the First Performance in 1732 to 1901*. Vol. 1. 1903. New York: Benjamin Blom, Inc., 1964. 3 vols.

Buckley, Peter George. "To the Opera House: Culture and Society in New York City, 1820–1860." Diss. State University of New York, Stony Brook, 1984.

Buntline, Ned. *The B'hoys of New York*. New York: Dick and Fitzgerald, 1848.

———. *The G'hals of New York*. New York: Dewitt and Davenport, 1850.

Burrows, Edwin G., and Mike Wallace. *Gotham: A History of New York City to 1898*. New York: Oxford University Press, 1999.

Butsch, Richard. "Bowery B'hoys and Matinee Ladies: The Re-Gendering of Nineteenth-Century American Theater Audiences." *American Quarterly* 46.3 (Sept. 1994): 374–405.

Cahan, Abraham. Letter to Hutchins Hapgood. February 1, 1918. Hapgood Family Papers. Yale Collection of American Literature. Beinecke Rare Book and Manuscript Library. New Haven, Conn.

———. *Yekl and the Imported Bridegroom and Other Stories of Yiddish New York*. Introduction by Bernard G. Richards. New York: Dover Publications, Inc., 1970.

Cain, William E. "Sensations of Style: The Literary Realism of Stephen Crane." *The Blackwell Companion to American Fiction, 1865–1914*. Eds. Robert Paul Lamb and G. R. Thompson. Oxford: Blackwell Publishers, 2005: 557–71.

Campbell, Helen. *Darkness and Daylight, or, Lights and Shadows of New York Life*. With Thomas W. Byrnes and Thomas W. Knox. 1891. Hartford, Conn.: A. D. Worthington and Co., 1895.

———. *The Problem of the Poor: A Record of Quiet Work in Unquiet Places*. New York: Fords, Howard, and Hulbert, 1882.

———. *Prisoners of Poverty: Women Wage-Workers, Their Trades and Their Lives*. 1887. Westport, Conn.: Greenwood Press, 1970.

Candela, Gregory L. "We Wear the Mask: Irony in Dunbar's *The Sport of the Gods*." *American Literature* 48.1 (March 1976): 60–72.

Carlin, Deborah. "'What Methods Have Brought Blessing': Discourses of Reform in Philanthropic Literature." *The (Other) American Traditions*. Ed. Joyce Warner. New Brunswick, N.J.: Rutgers University Press, 1993. 203–25.

Cataliotti, Robert H. *The Music in African American Fiction*. New York: Garland Publishing, 1995.

Chauncey, George. *Gay New York: Gender, Urban Culture, and the Making of the Gay Male World, 1890–1940.* New York: Basic Books, 1994.

Chesnutt, Charles W. "The Future American." *Chesnutt: Stories, Novels, and Essays.* Ed. Werner Sollors. New York: Library of America, 2002. 845–63.

———. *The Journals of Charles W. Chesnutt.* Ed. Richard H. Brodhead. Durham, N.C., 1993.

———. "Post-Bellum—Pre-Harlem." 1931. *Chesnutt: Stories, Novels, and Essays.* Ed. Werner Sollors. New York: Library of America, 2002. 906–12.

Colvert, James B. Introduction to *George's Mother. The University of Virginia Edition of the Works of Stephen Crane: Vol. 1.* Ed. Fredson Bowers. Charlottesville: University Press of Virginia, 1969. 101–8.

Cooper, Anna Julia. *A Voice from the South: By a Black Woman of the South.* 1892. Introduction by Mary Helen Washington. New York: Oxford University Press, 1988.

Cooper, Wayne F. Foreword. *Home to Harlem.* 1928. By Claude McKay. Boston: Northeastern University Press, 1987.

Crane, Stephen. *Crane: Prose and Poetry.* Ed. J. C. Levenson. New York: Library of America, 1984.

———. "An Experiment in Luxury." *Maggie, A Girl of the Streets and Other New York Writings.* Ed. Luc Sante. New York: Modern Library, 2001.165–73.

———. "An Experiment in Misery." *Maggie, A Girl of the Streets and Other New York Writings.* Ed. Luc Sante. New York: Modern Library, 2001. 152–64.

———. "In the 'Tenderloin.'" 1896. *New York Sketches* 166–69.

———. *George's Mother. Crane* 213–77.

———. *Maggie: A Girl of the Streets.* 1893. New York: D. Appleton and Co., 1896.

———. *Maggie: A Girl of the Streets. Crane* 5–78.

———. *The New York Sketches of Stephen Crane and Related Pieces.* Ed. R. W. Stallman and E. R. Hagemann. New York: New York University Press, 1966.

———. "Stephen Crane in Minetta Lane, One of Gotham's Most Notorious Thoroughfares." 1896. *New York Sketches* 178–84.

———. "The 'Tenderloin' as It Really Is." 1896. *New York Sketches* 162–66.

De Jongh, James. *Vicious Modernism: Black Harlem and the Literary Imagination.* Cambridge, U.K.: Cambridge University Press, 1990.

Den Tandt, Christophe. *The Urban Sublime in American Literary Naturalism.* Urbana: University of Illinois Press, 1998.

———. "American Literary Naturalism." *The Blackwell Companion to American Fiction, 1865–1914.* Eds. Robert Paul Lamb and G. R. Thompson. Oxford: Blackwell Publishers, 2005. 96–118.

Dickens, Charles. *American Notes.* 1842. Gloucester, Mass.: Peter Smith, 1968.

Dickstein, Morris, "The City as Text: New York and the American Writer," *Tri-Quarterly* 83 (Winter 1991–92): 183–205.

Douglas, Ann. *The Feminization of American Culture.* New York: Avon Books, 1978.

———. *Terrible Honesty: Mongrel Manhattan in the 1920s.* New York: Papermac, 1997.

Du Bois, W. E. B. "Chesnutt." 1933. *Du Bois* 1234–35.

———. "Criteria of Negro Art." 1926. *The Crisis Reader.* Ed. Sondra Kathryn Wilson. New York: Modern Library, 1999. 317–25.

————. *Du Bois: Writings*. 1986. Ed. Nathan Huggins. New York: Library of America, 1996.

————. "Howells and Black Folk." 1913. *Du Bois* 1147–48.

————. *The Souls of Black Folk*. 1903. *Du Bois* 357–547.

————. "Van Vechten's 'Nigger Heaven.'" *The Crisis* (Dec. 1926). 1216–18.

Dunbar, Paul Laurence. *The Sport of the Gods*. 1902. Introduction by William L. Andrews. New York: Signet Classics, 1999.

————. "The Negroes of the Tenderloin." 1898. *The Sport of the Gods and Other Essential Writings*. Ed. Shelley Fisher Fishkin and David Bradley. New York: Modern Library, 2005. 264–67.

Ewen, Elizabeth. *Immigrant Women in the Land of Dollars: Life and Culture on the Lower East Side, 1890–1925*. New York: Monthly Review Press, 1985.

Farrell, James T. *The Short Stories of James T. Farrell*. New York: Halcyon Press, 1941.

Ferens, Dominika. *Edith and Winnifred Eaton: Chinatown Missions and Japanese Romance*. Urbana: University of Illinois Press, 2002.

Fiedler, Leslie. *Love and Death in the American Novel*. 1960. New York: Anchor Books, 1992.

Floyd, Virginia, ed. *Eugene O'Neill at Work: Newly Released Ideas for his Plays*. New York: Ungar, 1981.

Foster, George G. *Celio: or, New York Above-Ground and Under-Ground*. New York: Dewitt and Davenport, 1850.

————. *New York by Gaslight and Other Urban Sketches*. Ed. Stuart Blumin. Berkeley: University of California Press, 1990.

Gandal, Keith. "Stephen Crane's 'Maggie' and the Modern Soul," *ELH* 60 (Fall 1993): 759–85.

————. *The Virtues of the Vicious: Jacob Riis, Stephen Crane, and the Spectacle of the Slum*. New York: Oxford University Press, 1997.

Garland, Hamlin. *Crumbling Idols*. Chicago: Stone and Kimball, 1894.

————. "From 'An Ambitious French Novel and a Modest American Story.'" 1893. *Wertheim* 6–7.

————. Manuscript note concerning Stephen Crane's *Maggie*. Signed and undated. Two pages. Berg Collection of English and American Literature. New York Public Library, the Astor, Lennox, and Tilden Foundations.

Gebhard, Caroline, and Barbara McCaskill, eds. *Post-Bellum, Pre-Harlem: The Achievement of African-American Writers, Artists, and Thinkers, 1880–1914*. New York: New York University Press, 2006.

Gelb, Arthur, and Barbara Gelb. *O'Neill: Life with Monte Cristo*. New York: Applause Cinema and Theater Books, 2000.

Gelfant, Blanche Housman. *The American City Novel*. Norman: University of Oklahoma Press, 1954.

Giamo, Benedict. *On the Bowery: Confronting Homelessness in American Society*. Iowa City: University of Iowa Press, 1989.

Giles, James Richard. *The Naturalistic Inner-City Novel in America: Encounter with the Fat Man*. Columbia: University of South Carolina Press, 1995.

Gilfoyle, Timothy J. *City of Eros: New York City, Prostitution, and the Commercialization of Sex, 1790–1920*. New York: W. W. Norton and Co., 1992.

Hadley, Samuel H. *Down in Water Street: A Story of Sixteen Years Life and Work in the Water Street Mission; A Sequel to the Life of Jerry McAuley.* New York: Fleming H. Revell Co., 1906.

Halttunen, Karen. *Confidence Men and Painted Women: A Study of Middle Class Culture in America, 1830–1870.* New Haven, Conn.: Yale University Press, 1982.

Hapgood, Hutchins. Letter to Abraham Cahan. Unsigned and unsent. October 22, 1942. Hapgood Family Papers. Yale Collection of American Literature. Beinecke Rare Book and Manuscript Library. New Haven, Conn.

———. "Realism on the Ghetto Stage." *Atlantic Monthly* 85 (June 1900): 839–43.

———. *The Spirit of the Ghetto.* 1902. Ed. Moses Rischin. Cambridge, Mass.: Belknap Press of Harvard University Press, 1967.

———. *Types from City Streets.* New York: Funk and Wagnall's Co., 1910.

———. *A Victorian in the Modern World.* New York: Harcourt, Brace and Co., 1939.

Hapke, Laura. *Girls Who Went Wrong: Prostitutes in American Fiction, 1885–1917.* Bowling Green, Ohio: Bowling Green State University Popular Press, 1989.

———. *Labor's Text: The Worker in American Fiction.* New Brunswick, N.J.: Rutgers University Press, 2001.

Howard, June. *Form and History in American Literary Naturalism.* Chapel Hill: University of North Carolina Press, 1985.

Howells, William Dean. *Criticism and Fiction and Other Essays.* New York: New York University Press, 1959.

———. "An East Side Ramble." *Impressions and Experiences.* New York: Harper and Brothers Publishers, 1896. 127–49.

———. *A Hazard of New Fortunes.* 1890. New York: New American Library, 1965.

———. Introduction. *Lyrics of Lowly Life.* By Paul Laurence Dunbar. 1896. Salem, N.H.: Ayer Co., Publishers, Inc.: 1991. xiii–xx.

———. "New York Low Life in Fiction." 1896. Stephen Crane. *Maggie: A Girl of the Streets.* 1893. Ed. Luc Sante. New York: Modern Library, 2001. 261–64.

———. "New York Streets." *Impressions and Experiences.* New York: Harper and Brothers Publishers, 1896. 245–81.

Hughes, Langston. *The Big Sea: An Autobiography.* New York: Alfred A. Knopf, 1945.

———. "The Negro Artist and the Racial Mountain." 1926. Ed. David Levering Lewis. *The Portable Harlem Renaissance Reader.* New York: Penguin Books, 1994. 91–95.

Hurd, Myles. "Blackness and Borrowed Obscurity: Another Look at Dunbar's *The Sport of the Gods.*" *Callaloo* No. 11/13 (February 1981): 90–100.

Ingraham, Thomas Allan, and Richmond Mayo-Smith. "Migration." *Encyclopedia Britannica.* 11th Edition. Vol. 18. Britannica: London, 1911: 431–33. 29 vols.

Jackson, Kenneth T., ed. *The Encyclopedia of New York City.* New Haven, Conn.: Yale University Press, 1995.

James, Henry. *The American Scene.* 1907. Bloomington: Indiana University Press, 1968.

James, William. *Pragmatism and Other Writings.* Introduction by Giles Gunn. New York: Penguin Classics, 2000.

Jameson, Frederic. *The Political Unconscious: Narrative as a Socially Symbolic Act.* Ithaca, N.Y.: Cornell University Press, 1981.

Johnson, Eloise. *Rediscovering the Harlem Renaissance: The Politics of Exclusion.* New York: Garland Publishing Inc., 1997.

Johnson, James Weldon. *Along This Way: The Autobiography of James Weldon Johnson.* 1933. Introduction by Sondra Kathryn Wilson. New York: Da Capo Press, 2000.

———. *The Autobiography of an Ex-Colored Man.* 1912. Introduction by William L. Andrews. New York: Penguin Books, 1990.

———. *Black Manhattan.* 1930. New York: Da Capo Press, 1991.

———, ed. *The Book of American Negro Poetry: Chosen and Edited, with an Essay on the Negro's Creative Genius by James Weldon Johnson.* New York: Harcourt, Brace, and Co., 1922.

———. *God's Trombones: Seven Negro Sermons in Verse.* New York: Viking Press, 1927.

———. "Romance and Tragedy in Harlem: A Review of Carl Van Vechten's *Nigger Heaven.*" 1926. *Selected Writings* 392–96.

———. *The Selected Writings of James Weldon Johnson.* Vol. 2. Ed. Sondra Kathryn Wilson. New York: Oxford University Press, 1995. 2 vols.

Kaplan, Amy. *The Social Construction of American Realism.* Chicago: University of Chicago Press, 1992.

Kazin, Alfred. *On Native Grounds: An Interpretation of Modern American Prose Literature.* 1942. New York: Harcourt, Brace and Co., 1995.

Kellner, Bruce. *Carl Van Vechten and the Irreverent Decades.* Norman: University of Oklahoma Press, 1968.

Kennedy, J. Gerald. *Imagining Paris: Exile, Writing, and American Identity.* New Haven, Conn.: Yale University Press, 1993.

Kennedy, Randall. Introduction. *Blacks at Harvard: A Documentary History of African American Experience at Harvard and Radcliffe.* Ed. Werner Sollors, Caldwell Titcomb, and Thomas A. Underwood. New York: New York University Press, 1993.

Labaree, Benjamin W. *America and the Sea: A Maritime History.* Mystic, Conn.: Mystic Seaport, 1998.

Lears, Jackson, T. J. "The Concept of Cultural Hegemony: Problems and Possibilities." *American Historical Review* 90 (June 1985): 567–93.

Leland, John. *Hip: The History.* New York: HarperCollins Publishers, 2004.

Levy, Eugene. *James Weldon Johnson: Black Leader, Black Voice.* Chicago: University of Chicago Press, 1973.

Lewis, David Levering. Introduction. *The Portable Harlem Renaissance Reader.* New York: Penguin Books, 1994.

———. *When Harlem Was in Vogue.* 1979. New York: Penguin Books, 1997.

Lippard, George. *New York: Its Upper Ten and Lower Million.* Cincinnati: E. Mendenhall, 1854.

Locke, Alain. "American Literary Tradition and the Negro." *Critical Temper* 433–38.

———. *The Critical Temper of Alain Locke: A Selection of His Essays on Art and Culture.* Ed. Jeffrey C. Stewart. New York: Garland Publishing, 1983.

———. "The Saving Grace of Realism: Retrospective Review of the Negro Literature of 1933." *Critical Temper* 221–25.

Lovett, Robert Morss. Introduction. In James T. Farrell. *The Short Stories of James T. Farrell.* New York: Halcyon Press, 1941: xv–xxvii.

Lowell, Amy. *Tendencies in Modern American Poetry.* New York: Macmillan Co., 1917.

Lueders, Edward. *Carl Van Vechten and the Twenties.* Albuquerque: University of New Mexico Press, 1955.

Martin, Jay. *Harvests of Change: American Literature, 1865–1914.* Englewood Cliffs, N.J.: Prentice-Hall, 1967.

Matthiessen, F. O. *Theodore Dreiser.* New York: William Sloan Associates, 1951.

Maxey, Duane V. "Conversion of McAuley's Irish Dialect into Proper English." Note to *Life Story of Jerry McAuley.* By Jeremiah McAuley. Edited by Duane V. Maxey. Atlanta: Repairer Publishing Co., 2000. http://wesley.nnu.edu/wesleyctr/books/1801-1900/HDM1855.PDF.

May, Henry F. *The End of American Innocence: A Study of the First Years of Our Own Time.* 1959. New York: Knopf, 1969.

McAuley, Jeremiah. *Transformed, or, the History of a River Thief: Briefly Told.* With a Preface by Mrs. Helen E. Brown. Self-published, 1876.

McKay, Claude. *Home to Harlem.* 1928. Foreword by Wayne F. Cooper. Boston: North-eastern University Press, 1987.

———. *The Passion of Claude McKay: Selected Poetry and Prose, 1912–1948.* New York: Schocken Books, 1973.

Mencken, H. L. "The Negro as Author." 1920. *Smart Set Criticism.* Ed. William H. Notle. Washington, D.C.: Regnery Publishing, 1987: 320–22.

Merton, Robert K. "Insiders and Outsiders: A Chapter in the Sociology of Knowledge." *Theories of Ethnicity: A Classical Reader.* Ed. Werner Sollors. 1972. New York: New York University Press, 1996. 325–69.

Miller, Kenneth D. and Ethel Prince Miller. *The People Are the City: 150 Years of Social and Religious Concern in New York City.* New York: Macmillan, 1962.

Monteiro, George. "The Drunkard's Progress: Bowery Plot, Social Paradigm in Stephen Crane's *George's Mother.*" *Dionysos: The Literature and Addiction TriQuarterly* 9.1 (1999): 5–16.

Morgan, Thomas L. "The City as Refuge: Constructing Urban Blackness in Paul Laurence Dunbar's *The Sport of the Gods* and James Weldon Johnson's *The Autobiography of an Ex-Colored Man.*" *African American Review* 38:2 (Summer 2004): 213–37.

Muller, Edward K. "From Waterfront to Metropolitan Region: The Geographical Development of American Cities." *American Urbanism: A Historiographical Review.* Eds. Howard Gillette Jr. and Zane Miller. New York: Greenwood Press, 1987.

Mumford, Kevin J. *Interzones: Black/White Sex Districts in Chicago and New York in the Early Twentieth Century.* New York: Columbia University Press, 1997.

Nilon, Charles. Introduction. *The Sport of the Gods.* By Paul Laurence Dunbar. 1902. London: Collier Books, 1970. 6–16.

Nord, Deborah Epstein. "The Social Explorer as Anthropologist: Victorian Travelers among the Urban Poor." *Visions of the Modern City: Essays in History, Art, and Literature.* Ed. William Sharpe and Leonard Wallock. New York: Heyman Center for the Humanities, Columbia University, 1983.

Norris, Frank. "Zola as a Romantic Writer." *Frank Norris: Novels and Essays.* Ed. Donald Pizer. New York: Library of America, 1986. 1106–8.

Offord, Rev. R. M., ed. *Jerry McAuley, His Life and Work; with an Introduction by the Rev. S. Iranaeus Prime: and Personal Sketches by A. S. Hatch.* New York: New York Observer, ca. 1885.

O'Neill, Eugene. *The Hairy Ape.* Ed. Travis Board. 1922. New York: Library of America, 1988.

Orlov, Paul A. "Psychology, Style, and the Cityscape in Stephen Crane's *George's Mother.*" *CLA Journal* 34 (Dec. 1990): 212–27.

Orvell, Miles. *The Real Thing: Imitation and Authenticity in American Culture, 1880–1940.* Chapel Hill: University of North Carolina Press, 1989.

Osofsky, Gilbert. *Harlem: The Making of a Ghetto, Negro New York, 1890–1930.* 1963. New York: Harper Torchbooks, 1968.

Ostendorf, Berndt. "Literary Acculturation: What Makes Ethnic Literature 'Ethnic.'" *Callaloo* 25. *Recent Essays from Europe: A Special Issue* (Autumn 1985): 577–86.

Park, Robert E. "The City: Suggestions for the Investigation of Human Behavior in the Urban Environment." *The City: Suggestions for the Investigation of Human Behavior in the Urban Environment.* Robert E. Park and Ernest W. Burgess. 1925. Chicago: University of Chicago Press, 1967: 1–46.

———. "Human Migration and the Marginal Man." *Theories of Ethnicity: A Classical Reader.* Ed. Werner Sollors. 1928. New York: New York University Press, 1996. 156–67.

Parrington, Vernon L. *Main Currents in American Thought. Vol. 3.* New York: Harcourt, Brace and Co., 1930.

Peck, Harry Thurston. Rev. of *George's Mother* by Stephen Crane. 1896. *The Merrill Studies in* Maggie *and* George's Mother. Ed. Stanley Wertheim. Columbus, Ohio: Charles E. Merrill Publishing, 1970. 115–17.

Pfeiffer, Kathleen. "Individualism, Success, and American Identity in *The Autobiography of an Ex-Colored Man.*" *African American Review* 30.3 (1996). 403–19.

Pfister, Joel. *Staging Depth: Eugene O'Neill and the Politics of Psychological Discourse.* Cultural Studies of the United States. Chapel Hill: University of North Carolina Press, 1995.

Poole, Ernest. *The Harbor.* 1915. New York: Sagamore Press Inc., 1957.

Posnock, Ross. "Affirming the Alien: The Pragmatist Pluralism of *The American Scene.*" *The Cambridge Companion to Henry James.* Ed. Jonathan Freedman. New York: Cambridge University Press, 1998. 224–46.

Rabinowitz, Paula. "Margaret Bourke-White's Red Coat; or, Slumming in the 1930s." *Radical Revisions: Rereading 1930s Culture.* Ed. Bill Pullen. Urbana: University of Illinois Press, 1996. 187–207.

Reynolds, David S. *Beneath the American Renaissance: The Subversive Imagination in the Age of Emerson and Melville.* Cambridge, Mass.: Harvard University Press, 1988.

———. *Walt Whitman's America: A Cultural Biography.* 1995. New York: Vintage Books, 1996.

Richards, Bernard G. Introduction. *Yekl and the Imported Bridegroom and Other Stories of Yiddish New York.* By Abraham Cahan. New York: Dover Publications, 1970.

Richter, Robert A. *Eugene O'Neill and Dat Ole Davil Sea: Maritime Influences in the Life and Works of Eugene O'Neill.* Mystic, Conn.: Mystic Seaport, 2004.

Riis, Jacob. *How the Other Half Lives.* 1890. Introduction by Luc Sante. New York: Penguin Classics, 1997.

Rischin, Moses. "Abraham Cahan and the New York *Commercial Advertiser*." *Publications of the American Jewish Historical Society* 43 (Sept. 1953): 10–36.

———. Introduction. *The Spirit of the Ghetto*. By Hutchins Hapgood. 1902. Cambridge, Mass.: Belknap Press of Harvard University Press, 1967.

Rosenberg, Caroll Smith. *Religion and the Rise of the American City: The New York City Mission Movement, 1812–1870*. Ithaca, N.Y.: Cornell University Press, 1971.

Rusch, Frederic E., and Donald Pizer, eds. *Theodore Dreiser: Interviews*. Urbana: University of Illinois Press, 2004.

Sanders, Ronald. "Reformers in the Ghetto." *Commentary* 40 (1965): 78–93.

Sante, Luc. Introduction. *How the Other Half Lives*. By Jacob Riis. 1890. New York: Penguin Classics, 1997.

———. Introduction. *Maggie, A Girl of the Streets and Other New York Writings*. Ed. Luc Sante. New York: Modern Library, 2001.

———. *Low Life: Lures and Snares of Old New York*. New York: Vintage Books, 1992.

Schocket, Eric. "Undercover Explorations of the 'Other Half,' or the Writer as Class Transvestite." *Representations* 64 (Fall 1998): 109–33.

Scruggs, Charles. "H. L. Mencken and James Weldon Johnson: Two Men Who Helped Shape a Renaissance." *Critical Essays on James Weldon Johnson*. Ed. Kenneth M. Price and Lawrence J. Oliver. New York: G. K. Hall and Co., 1997. 174–90.

Sharpe, William, and Leonard Wallock. Introduction. *Visions of the Modern City: Essays in History, Art, and Literature*. New York: Heyman Center for the Humanities, Columbia University, 1983.

Simoneaux, Katherine G. "Color Imagery in Crane's *Maggie: A Girl of the Streets*." By Stephen Crane. Ed. Thomas A. Gullason. 1893. New York: W. W. Norton, 1979. 222–30.

Sollors, Werner. *Beyond Ethnicity: Consent and Descent in American Culture*. New York: Oxford University Press, 1986.

———. *Neither Black nor White nor Both: Thematic Explorations of Interracial Literature*. New York: Oxford University Press, 1997.

———. *Theories of Ethnicity: A Classical Reader*. New York: New York University Press, 1996.

Stansell, Christine. *American Moderns: Bohemian New York and the Creation of a New Century*. New York: Metropolitan Books, 2000.

Steffens, Lincoln. *The Autobiography of Lincoln Steffens*. New York: Harcourt, Brace, and Co., 1931.

Taylor, William R. *In Pursuit of Gotham: Culture and Commerce in New York*. New York: Oxford University Press, 1992.

Toomer, Jean. "The Negro Emergent." Ca. 1924. *A Jean Toomer Reader: Selected Unpublished Writings*. Ed. Frederik L. Rusch. New York: Oxford University Press, 1993. 86–93.

Trachtenberg, Alan. "American Studies as a Cultural Program." *Ideology and Classic American Literature*. Ed. Sacvan Bercovitch and Myra Jehlen. New York: Cambridge University Press, 1986. 172–87.

Van Vechten, Carl. *Nigger Heaven*. 1926. Introduction by Kathleen Pfeiffer. Urbana: University of Illinois Press, 2000.

————. Introduction. *The Autobiography of an Ex-Colored Man*. Ed. Kenneth M. Price and Lawrence J. Oliver. New York: G. K. Hall and Co., 1997. 25–27.

————. *Letters of Carl Van Vechten*. Ed. Bruce Kellner. New Haven, Conn.: Yale University Press, 1987.

Vose, John D. *Seven Nights in Gotham*. New York: Bunnell and Price, 1852.

————. *The B'hoys of Yale, or, The Scraps of a Hard Set of Collegians*. New York: Beadle and Adams, 1878.

Ward, David. *Poverty, Ethnicity, and the American City, 1840–1925*. New York: Cambridge University Press, 1989.

Weatherford, Richard M., ed. *Stephen Crane: The Critical Heritage*. London: Routledge and Kegan Paul, 1973.

Wertheim, Stanley, ed. Introduction. *The Merrill Studies in* Maggie *and* George's Mother. Columbus, Ohio: Charles E. Merrill Publishing, 1970.

Whitman, Walt. *Democratic Vistas*. 1871. 1885. *Poetry and Prose*. Ed. Justin Kaplan. New York: Library of America, 1996. 953–1018.

————. "The Old Bowery." 1885. *Poetry and Prose*. Ed. Justin Kaplan. New York: Library of America, 1996. 1209–16.

————. "Why Do the Theatres Languish? And How Shall the American Stage Be Resuscitated?" 1847. *The Uncollected Poetry and Prose of Walt Whitman*. 2 vols. Ed. Emory Holloway. Gloucester, Mass.: Peter Smith, 1992. 152–54.

Wittke, Carl. "The Immigrant Theme on the American Stage." *Mississippi Valley Historical Review* 39.2 (Sept. 1952): 211–32.

Wonham, Henry B. *Playing the Races: Ethnic Caricature and American Literary Realism*. New York: Oxford University Press, 2004.

Woolston, Howard. *Metropolis: A Study of Urban Communities*. New York: D. Appleton-Century Co., 1938.

Worth, Robert F. "*Nigger Heaven* and the Harlem Renaissance." *African American Review* 29.3 (Fall 1995): 461–73.

INDEX

Abbott, Lyman, 24, 34
Abell, Aaron Ignatius, 36
Addams, Jane, 7
Adler, Jacob, 119–20
African Americans: African American
intellectualism, 141, 142–43, 165–66;
"black and tan" clubs, 91; cabarets as
slumming destinations, 97–98, 152, 157,
180n4; Chesnutt as racial insider, 86; civil
rights movement, 136, 141; in Greenwich
Village, 79, 81–82; Howells on, 82–83,
85–86; Johnson on racial awareness,
94, 96–97, 106; Mencken on, 106, 155;
"Nigger Heaven" term, 146, 148, 149, 151,
157–59; as outsider literature subjects,
82, 96–97, 150–51, 154, 156–61, 162–63, 173;
racial ambiguity and, 91, 96–99, 100–101;
ragtime as cultural ascendancy vs. appropriation, 99–105, 107–9; reception of
Van Vechten, 145–50; Riis on, 80–81, 110;
skin color as literary device, 152, 164–65;
Tenderloin neighborhood and, 3, 10–11,
79–88, 97–98; traditional dialect and,
108; turn-of-the-century bohemianism and, 138. *See also* Great Migration;
Harlem neighborhood; Tenderloin
neighborhood
Algren, Nelson, 12–13
alienation, 12–13, 23, 61, 161
Allen, Gay Wilson, 54
Allen, John, 29, 31–32

Americanization movement, 114–15, 125,
131, 136
anarchism, 13–14, 40
Andrews, William L., 87
Antin, Mary, 2
Arnold, Rev. A. C., 29
Asbury, Herbert, 175
authenticity: background as literary component, 9–10; in Bowery "B'hoy/G'hal"
literature, 56–57, 178nn3–4; as city-mysteries concern, 4; converted outsiders
and, 6, 93; moral regions and, 11–12; New
Negro primitivism and, 153; representation of Harlem and, 138, 180n10, 199

Baker, Benjamin A., 53–54
Baker, Kevin, 174
Bakhtin, Mikhail, 108
Barnum, P. T., 62
Battan, Jesse, 13
Beer, Thomas, 49
Benfey, Christopher, 52
Bergson, Henri, 116
Berlin, Edward A., 101–2
Berlin, Irving, 105
Bernard, Emily, 150
"black and tan" clubs, 91
boarding houses, 26–27
Boas, Franz, 10
Bohemians, 20
Borges, Jorge Luis, 175

ROBERT M. DOWLING received his Ph.D. in English and American Studies from the Graduate Center of the City University of New York. He is an associate professor of English at Central Connecticut State University and author of numerous articles in journals and critical anthologies on late nineteenth and early twentieth-century American literature and cultural history. His next book project is on the playwright Eugene O'Neill.

The University of Illinois Press
is a founding member of the
Association of American University Presses.

—————————————————————

Composed in 10.5/13 Adobe Minion
by Jim Proefrock
at the University of Illinois Press
Manufactured by Thomson-Shore, Inc.

University of Illinois Press
1325 South Oak Street
Champaign, IL 61820-6903
www.press.uillinois.edu